My
PowerPoint® 2016

Echo Swinford

800 East 96th Street,
Indianapolis, Indiana 46240 USA

ii

My PowerPoint 2016

Copyright © 2016 by Pearson Education

ISBN-13: 978-0-7897-5568-1
ISBN-10: 0-7897-5568-8

Library of Congress Control Number: 2015950784

Printed in the United States of America

First Printing: November 2015

Trademarks

Warning and Disclaimer

Special Sales

For information about buying this title in bulk quantities, or for special sales opportunities (which may include electronic versions; custom cover designs; and content particular to your business, training goals, marketing focus, or branding interests), please contact our corporate sales department at corpsales@pearsoned.com or (800) 382-3419.

For government sales inquiries, please contact governmentsales@pearsoned.com.

For questions about sales outside the U.S., please contact international@pearsoned.com.

Editor-in-Chief
Greg Wiegand

Acquisitions Editor
Laura Norman

Development Editor
Joyce Neilsen

Managing Editor
Kristy Hart

Project Editor
Elaine Wiley

Copy Editor
Cheri Clark

Senior Indexer
Cheryl Lenser

Proofreader
Chrissy White

Technical Editor
J. Boyd Nolan

Cover Designer
Mark Shirar

Compositor
Trina Wurst

Contents at a Glance

Table of Contents

3   Creating and Working with Shapes   81

7 Creating and Formatting Charts   181

x My PowerPoint 2016

About the Author

A Microsoft PowerPoint MVP since 2000, Echo Swinford began her PowerPoint career in 1997 working for a medical education communications company, where she was responsible for the development of enduring materials and stand-alone modules for continuing medical education programs.

Echo holds a master's degree in New Media from the Indiana University–Purdue University at Indianapolis School of Informatics. She is self-employed, specializing in developing PowerPoint templates, presentation creation and makeovers, and training for large and small corporate clients. Echo has been a featured speaker for the Presentation Summit (formerly PowerPoint Live) user conference since its inception.

Echo's first book, *Fixing PowerPoint Annoyances*, was published by O'Reilly Media in February 2006, and *The PowerPoint 2007 Complete Makeover Kit*, co-authored with Geetesh Bajaj, was published by Que in November 2008. Her third book, *Building PowerPoint Templates: Step by Step with the Experts* (co-authored with Julie Terberg), came out in fall 2012 and was also published by Que. Video publications for Que include LiveLessons for PowerPoint 2010, 2013, and 2016, and PowerPoint for iPad. Echo also has a string of tech editing credits with these and other publishers.

Visit Echo's website at www.echosvoice.com.

Acknowledgments

A huge, heartfelt thank you goes to the team at Que who always manages to make me look and sound good, no matter what: Laura Norman, Todd Brakke, Joyce Neilsen, J. Boyd Nolan, Elaine Wiley, Cheri Clark, Chrissy White, Cheryl Lenser, Trina Wurst, and Mark Shirar. I couldn't ask for a better team supporting me.

Thank you also to friend and colleague Julie Terberg for the cover photo as well as the beautiful animal and flower pictures featured throughout.

We Want to Hear from You!

As the reader of this book, you are our most important critic and commentator. We value your opinion and want to know what we're doing right, what we could do better, what areas you'd like to see us publish in, and any other words of wisdom you're willing to pass our way.

We welcome your comments. You can email or write to let us know what you did or didn't like about this book—as well as what we can do to make our books better.

Please note that we cannot help you with technical problems related to the topic of this book.

When you write, please be sure to include this book's title and author as well as your name and email address. We will carefully review your comments and share them with the author and editors who worked on the book.

Email: feedback@quepublishing.com

Mail: Que Publishing
            ATTN: Reader Feedback
            800 East 96th Street
            Indianapolis, IN 46240 USA

Reader Services

Visit our website and register this book at quepublishing.com/register for convenient access to any updates, downloads, or errata that might be available for this book.

Customize the Quick Access Toolbar

Review new features in PowerPoint 2016

Tour the PowerPoint interface

In this chapter, you will become familiar with the PowerPoint interface and learn to customize your Quick Access Toolbar. Specific topics in this chapter include the following:

→ PowerPoint everywhere
→ Looking at the new features
→ Installing Microsoft Office 2016
→ The PowerPoint 2016 interface
→ Customizing the Quick Access Toolbar

Getting Started

Before you learn how to perform specific tasks in PowerPoint, you should become familiar with the interface. If you've used PowerPoint, Word, or Excel 2007, 2010, or 2013, you'll already know many of the basics. But if you've been using an older version, or if PowerPoint 2016 is your first experience with PowerPoint, it can be helpful to know some tricks for interacting with it.

PowerPoint Everywhere

Microsoft has made huge efforts in the past few years to introduce Office everywhere. We now have Office applications—which include Word, Excel, and PowerPoint—available on our phones, our tablets, and our browsers, as well as on our desktop and laptop computers. Keep an eye out for these different PowerPoint options on your various devices:

- Office 2016. This is the full-featured installed set of programs that run on your desktop or laptop computer. Office 2016 usually includes at least Word, Excel, and PowerPoint, but depending on the plan you purchase, it may also include OneNote, Outlook, Access, Publisher, and other applications. Office 2016 is available for both Windows and Mac operating systems.

Office 2016 or Office 365?

Sometimes Office 2016 is called Office 365. The difference between them is that Office 365 is a subscription, and Office 2016 is a one-time purchase. Most of the Office 365 subscription plans allow you to install the applications (Word, Excel, PowerPoint, and so on) on up to five devices, which includes other computers (both Mac and PC), phones, tablets, and iPads. You truly get access to Office everywhere! With Office 2016, you can usually install it on only one computer and not on any other device. Office 365 also keeps itself up-to-date so you always have the latest features. It doesn't matter whether you're using Office 2016 or Office 365—the exercises in this book will apply to both as long as you installed PowerPoint on your laptop or desktop computer.

- Office Universal for Windows 10. These are Office applications that you can download and install on Windows 10 through the Windows Store. On phones and tablets you can view, create, and edit presentations free, but you need your Office 365 subscription to use some of the advanced features. On larger tablets, laptops, and desktops, you can view and show presentations free, but you'll need your Office 365 subscription to create and edit presentations. You can sign in with your Office 365 account to use one of your device installs for the Office Universal apps. If you don't already have an Office 365 account, you can sign up for one from within the Office Universal apps. On some devices, Office Universal is called Office Mobile, but it's really the same thing. Office Universal apps don't have the complete set of features that the full-featured Office 2016 or Office 365 programs do.

- Office for Android. These apps are similar to Office Universal, but of course, they're designed to work on Android tablets and phones. You can use one of your Office 365 device installs on the Office for Android apps.

- Office for iPad and iPhone. This is the same as Office Universal and Office for Android, discussed previously, but for iOS devices.

- Office Online. These are the free browser-based versions of PowerPoint, Word, and Excel. They work in major browsers such as Internet Explorer 9 and higher, Chrome, Firefox, Safari, Safari for iOS, and Chrome for Android. If you open a PowerPoint file in OneDrive or Dropbox and it opens in your browser, then you're using Office Online.

When you search the app store for Microsoft Office on most, if not all, of your devices, the results will give you the individual applications. That's okay. Install PowerPoint, Word, and Excel separately and use your Office 365 account to sign in. The applications together count as one device installation, not three individual installations. And one more thing: You can still use the applications on the various devices even without an Office 365 account, but some features may not be available.

Which PowerPoint Version Does This Book Cover?

This book covers the full-featured version of PowerPoint 2016 that comes as part of Office 2016 or Office 365 and that you install on your desktop or laptop computer.

Looking at the New Features

PowerPoint 2016 isn't extremely different from the previous version, PowerPoint 2013, but there are a few new features to be aware of.

Improved Office Themes

In this case, "Office themes" doesn't refer to the themes (.thmx files) you use for PowerPoint slides and presentations. Instead, these Office themes refer to the Colorful, Dark Gray, or White options you can choose for the interface. You can access these by going to File, Account and selecting an option from the Office Theme drop-down list.

Colorful is the default Office Theme selection. With the Colorful interface, you get a dark orange strip starting with the Ribbon tabs at the top of the screen, and the workspace is light gray.

Colorful theme

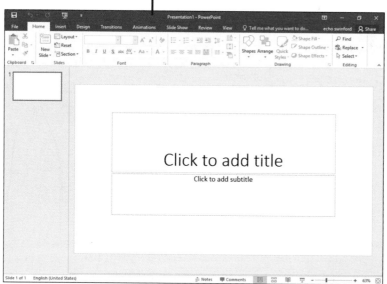

The White theme is similar to Colorful, but it's brighter. The workspace and Ribbon tabs are white, and the status bar at the bottom of the screen is bright orange. The tabs on the Ribbon are highlighted with orange text when they're active.

White theme

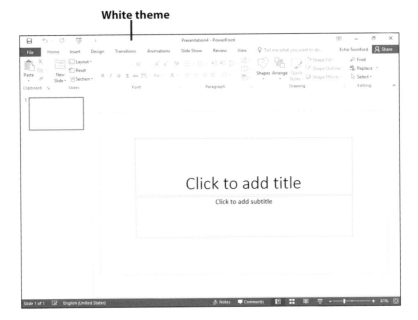

The Dark Gray theme mutes the entire workspace to shades of gray. This look is especially nice when you're working in a very dark environment (such as backstage) because staring at a bright screen for a long time while working in the dark is a recipe for headache and eyestrain.

Dark Gray theme

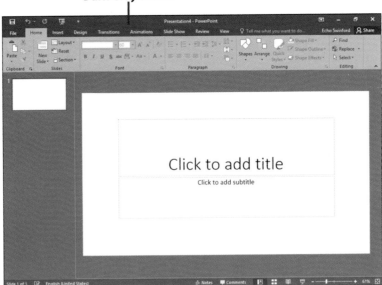

New "Modern" Chart Types

Office 2016 has introduced five new chart types: treemap, sunburst, histogram, box & whisker, and waterfall. Pareto charts are also included in the histogram category.

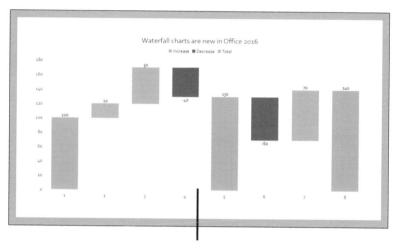

New waterfall chart type

Improved Smart Guides

Smart Guides now work with tables, making it easier to perfectly align everything on your slides.

	2014	2015	2016
	1000	1250	1300
Product A	2345	2658	2197
	4621	4342	4879

Smart Guides for tables

More Picture-Quality Options

The picture compression options now include 330 ppi (pixels per inch), which is a good resolution for high-definition displays.

Compress Pictures   ?   ×

Compression options:
☑ Apply only to this picture
☑ Delete cropped areas of pictures

Target output:
◉ HD (330 ppi): good quality for high-definition (HD) displays
○ Print (220 ppi): excellent quality on most printers and screens
○ Web (150 ppi): good for web pages and projectors
○ E-mail (96 ppi): minimize document size for sharing
○ Use document resolution

[OK]   [Cancel]

Improved Video Resolution

High-quality video now uses 1080p, medium-quality uses 720p, and low-quality uses 480p.

Presentation Quality
Largest file size and highest quality (1920 x 1080)   ▾

Presentation Quality
Largest file size and highest quality (1920 x 1080)

Internet Quality
Medium file size and moderate quality (1280 x 720)

Low Quality
Smallest file size and lowest quality (852 x 480)

Video

Record Ink

Now when you record your slide show using Slide Show, Record Slide Show, inking activity (which includes a pen and highlighter) will also be recorded. This feature has also been added retroactively to PowerPoint 2013.

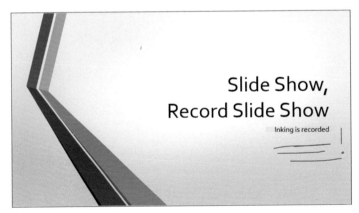

Ink Equations

Ink equations lets you input mathematical formulas and symbols in your own handwriting and insert them on the slide as typed text. The easiest way to get started with ink equations is to type Ink into the Tell Me box and select Ink Equation from the results.

Insert Screen Recording

Screen recording has been added to the Insert tab. It has been retroactively added to PowerPoint 2013 as well.

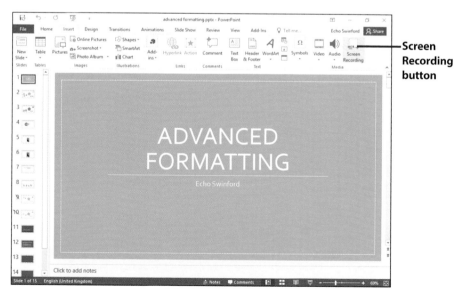

Screen Recording button

Tell Me

The Tell Me feature is located at the end of the tabs on the Ribbon. This feature makes it easier to get information on the task at hand rather than having to poke around until you find it. Want to know the fastest way to get a highlighter when you're editing a slide? Type ink into the Tell Me box and click the first result, Ink Annotations, to open the Ink Tools tab, complete with highlighters and pens!

Type text here...

...to see a list of tasks and access to Help info

Insights

Right-click any text and click Smart Lookup to access the new Insights feature. You'll see a definition and pronunciation information from Bing at the top of the Define tab on the Insights pane. On the Explore tab, you'll be able to check further information pulled from Wikipedia and other places on the Web.

**Insights pane
(Explore tab)**

**New Smart Lookup
command**

Installing Microsoft Office 2016

The most common way to install Office 2016 is to purchase an Office 365 subscription or let your existing Office 365 subscription update. To purchase a new subscription, head to office.microsoft.com, choose the plan you want, and click Buy. You can also click the Get Office tile on the Windows 10 Start menu and sign in with your Office 365 account or try it free. After the trial is complete, you can cancel or choose which Office 365 plan best meets your needs.

After you've completed the payment or trial sign-up process, you'll be able to download Office, which automatically begins the streaming installation process (also known as Click to Run). It doesn't usually take too long to install Office, and the best part is that you'll be able to use your programs and activate Office while it installs by clicking any of the applications when its tile appears in color.

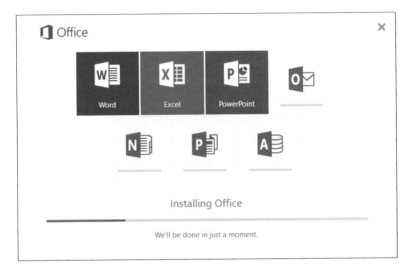

You may be prompted to make PowerPoint the default application for opening presentations. Go ahead and click Yes or OK, and if you don't want to be bothered again, check the Don't Show This Again box. You'll see a message telling you where you can specify default application settings. Make a note of it so you can do this later if you want. You may also be presented with a screen with options for Default File Types. In that case, choose Office Open XML formats.

At some point you'll need to activate Office. Enter the Microsoft account email associated with your Office 365 subscription and click Next. If you don't yet have a Microsoft account or an email associated with your subscription, just click Next. You can sign in or create a new account on the following screen.

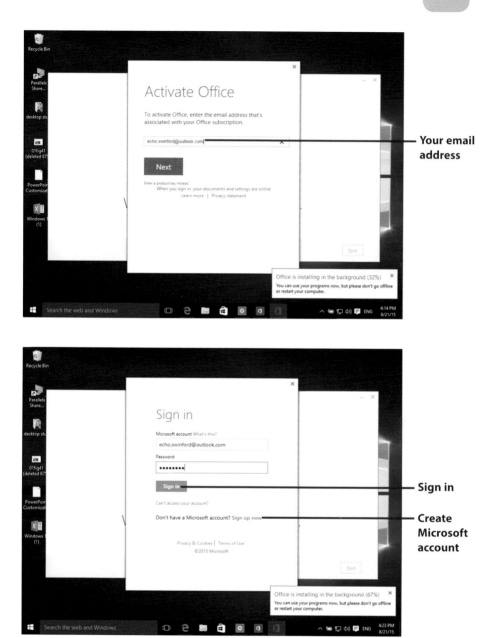

Your email address

Sign in

Create Microsoft account

After you've signed in, accept any licensing agreements such as the one which explains that Office 2016 comes with automatic updates and activation prompts.

When you're able to, open PowerPoint. On Windows 10, do this by clicking the Start button, then All Apps. Scroll down and click the PowerPoint 2016 menu option or, if there is one, click the icon on the Windows taskbar.

PowerPoint 2016   **Get Office 365**

Start button   **Windows taskbar**

One last thing to note: Office 2016 and Office 365 use OneDrive for cloud storage and syncing files across devices. You can access OneDrive from within PowerPoint on the Start screen or from the Open, Save, or Save As screens in Backstage view. Or you can go directly to onedrive.com in your browser. Sign in with the Microsoft account that's associated with Office 2016 or Office 365 to upload files and see the features available on OneDrive.

The PowerPoint 2016 Interface

The PowerPoint interface might be a little intimidating at first, but it's really pretty straightforward after you get used to it.

The Start screen lets you choose a look for your presentation, or you can simply start with a Blank Presentation and worry about the look later. Most of your work will be done in Normal view, and you can access many of the tools you'll need right from the Home tab on the Ribbon. And finally, you can always start your slide show from the shortcut button on the status bar at the bottom of the screen. That's pretty much it. Ready? Let's take a look around....

The Start Screen

When you open PowerPoint, you'll first see the Start screen.

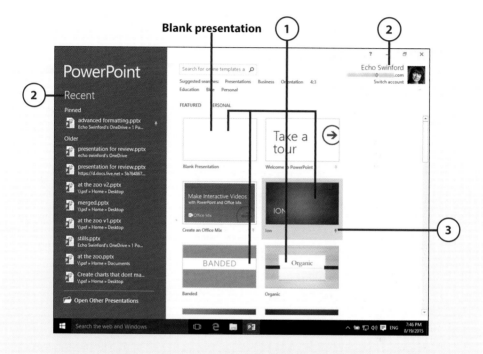

Blank presentation

1. On the Start screen, you'll see a number of Office themes (.thmx files) you can choose to base your presentation on. These themes may change periodically—which ones you see depends on what Microsoft chooses to display, which ones you've used recently, and whether you're signed into your Microsoft account.

2. If you have signed into your Microsoft account, your username will display in the upper-right corner, and you'll see your files in the Recent files list on the left. You may have opened them on a different device, but signing in syncs all that information across devices.

3. To make sure a particular theme is always available on the Start screen, hover over its thumbnail and click the thumbtack icon to "pin" it in place. When you pin a theme, it will jump to the top of the list.

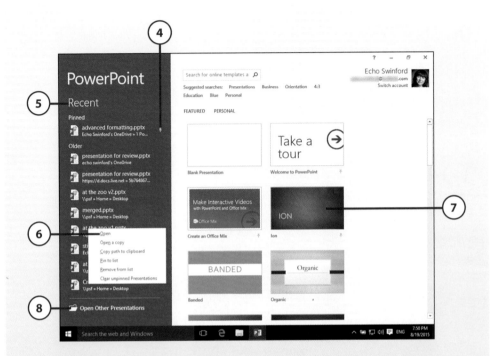

4. Notice that you can also pin files to the Recent Files list.

5. You can click any file in the Recent Files list to open it.

6. Or you can right-click any file in the Recent Files list to open it, open a copy of it, copy its file path to the Clipboard, pin it to the list, remove it from the list, or clear any unpinned presentations from the list. Clearing and removing files from the list doesn't delete them; it just removes them from the Recent Files list.

7. Or click a thumbnail to start a new presentation based on that theme.

8. Or click Open Other Presentations to navigate to other presentations on OneDrive or on your hard drive. This takes you to the Open screen, which you can access at any time by clicking the File tab, then Open.

Files and folders

9. In the Open screen, click Recent to see the same set of Recent files as on the Start screen.

10. Click OneDrive to see your files and folders that are stored on OneDrive.

11. Or click This PC to see files and folders on your hard drive.

12. Or click Browse or the file path at the top of the This PC list to open a File Explorer folder and browse your hard drive.

13. Or click Add a Place to add additional online storage locations such as an Office 365 SharePoint site.

The Ribbon

The Ribbon is the heart of the PowerPoint interface. The Ribbon is made up of tabs, and each tab consists of tools and buttons arranged into groups. Tabs are labeled at the top of the Ribbon; groups are labeled at the bottom. Click a tab to make it active and see the tools on it.

Many of the tools available on the Home tab also appear on other tabs of the Ribbon. The thought here is that the tools you need most often to create a basic presentation can be accessed from right here at home base.

Some tabs are contextual. That is, they become available when you select an object that can use those tools. For example, if you select a shape, the Drawing Tools Format tab appears so you will have a wide selection of formatting tools. Double-click the shape, and the Drawing Tools Format tab becomes the active tab.

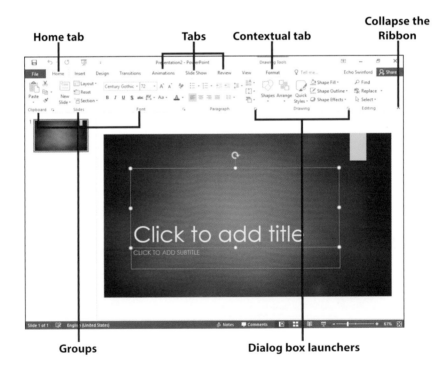

Depending on what you've selected, sometimes you'll see more than one contextual tab. If you fill a shape with a picture, you'll see both the Drawing Tools Format tab and the Picture Tools Format tab.

The small arrow icons in the corner of some groups are dialog box launchers. Click them to open formatting panes or dialog boxes where you can access more tools and settings related to that group.

Click the caret at the far right to collapse the Ribbon and streamline your workspace. Double-click any tab to restore a collapsed Ribbon. Alternatively, single-click a tab and then click the thumbtack icon that appears where the Collapse the Ribbon caret was.

There are various kinds of buttons on the Ribbon. You can click either the top or the bottom of split buttons, such as the New Slide button or the Crop button. Click the top for the default behavior (such as add a new slide); click the bottom to open a gallery or options (such as different slide layouts).

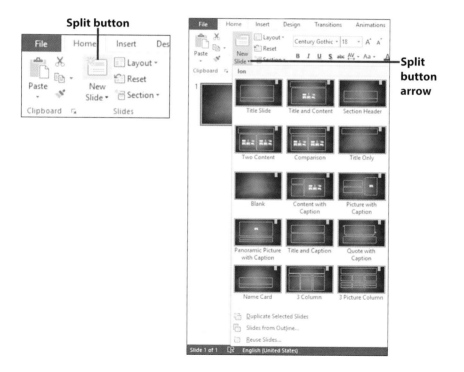

An arrow next to a button indicates there are more options or a gallery. Click the arrow to expand them.

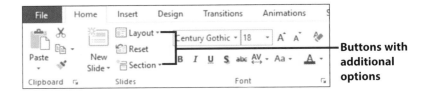

Buttons with additional options

Click a button with a color strip, and that color will be applied. Click the arrow next to these buttons to choose a different color from a palette.

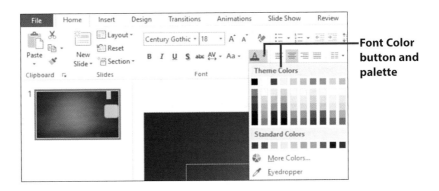

Font Color button and palette

You can type in some tools, such as the Shape Height and Shape Width boxes in the Size group on the Drawing Tools Format tab or the Font Size tool on the Home tab. Use the up and down arrows to scroll through a gallery row by row. Click the More button to expand a gallery and see all choices.

Shape Height box

More button

Scroll arrow

Three dots at the end or corner of a gallery indicate that you can click and drag the edge to resize the gallery. Sometimes this makes it easier to see the content in your workspace.

WordArt gallery

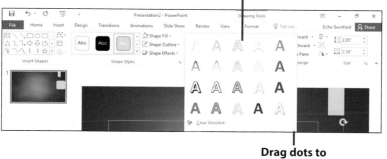

Drag dots to resize gallery

At the bottom of many galleries is an Options button. Click this to open the Formatting pane, where you can access more settings related to the tool. See more about the Formatting pane later in this chapter.

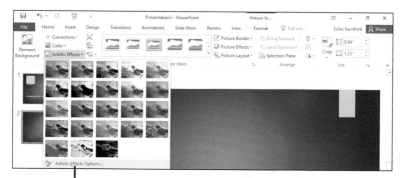

Click for additional options

On the Insert tab, click the Add-ins button. Add-ins are tools that extend PowerPoint's capabilities. To see examples, click the Store option and check out the available Office Add-ins.

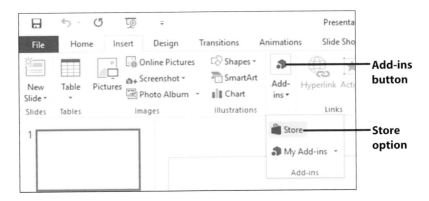

Select an add-in and click Trust to open a pane with the add-in tools. The next time you want to use it, click the Insert tab and then choose Add-ins, My Add-ins and select it from the list.

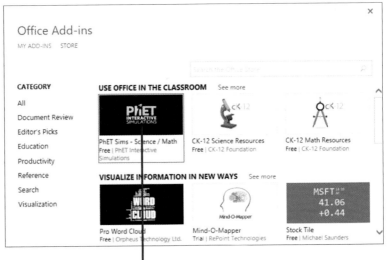

Screen Size Affects the Ribbon

Your Ribbon might look different than those pictured. It will adjust and expand or collapse some tool sets depending on your screen size and resolution.

The Shortcut Menu and Mini Toolbar

You can right-click text, an object on a slide, or other screen elements to see a shortcut menu with context-sensitive commands. If you right-click text on a slide, you'll also see a Mini Toolbar that provides quick access to common formatting commands. Right-click is your friend. You never know what you'll find!

1. Right-click text, and a Mini Toolbar with a full complement of text formatting options will appear. Click any tool on the Mini Toolbar to apply it to the text.

Select Text First

It's usually best to select text and then right-click to access the formatting options; otherwise, the formatting will be applied to a single word, which may not be what you want.

2. Right-click a shape or another object, and a Mini Toolbar with a Style gallery and Fill and Outline options appears.

3. Notice that the selection of tools that appears on the shortcut menu depends on the object you're right-clicking.

4. At the bottom of the shortcut menu is usually a Format <object> option. If you're right-clicking a shape, it will be Format Shape; if you're right-clicking a picture, it will be Format Picture; and so on. Click this to open the Formatting pane, where you will be able to access more formatting tools related to the object.

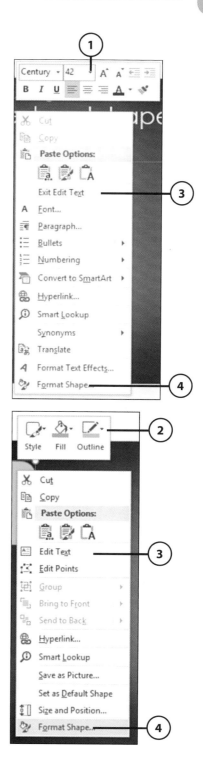

Backstage View

Click the File tab to access all file management tools. This is known as the Backstage view, and it's where you go to do things like open existing files, start new presentations, set PowerPoint options, print, and change the PowerPoint interface.

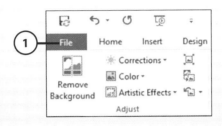

1. Click the File tab and you'll be taken to the Info screen, where you can see basic file properties and inspect your document or check for accessibility and compatibility issues. See Chapter 10, "Printing and Finalizing Your Presentation," for more on these options.

2. Click New to start a new presentation based on one of the themes when you already have PowerPoint open. This screen is similar to the Start screen, but it doesn't include the Recent Files list.

3. Click Open to open an existing presentation.

4. Click Save to save your presentation. By default, PowerPoint saves to OneDrive, but you can save to your hard drive or add another online location.

5. Click Save As to save your presentation with a different name or to a different location. As with Save, you'll have options to save to OneDrive, to your hard drive, or to add another online location.

6. Click Print to print your files. See Chapter 10 for more about printing.

7. Click Share to share your presentation with others. See Chapter 10 for more about sharing options.

8. Click Export to save your presentation as a PDF or XPS file, create a video or handouts, or save as a different file format. See Chapter 11, "Setting Up Your Slide Show," for more about exporting options.

9. Click Close to close the presentation without closing PowerPoint.

10. Click Account to change your Office background or theme, check for updates, check which version of PowerPoint you're using, sign out of your Microsoft account, or add a service such as YouTube, Facebook, or SharePoint.

11. Click Options to display the PowerPoint Options dialog box. Here, you can set various options, customize your Quick Access Toolbar, or access the Trust Center.

12. Click Feedback to send Microsoft your thoughts on Windows or Office.

>>>Go Further

WHICH OPTIONS DO I NEED TO SET?

Most of the PowerPoint settings available in the PowerPoint Options dialog box (choose File, Options) are optional, but there are a few you definitely want to set or change.

On the General tab, you can choose to bypass the Start screen when you start PowerPoint. If you do this, PowerPoint will open to a presentation based on the default theme.

On the Advanced tab, uncheck When Selecting, Automatically Select Entire Word. Otherwise, PowerPoint is liable to drive you batty when you can't select a single letter!

You can choose a different default image compression target or turn it off altogether in the Image Size and Quality section on the Advanced tab, but you'll have to remember to do this for every file. See Chapter 5, "Working with Pictures," for more about image compression settings.

Click the Quick Access Toolbar tab to customize the Quick Access Toolbar. This will help you tremendously and is covered later in this chapter. Customizing the Ribbon via the Customize Ribbon tab works similarly, but isn't usually necessary.

If you use Add-ins, you can manage them on the Add-Ins tab.

The Trust Center is where you can change settings related to macros and trusted locations and publishers. PowerPoint's settings are secure yet easy to work with, so you would rarely need to do anything here. For example, macros are set to be disabled with a notification. When you see the notification bar, you'll have the option to enable the macro.

The Editing Workspace (Normal View)

The Normal view is where you'll perform most editing tasks in PowerPoint.

The Ribbon appears at the top of Normal view. (You already know this!) The pane to the left with slide thumbnails is the Slides pane. The selected slide is highlighted in the Slides pane, and you edit the selected slide in the workspace. The status bar is at the bottom of Normal view. Right-click the status bar and uncheck items you don't want to show.

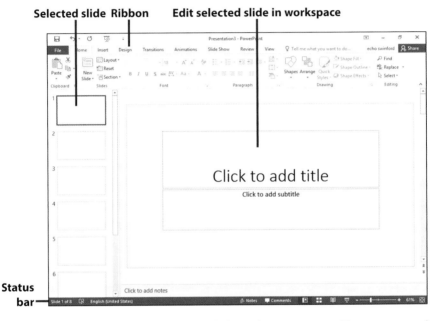

Click the Notes button to open and close the Notes pane. Type your speaker notes here, and they'll appear in Notes Page view (which you can print) and in Presenter view (which you can see while you present).

Click the Comments button to open and close the Comments pane. You can click and drag the edge of the various panes to resize them.

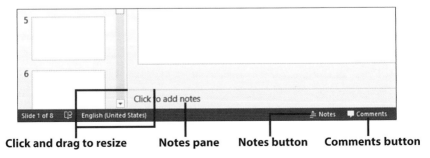

Click the Normal button to return to Normal view. Click the Slide Sorter button to switch to Slide Sorter view, where you see all the slides. This is a great view to use when you're rearranging slides in your presentation. Click the Reading View button to open Reading view. Click the Slide Show button to start a slide show from the selected slide.

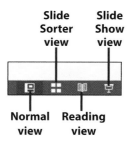

Use the Zoom slider or the +/– buttons to zoom in and out. Click the zoom level percent to open a dialog box where you can specify the zoom level. Click the last button to fit the slide to the current window. Think of this as a one-click "zoom to fit" button you can use when you're zoomed very far in or out.

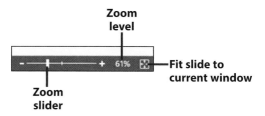

Other PowerPoint Views

You just learned about Normal view, but PowerPoint has a whole bunch of other views too. Head to the View tab to access most of them.

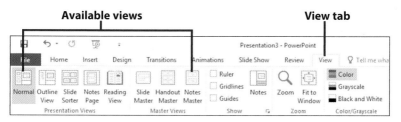

Click Outline view to open a pane similar to the Slides pane where you can type slide text in outline form. Type text for the slide title and then press Enter and Tab to create body text. Right-click in the outline to access additional outlining tools on the shortcut menu.

Slide Sorter view shows all your slides as thumbnails. You can also use the shortcut button on the status bar to access Slide Sorter view. You cannot edit slides in Slide Sorter view, but you can add transitions, create sections, and rearrange, hide, and delete slides. Use the Zoom slider on the status bar to resize the thumbnails.

Notes Page view shows you a slide thumbnail and a placeholder you can add notes to. Any notes already added in the Notes pane will appear in the placeholder. You cannot edit the slide in Notes Page view. Also, if you receive a prompt saying that changes you make in this view won't be saved, click Check Out or Save As to enable changes in Notes Page view to be saved.

Slide Sorter view

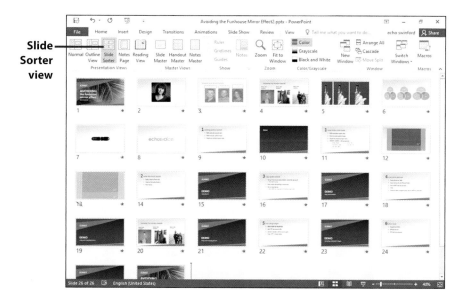

Reading view shows your presentation in a window. You can use it to play two presentations side by side, for example. Press Esc on your keyboard to exit Reading view.

Notes Page view

Reading View button

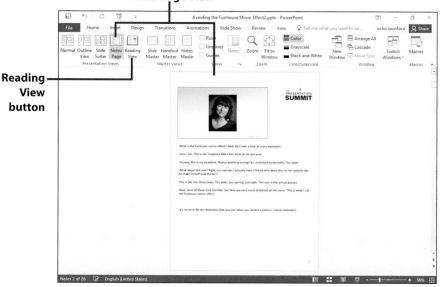

Returning to Normal View

From all other views, click the Normal button on the View tab or status bar to return to the typical PowerPoint editing workspace.

The slide master controls the overall look of your presentation. Slide Master view is where you can tweak background graphics, control placeholder formatting and positioning, and add things that should appear on every slide (such as your logo or a confidentiality statement). Learn more about slide masters, layouts, and Slide Master view in Chapter 12, "Creating Your Own Theme."

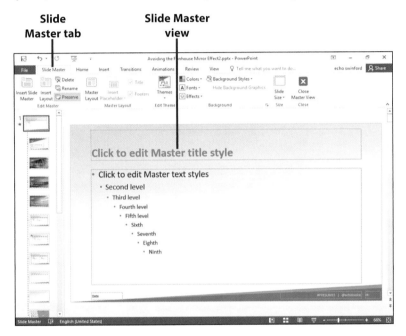

The handout master controls what printed handouts look like. Handout Master view is where you add any graphics that should appear on the handouts, such as a corporate logo. You cannot resize or reposition the slide thumbnails on the handout master; they are simply placeholders to show you where slides will appear on the printed handouts. Click the Slides Per Page button on the Handout Master tab of the Ribbon to see the other handout layouts.

The notes master controls what the notes pages look like. Notes Master view is where you add any graphics that should appear on all the notes pages. You can resize and reposition the slide thumbnail and notes text placeholder on the notes master.

Slide Show view is what your audience sees when you're presenting. In Slide Show view, your presentation is usually full-screen. Start your presentation from the Slide Show tab or from the Slide Show shortcut on the status bar. See Chapter 11 for more information about starting your presentation.

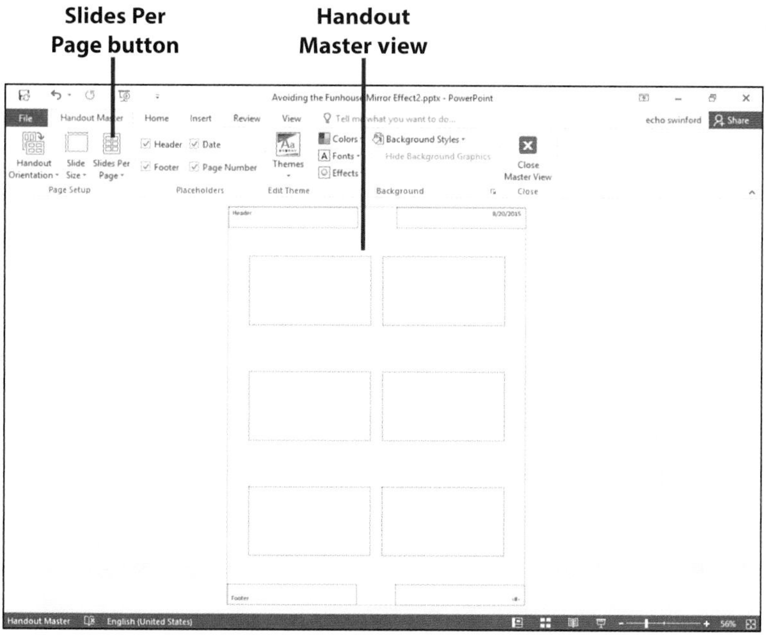

**Slides Per
Page button**

**Handout
Master view**

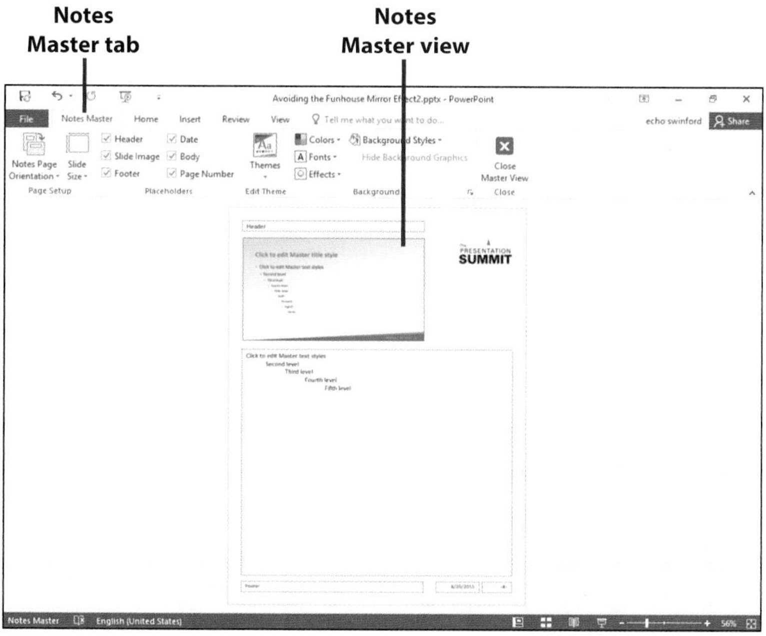

**Notes
Master tab**

**Notes
Master view**

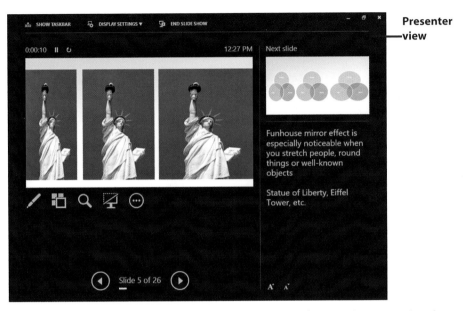

Presenter view

Presenter view is an optional view you can use when you're presenting. It shows your notes, slide thumbnails, and other features on your laptop while the Slide Show view displays on the screen your audience sees. See Chapter 11 for more information about Presenter view.

Formatting Panes

Formatting panes give you access to more tools than are available on the Ribbon. It's often a good practice to start the formatting with the tools on the Ribbon and then access the Formatting pane to perform any final tweaks that might be necessary. Use the dialog box launchers on the Ribbon or right-click and choose Format at the bottom of the shortcut menu to access a Formatting pane.

1. Insert a shape on a slide. Right-click it and choose Format Shape to open the Format Shape pane.

2. Click either of the tabs (headings) to access related tools. For example, click Shape Options to open tools related to the shapes. Click Text Options to open tools related to the text inside a shape.

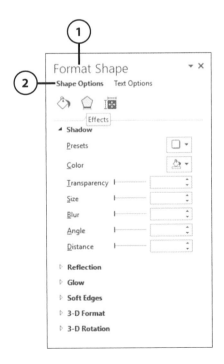

3. Hover over the icons to see what types of tools are in that group. The paint bucket represents Fill & Line options, the shape with a reflection represents Effects, and the measuring square represents Size & Properties. Click an icon to access those tools.

4. Click any heading in a pane to expand or collapse it.

5. Click Text Options to access settings that apply to text instead of to the shape. The icons that label each group of tools can help you distinguish. You can also choose Format Text Effects from the shortcut menu to directly access this heading in the Format Shape pane.

6. Explore the formatting panes for various objects. For example, the Format Picture pane adds a Picture group with tools for picture corrections, recoloring, and cropping. It also adds Artistic Effects in the Effects group since those tools can be used to format pictures.

Format Shape

Shape Options · · · Text Options

(3)

Effects

▲ Shadow

 Presets

 Color

 Transparency

 Size

(4) Blur

 Angle

 Distance

▷ **Reflection**

▷ **Glow**

▷ **Soft Edges**

▷ **3-D Format**

▷ **3-D Rotation**

Format Shape

Shape Options · · · **Text Options** — (5)

Text Effects

▲ Shadow

 Presets

 Color

 Transparency

 Size

 Blur

 Angle

 Distance

▷ **Reflection**

▷ **Glow**

▷ **Soft Edges**

▷ **3-D Format**

▷ **3-D Rotation**

Format Picture

(6)

▷ **Picture Corrections**

▷ **Picture Color**

▷ **Crop**

Dynamic Paste Preview

One of the really great features in more recent versions of PowerPoint is called dynamic paste preview. If you copy an object and then right-click to paste it, you'll be able to see how various paste options treat your content.

1. Insert a text box on a slide and type some text in it. Use the WordArt Styles on the Drawing Tools Format tab to quickly apply some formatting.

2. Select the text and either press Ctrl+C to copy it or click the Copy button on the Home tab.

3. Right-click the slide and hover over each of the Paste Options in turn to see how it treats your text. You'll see a preview of each option as you hover over it, and a ScreenTip will give you more information.

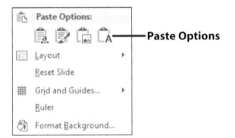 **Paste Options**

What Are the Different Paste Options?

The Paste Options you have will depend on the object you copied. It's pretty common to have Use Destination Theme as the first option. This means if you copy text or objects from another presentation, PowerPoint will use the formatting from the current (destination) presentation, not from the original one.

Keep Source Formatting is usually the next option. This means PowerPoint will retain the original formatting instead of using the current presentation's formatting. With Picture, the text or object will be pasted as a picture so it won't be editable. The Keep Text option only means that the text will be pasted without any formatting.

Customizing the Quick Access Toolbar

The Quick Access Toolbar helps you customize your PowerPoint interface for maximum productivity. As you get used to the tools on the Ribbon, you might find yourself clicking around trying to find certain tools.

Although the new Tell Me feature can certainly help with that, you don't want to use it all the time. Also, there are always tools you use all the time that you might want keep right at your fingertips. That's where the Quick Access Toolbar comes in. Your productivity will increase because you'll develop muscle memory as you use the tools on your Quick Access Toolbar instead of fumbling around on the Ribbon.

The Quick Access Toolbar appears by default in the upper-left corner of the PowerPoint interface, above the Ribbon. You can set it to show below the Ribbon so you don't have to travel your mouse quite so far to click its buttons. Also, if you have many tools on your Quick Access Toolbar, it will crowd against the presentation name and tabs at the top of the screen and be a hassle to work with.

Customize Your Quick Access Toolbar

You can right-click any button on the Ribbon and add it to your Quick Access Toolbar, or you can use the Quick Access Toolbar tab in the PowerPoint Options dialog box, where you'll have more options. A combination of both is what most people end up using.

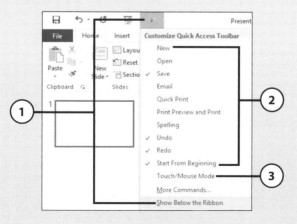

1. Click the arrow at the end of the Quick Access Toolbar and choose Show Below the Ribbon.

2. You can also check or uncheck any of the shortcuts on that menu to quickly add or remove them from the Quick Access Toolbar.

3. If you're using a touch-enabled device, the Touch/Mouse Mode button will appear on the default Quick Access Toolbar.

4. Right-click any tool on any tab of the Ribbon and choose Add to Quick Access Toolbar. The tool will appear at the end of the Quick Access Toolbar.

5. You can add galleries or individual tools from drop-down menus to the Quick Access Toolbar. For example, on the Home tab click Arrange, Align, and then right-click Align Center and choose Add to Quick Access Toolbar.

6. To remove a tool from the Quick Access Toolbar, right-click it and choose Remove from Quick Access Toolbar.

7. To rearrange tools on your Quick Access Toolbar, right-click anywhere on the Quick Access Toolbar and choose Customize Quick Access Toolbar. You can also click the File tab, Options, Quick Access Toolbar to access the customization dialog box.

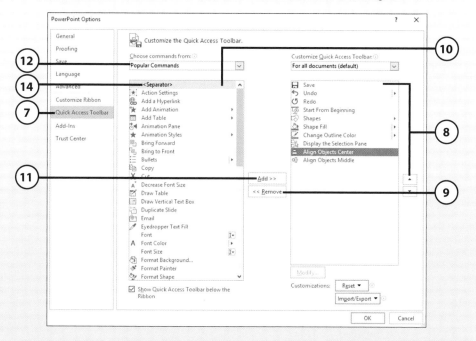

8. Notice that the current tools on your Quick Access Toolbar appear in the list box on the right. Select a tool and move it up or down using the arrows to the right of the list box.

9. Select a tool on the Quick Access Toolbar (in the list box on the right) and click Remove to delete it from the Quick Access Toolbar.

10. Notice that tools you can add to the Quick Access Toolbar appear in the list box on the left.

11. Select a tool in the list box on the left and click Add to add it to the Quick Access Toolbar. When you add a tool this way, it will be placed immediately after whichever tool you have selected on the right. Use the arrows to move it, if necessary. If nothing is selected on the right, the tool will be placed at the end of the list.

12. The available tools you see depend on the category selected in the Choose Commands From drop-down list. The default selection is Popular Commands.

13. Click the Choose Commands From arrow to choose from a different category. All Commands is an alphabetical list of every tool available. If you know where the tool you want to add is located, click that tab in the list. If you can't find a command you're looking for, select Commands Not in the Ribbon or All Commands.

14. The <Separator> option appears as an available tool at the top of every category. Separators are small vertical lines you can add to the Quick Access Toolbar as visual separators between groups of tools.

15. To restore the default Quick Access Toolbar, click Reset. If you've customized your Ribbon and don't want to reset those, choose Reset Only Quick Access Toolbar. Otherwise, you can choose Reset All Customizations.

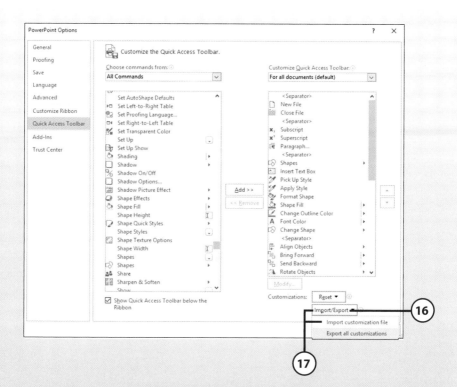

16. To save your Quick Access Toolbar as a backup or to use on a different computer, click Import/Export and choose Export All Customizations. (You can rename the file that's saved but leave the extension as .exportedUI.)

17. To import a Quick Access Toolbar, click Import/Export and choose Import Customization File. Navigate to a Quick Access Toolbar file you exported earlier and insert!

>>>Go Further

WHAT'S WITH ALL THE DIFFERENT SYMBOLS?

If you look in the list boxes in the PowerPoint Options dialog box, you'll see different symbols following many of the commands. Hover over a command to see the ScreenTip explaining what command it is.

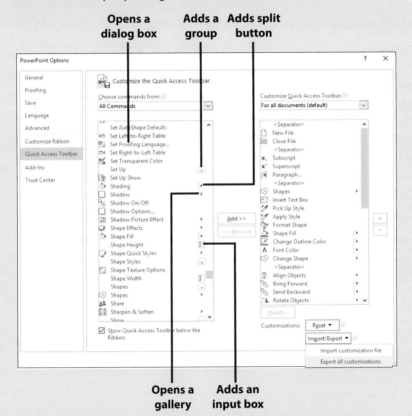

For example, if you see something like Animations Tab | Animation (GroupAnimations), you'll know that this command adds the entire Animation group to the Quick Access Toolbar. Click the button on the Quick Access Toolbar, and the group will appear under it.

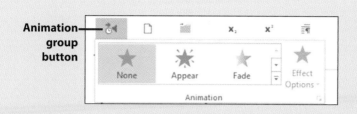

Command names ending in an ellipsis (…) open a dialog box. Those with arrows add split buttons or galleries. Boxes with "I" symbols are input boxes (like Shape Height and Shape Width) where you can type values.

A number of tools may seem to be the same at first glance. If you still can't tell the difference after reading the ScreenTip, just add the button to the Quick Access Toolbar and test it to see what it does. If it's not what you wanted, right-click the button and remove it!

Save your
presentation

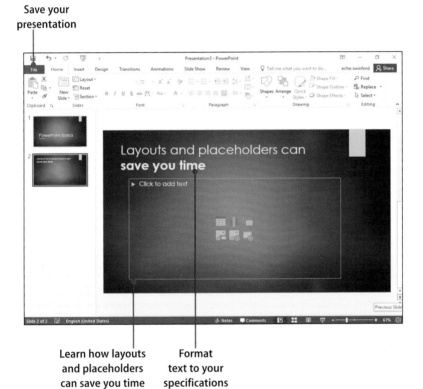

Learn how layouts
and placeholders
can save you time

Format
text to your
specifications

In this chapter, you will learn the basics of starting and saving a presentation and formatting text. Specific topics in this chapter include the following:

→ Starting a presentation
→ Formatting text
→ Changing slide size
→ Inserting existing slides
→ Saving your presentation

PowerPoint Basics

PowerPoint is so easy to use that often people don't learn the basics of PowerPoint and how placeholders and layouts can save them time. In this chapter, we'll cover the basics of starting a presentation, choosing a layout, entering text and other content into placeholders, and reusing existing slides. If you need to customize the underlying presentation theme, refer to Chapter 12, "Creating Your Own Theme."

Starting a Presentation

You learned in Chapter 1, "Getting Started," that when you open PowerPoint you'll see the Start screen, where you can opt to open an existing presentation or start a new one based on one of the stock theme designs. If you already have PowerPoint open, click the File tab and then click New to start a new presentation. You'll have access to the same stock theme designs as on the Start screen. Don't forget, to open an existing presentation, click File, Open as you learned in Chapter 1. Or from the Start screen, click Open Other Presentations.

Choose a Look for Your Presentation

All presentations are based on a theme. Even the Blank Presentation is based on a theme named "Office Theme." To begin this exercise, close and reopen PowerPoint if necessary so that you're looking at the Start screen.

Search for online themes

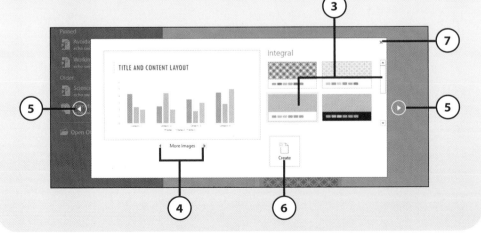

1. On the Start screen, scroll through the available themes. Click a theme once to select it and open the preview window.

2. Or double-click a theme thumbnail to bypass the preview window and create the presentation.

3. In the theme preview window, click any variant on the right to preview. Most stock themes have at least four variants. Some, like Integral, have more. Use the scrollbar to see them all. You can double-click any variant to create the presentation.

4. Each stock theme has five slide preview images. To see more previews for the selected variant, click the More Images arrows below the slide preview.

5. Click the arrows next to the large preview window to see a different theme.

6. Click the Create button to create the presentation based on the selected variant.

7. Or click the X to close the preview window and return to the Start screen.

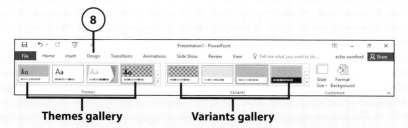

Themes gallery   **Variants gallery**

8. If you jump the gun and create the presentation before selecting the theme or variant you wanted, click the Design tab and choose a theme or variant from the galleries. You can always change the theme and variant for any presentation on the Design tab, but it's generally easier if you start the presentation based on the theme you plan to use.

Now You See It, Now You Don't

As you learned in Chapter 1, the themes that appear on the Start screen and the File, New screen may change. Pin a theme into place if you want to make sure it's available. If you don't see the theme you want, or if you'd just like to see what else might be an option, you can search for other themes online. Click a category in the Suggested Searches or input your own term in the search box.

By the way, you may already be familiar with the concept of a PowerPoint template, which provides formatting and layouts for your presentation. A theme is essentially the same as a template, but a theme can be applied to PowerPoint files, Word files, and Excel files. If you're curious about other differences between themes and templates, head to Chapter 12.

Add Slides

When you begin a new presentation, PowerPoint supplies the title slide by default. You can add as many slides as you need to a presentation.

1. Click in the title placeholder and type your presentation title.

2. Click in the subtitle placeholder and type a subtitle or other text, such as your name. Or don't type anything and just leave it blank.

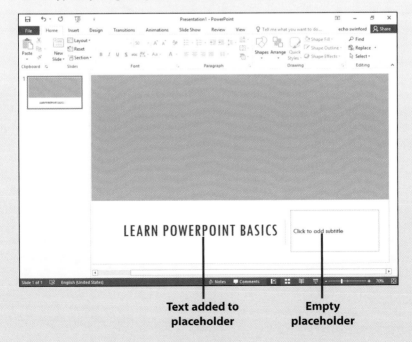

Text added to placeholder

Empty placeholder

Empty Placeholders

Empty placeholders won't show in Slide Show view. You can tell an empty placeholder by its dotted outline. You won't see this outline on a placeholder you've added text to. An empty placeholder displays text such as "Click to add title" or "Click to add subtitle." This promt text also won't show in Slide Show view.

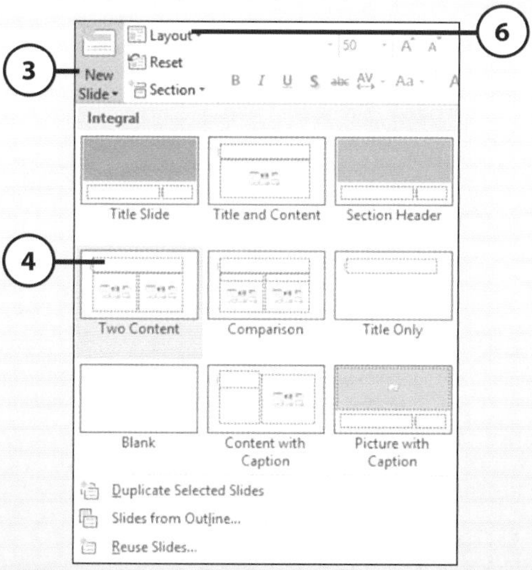

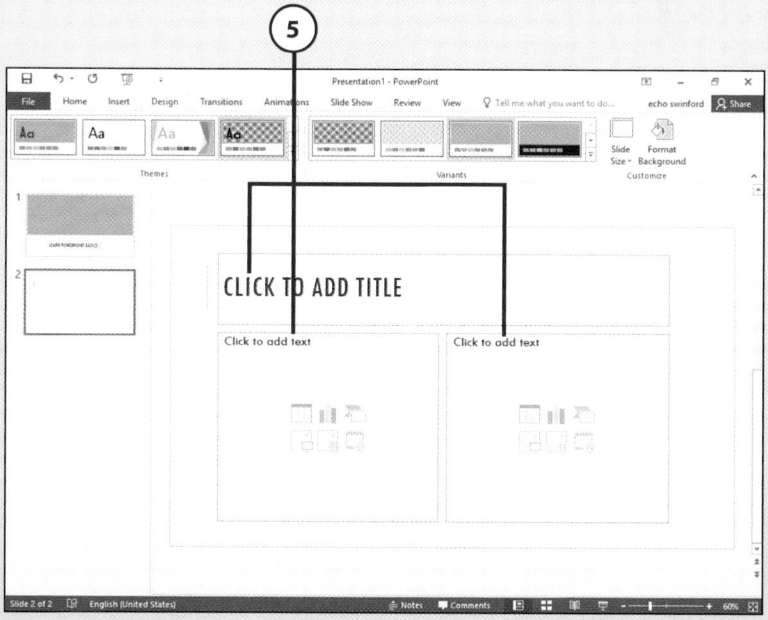

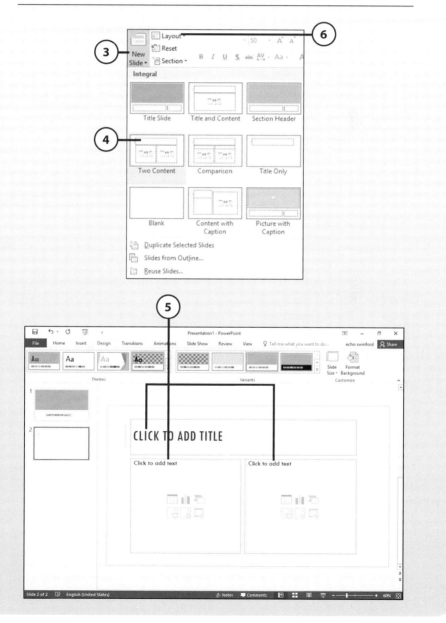

3. On the Home tab, click the bottom of the New Slide button to open the gallery.

4. Click the layout thumbnail to add a slide based on that layout.

Choosing a Slide Layout

If you know you need a slide with text beside a chart or diagram, choose the Two Content layout. If you plan to add a slide title and a large chart, choose Title and Content. For a large diagram or image with no slide title, choose Blank.

---

5. Click in each placeholder to add text or other content.

6. To change the layout of an existing slide, click the Layout button and choose a different layout. For example, change from a Title and Content layout to the Two Content layout. The placeholders will reposition themselves.

>>>Go Further
PLACEHOLDERS CAN SAVE YOU TIME

Placeholders are preformatted, prepositioned repositories for your content. Rather than deleting them and starting over from scratch with a text box from the Shapes gallery, let the placeholders work for you. If you don't like the way a placeholder is formatted or positioned by default, you can change that in Slide Master view. Chapter 12 teaches you how.

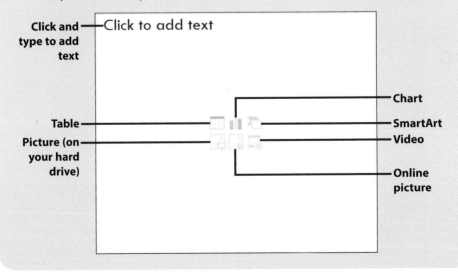

There are different kinds of placeholders. Title placeholders are used for title text. Content placeholders can hold seven kinds of content: text, table, chart, SmartArt graphic, picture (on your hard drive), online picture, or video. Click in a placeholder and type to add text or click the appropriate icon to add that type of content.

Using the Top of the New Slide Button

When you click the top of the New Slide button (or press Ctrl+M), PowerPoint will bypass the New Slide gallery and add a slide after the slide you've selected. The new slide will use the same layout as the selected slide. There's one exception: If the slide you've selected uses the Title Slide layout, PowerPoint will add a Title and Content slide next.

Changing Layouts

When you change a slide's layout, sometimes you'll end up with "orphaned" placeholders. For example, let's say you created a slide using a Two Content layout and added text on the left and a chart on the right. When you change to a Title and Content layout, the left placeholder will reposition and reformat itself into the one wide content placeholder that the Title and Content layout has. The chart in the right placeholder will become "orphaned" and will probably jump to the left or right edge of the slide.

You can still resize, move, and format the placeholders and content on the slide, but if you click Reset, the placeholders will reposition themselves to their default position and formatting. If you change back to a Two Content layout, PowerPoint will recognize the orphaned placeholder and treat it as a related placeholder again.

Formatting Text

Although placeholders provide the initial formatting, you may find that you want to apply additional formatting to your text. Bold, italics, and shadows are common additions, as are changing the font color and size.

You may also find that you want to tweak the line spacing or add tabs. Those settings are available in the Paragraph group of the Home tab.

If you find that you're changing these settings on all your text slides, make your life easier and apply that formatting to the placeholders in Slide Master view. The formatting will be preapplied when you create slides, and you won't have to spend the time and effort to format every slide as you build it. See Chapter 12 to learn how to customize the placeholders on the slide master.

Add Text in a Placeholder

Use your Tab key or the Increase List Level and Decrease List Level buttons on the Home tab to indent and unindent your text in a content placeholder.

1. Start a new presentation based on the Organic theme and then add a new slide based on the Title and Content layout.

2. Click in the body content placeholder (where it says, "Click to add text") and type some text. Press Enter to begin a new line of text.

3. Before typing the next line, press Tab to demote the text to second-level text. The bullet point will indent. Type some text for the second level and press Enter.

4. Continue typing text, pressing Enter each time you want to create a new bullet point.

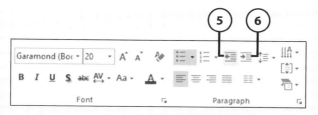

5. Use the Decrease List Level button to promote (unindent) text.

6. Use the Increase List Level button to demote (indent) text.

If the Primary Bullet Doesn't Have a Bullet

On some templates, the first-level text doesn't have a bullet point. In that situation, you'll need to use the Decrease List Level button or the shortcut Alt+Shift+right keyboard arrow to indent the text because Tab will move the text over but won't actually demote and format it like a second- or lower-level bullet.

7. If you place the insertion point between the bullet point and the first text character, you can use Shift+Tab to promote or Tab to demote the bullet point.

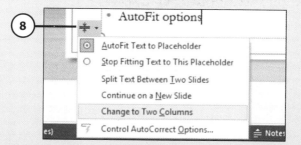

8. If you type enough text to fill the body placeholder, often the AutoFit setting will kick in. This setting automatically decreases the font size and sometimes adjusts the line spacing to fit more text in the placeholder. Click the AutoFit Options button to choose a different behavior.

Don't Brain Dump on Your Slides

Bulleted text is designed to be short phrases, not entire sentences, and certainly not a complete brain dump. If you're worried you're going to forget to say something, type that information in the Notes pane, which houses your speaker notes. You'll be able to print the notes pages or see the notes in Presenter view, so you won't need to have every little thing on the slide. In fact, sometimes it's helpful to start by typing everything you want to say in the Notes pane and then copying the necessary bits of text to your slide.

Streamlining your text is a good practice for your entire presentation, not just the text slides. You want the audience to listen to what you're saying and not have to spend a lot of time reading every bit of text on the slide.

On that note, it's also important to make sure the text that is on your slide is readable. Generally, the more text crammed on your slide, the smaller the font must become. Text that is too small to be read does nobody any good.

Format Text

Text formatting options are available on the Home tab and on the Mini Toolbar that appears when you right-click text on a slide. Continue using the Organic theme for this exercise.

1. Create a slide using the Title and Content layout and type some text in the content placeholder.

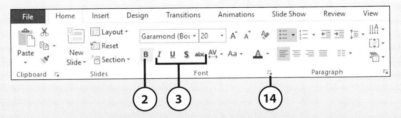

2. Select a word or phrase and then click the B button on the Home tab to make the text bold.

3. Click the I button to apply italics, the U to add an underline, or the S to add a text shadow. Click the Strikethrough button to add strikethrough to the text.

A Few Formatting Tips

Usually you'll want to apply the shadow to all text in a placeholder. If you want to add a shadow to all placeholders throughout the presentation, you can do so on the slide master.

Generally, you'll apply bold or italics to a word or phrase to highlight it. Changing color is another good way to highlight specific text. Use underlines sparingly—they usually look old-school.

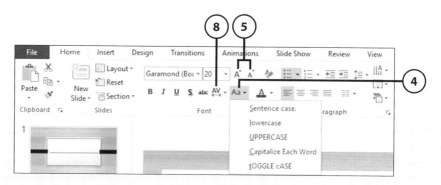

4. Click the Change Case button and then select an option.

Don't Capitalize Every Word

You'll almost always want to use sentence case (in which only the first letter of the first word is capitalized) for body text. It's also common to use sentence case for slide titles. Capitalizing every word of the titles can often make your slides look dated.

5. Click the Increase Font Size and Decrease Font Size buttons to make the selected text larger or smaller. If you want to apply this to all the text in a placeholder, select the entire placeholder by clicking its edge.

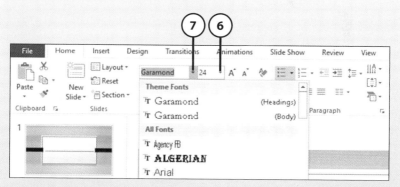

6. Change the font size by clicking the Font Size arrow and choosing a different size from the list. You can also click in the Font Size box and input your own font size value.

7. You can change the font face by clicking the Font arrow and choosing a different font. Changing the font generally isn't recommended except for small bits of text.

8. Click the Character Spacing button to widen or tighten the space between letters. Click More Spacing at the bottom of the drop-down list to open a dialog box with additional settings. Be careful here—a tiny bit of character space change goes a very long way. You don't want your letters to look smooshed together!

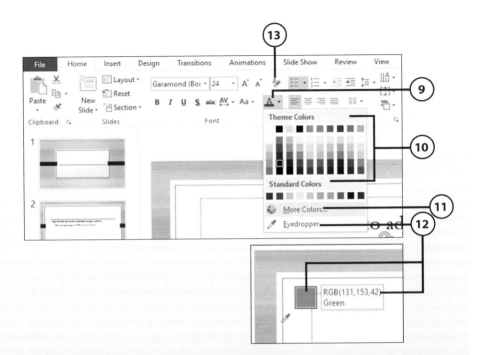

9. Click the Font Color button to apply the color you see in the strip on the button. Or click the Font Color arrow to open the color palette with additional choices.

10. Choose a font color by clicking a swatch under Theme Colors or Standard Colors.

11. Or click More Colors to input your own RGB or HSL colors for the font.

12. Or click the Eyedropper and then hover over any other object in the workspace. A preview color and ScreenTip will tell you which color is selected. Click to apply this color to the font.

Select Any Color with the Eyedropper

To select a font color from outside of the workspace, click the Eyedropper and don't release the mouse button. Move the mouse anywhere on your screen (even to other programs or the desktop). When the ScreenTip and preview indicate the color you want to select, release the mouse button.

---

13. Click the Clear Formatting button to clear all formatting from the selected text.

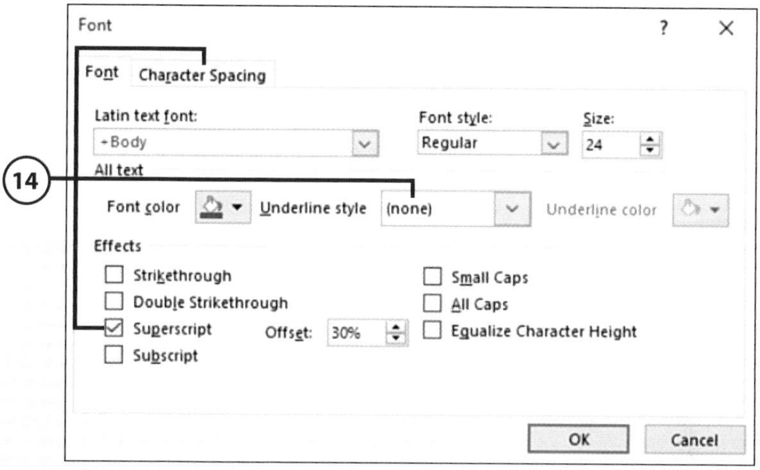

14. Click the Font dialog box launcher to access additional settings you can apply to the selected text, such as underline color and style, small caps, and superscript and subscript. You can get to the Character Spacing settings here as well.

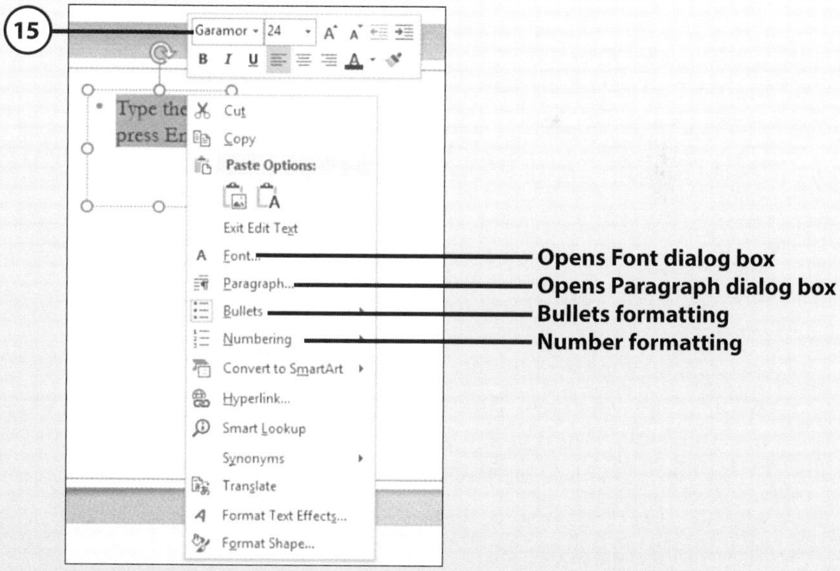

Opens Font dialog box
Opens Paragraph dialog box
Bullets formatting
Number formatting

15. When you select text, the Mini Toolbar will appear briefly. Or right-click text and the Mini Toolbar will appear above the shortcut menu. Click any of the tools on the Mini Toolbar or shortcut menu to use them.

Selecting Text

Here are some tips for selecting text:

- Click inside a text box or placeholder and then drag your mouse to select the text you want.
- Double-click inside the placeholder to select an entire word.
- Triple-click to select an entire "paragraph" or bulleted line of text.
- If you're having trouble selecting letters or parts of words, check File, Options, Advanced to make sure you have unchecked the option When Selecting, Automatically Select Entire Word.
- You can also use the same keyboard shortcuts you use in Word. Click inside a text box, press Shift, and then press any of the four arrow keys to select letters in that direction. Press Ctrl+Shift and then press the arrows to select entire words. Ctrl+B applies bold, Ctrl+I applies italics, and Ctrl+U applies underlining to the selected text.

>>>*Go Further*

STICK WITH THEME FONTS

Fonts can be tricky in PowerPoint. Here's the scoop.

Every presentation includes a set of theme fonts. You can see which ones these are by clicking the Font arrow and looking for the two at the top labeled Headings and Body.

All of the stock themes in PowerPoint use the font marked Headings in their slide titles. All other text is considered body text and is formatted with the font marked Body. Sometimes a theme (Organic, for example) uses the same font for Headings and Body. Others use different fonts for each. If you apply a different theme to the presentation, the Headings font in that theme will be applied to your slide titles, and the Body font in that theme will be applied to the rest of the text. It's a quick way to change the look of your whole presentation because everything uses the theme font—even charts, SmartArt, tables, and so on.

You can select a different set of theme fonts on the Design tab. Chapter 12 gives you more information about this.

If you apply a different font to text using the Font drop-down list on the Home tab, that text is now using a font that's "off theme." When you apply a different theme to the presentation, that font won't be replaced. Because of this, it's really best to use the Font drop-down list to replace only small bits of text that you know should look different from everything else.

One last thing. If you choose File, Options, and click the Save tab, you'll see a check box labeled Embed Fonts in the File. Unfortunately, only TrueType fonts (with the extension .ttf) can be embedded, and even some TrueType fonts cannot be. Even more important, Mac PowerPoint doesn't recognize embedded fonts, so any users who open your presentation in Mac PowerPoint will see a different font applied to that text. As frustrating as it is, it's best to stick with safe fonts such as Arial, Calibri, and Times New Roman. If you want to use a different font, at least test to see what your presentation looks like on a computer without that font installed.

Format Paragraphs

In addition to formatting text, you can format other settings that affect text but that are considered paragraph settings. These include things like bullets and numbering, indents, horizontal and vertical alignment, and line spacing.

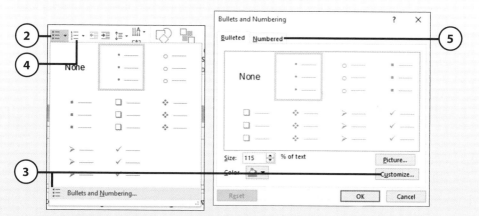

1. Using any theme, create a slide using the Title and Content layout and type some text in the content placeholder.

2. Click the Bullets button to turn the bullet points on or off. Click the Bullets button arrow to select another type of bullet from the stock sets.

3. Click Bullets and Numbering at the bottom of the gallery to open the Bullets and Numbering dialog box, where you can specify the color and size of bullets. Click the Customize button to choose a different bullet character altogether. Usually you'll do this on the slide master.

4. Click the Numbering button on the Home tab to change from a bullet point to a number. Click the Numbering button arrow to open a gallery with different numbering options.

5. Click Bullets and Numbering at the bottom of the Numbering gallery to open the Bullets and Numbering dialog box, where you'll use the Numbered tab to specify color, size, and what number to start with.

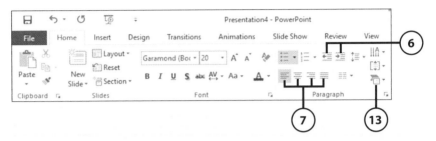

6. Click the Decrease List Level and Increase List Level buttons to indent and unindent text. See "Add Text in a Placeholder," earlier in this chapter, for specifics.

7. Click the Align Left, Center, Align Right, or Justify buttons to left-align, center, right-align, or justify text.

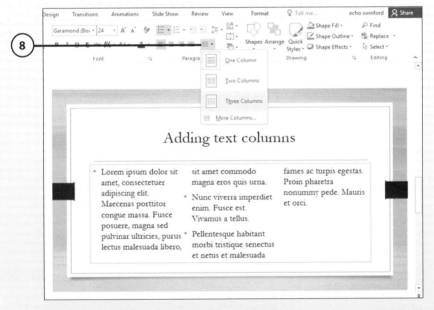

8. Click the Add or Remove Columns button to change your text into columns. This setting applies to the entire placeholder regardless of the specific text you've selected. Click More Columns at the bottom of the drop-down list to set gutter widths.

9. Click the Line Spacing button to select a different line spacing. Choose Line Spacing Options at the bottom if you need to tighten the line spacing. (The dialog box launcher on the Paragraph group also opens this dialog box.)

10. Click the Text Direction button to rotate text 90 degrees clockwise or counterclockwise or to stack it. This tool is used more often with small bits of text in shapes than with text in placeholders.

11. Click the Align Text button to vertically align the text to the top, bottom, or middle of the text box or placeholder.

12. Click More Options at the bottom of the Align Text drop-down list to access the text options in the Format Shape pane, where you can turn off the Autofit setting.

Shapes and Text Boxes Won't Resize?

Sometimes when you try to resize a shape, text box, or placeholder by dragging the bottom edge to make it longer, it snaps back into place and won't ever get bigger. That's usually because the Resize Shape to Fit Text setting has been turned on. To fix it, open the Format Shape pane, click Text Options, and select Do Not Autofit.

13. Click the SmartArt button to turn your text into a SmartArt graphic. See Chapter 6, "Creating Diagrams and Tables," for specifics.

>>>Go Further

HOW TO TIGHTEN UP LINE SPACING

The line spacing settings in the Paragraph dialog box are similar to those used in Word, so you need to know some tricks to use it more effectively in PowerPoint.

Line spacing refers to how much space is between lines of text in the same paragraph. In PowerPoint's case, this usually refers to the lines of text within a single bullet point.

The Space Before and Space After settings refer to how close or far away the next lines of bulleted text will be.

When you select Line Spacing from the Ribbon, you see 1.0 for single space, 2.0 for double space, and so on. You'll rarely need a double or triple space in PowerPoint; unfortunately, there's no option there to tighten the line space.

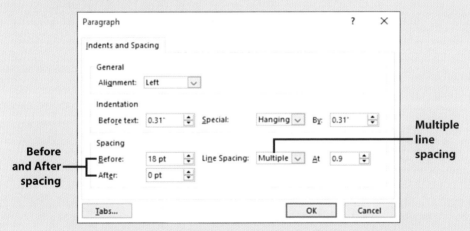

To tighten the line space, select Line Spacing Options at the bottom of the Line Spacing drop-down list. Change Single to Multiple, and then type .9 for the value to represent nine-tenths of the single line space. Finally, increase the Before spacing to at least half the font size so there's at least half a line between bullets. For example, if the font is 24-point, click and type 12 or 15 (or more!) in the Before text box.

Tightening the line space itself and then increasing the space before or after the text can help visually separate it and make it easier to read. If you use single spacing and don't put enough space before and after, sometimes all the text tends to run together.

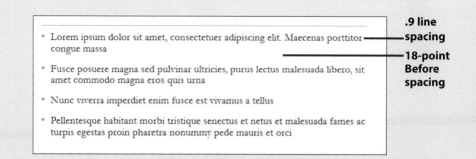

.9 line spacing

18-point Before spacing

Generally speaking, you won't want to go below .75 for a tight line, or the ascenders and descenders of letters may be cut off. Also, it's easier to adjust the before and after line spacing for a single bit of text on a slide if you use only the Before spacing setting. In printed documents with styles (like you have in Word or InDesign), it makes sense to use both, but that's rarely the case in PowerPoint.

On occasion you'll need to tweak line spacing on a particular slide or text box to make text fit or look more balanced, but usually you'll want to do this once on the slide master. Changing line spacing on all text in a presentation just isn't an efficient use of time.

Format Indents and Tabs

PowerPoint actually has pretty good tab control. You can set left, right, center, and decimal tabs. Control indents and tabs on the ruler or in the Paragraph dialog box.

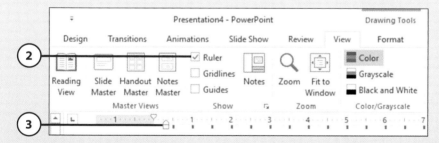

1. Create a slide using the Title and Content layout and type some text in the content placeholder.

2. Turn on the ruler by going to the View tab and clicking the Ruler option.

3. Click inside your text to see the indent markers on the Ruler.

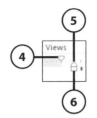

4. The downward-pointing indent marker on the top of the ruler indicates where the bullet is placed. Drag it to another position on the ruler to reposition the bullet.

5. The upward-pointing indent marker indicates where the text begins (the hanging-indent setting). Drag it into position on the ruler to change the indent.

6. The square below the two indent markers moves the other two together as one unit rather than independently.

Working with Indent Markers

Changes to the indent-marker positions apply only to the bullet points you've selected. Press Ctrl while dragging an indent marker for finer control over its positon.

7. Click the Paragraph dialog box launcher on the Home tab to create indents "by the numbers." The Before text value is the equivalent of the downward-pointing indent marker that determines where the bullet point is positioned. The Hanging indent setting is the distance between the text and the bullet, which is the same as the upward-pointing indent marker.

8. The gray marks under the ruler show the default tab stops. Click the Tabs button in the Paragraph dialog box to access these settings.

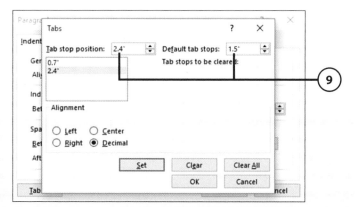

9. Change the Default tab stops setting by typing a value in the box or using the up and down arrows. You can also specify any specific tab stop using the Tab Stop Position setting.

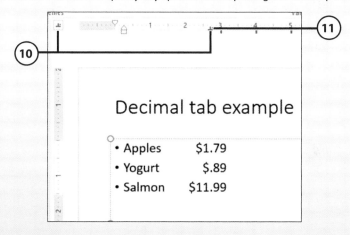

10. Sometimes the easiest way to add a tab is visually. Click the tab type button to the left of the ruler until you see the type of tab you want to add (left, center, right, or decimal) and then click on the ruler where you want to position the tab.

11. Click and drag the tab indicator on the ruler to reposition it. Click and drag it off the bottom edge of the ruler to remove it.

Tips on Working with Tabs

If there's already text in the placeholder, select all the text before adding a tab so that it applies to all the text. Otherwise, the tab stop will apply only to the paragraph of text your insertion point is in when you set the tab.

If there's not already text in the placeholder, any tab added to the first empty bullet will apply to all the text.

To add a tab to text when typing in a table, press Ctrl+Tab. Otherwise, pressing Tab will just move you to the next cell.

Changing Slide Size

One of the first things you might notice when you start a new presentation based on a stock theme is the widescreen slide. It's true! PowerPoint has been using a 16:9 aspect ratio by default since Office 2013 was released. This actually makes a lot of sense because most laptops and newer projectors are designed as 16:9 widescreens rather than the old 4:3 we used back in the Office 2010 days.

The actual size of the slide in PowerPoint 2016 is 7.5" tall x 13.33" wide. There's a good reason for this. The old 4:3 slide was also 7.5" tall (x 10" wide). Because these two different aspect ratios share the same slide height, it makes it easier for you when you're reusing slides or converting them from 4:3 to 16:9 (and vice versa) because you don't have to resize text or other content as much.

Change Slide Size Without Distorting Content

PowerPoint has a slide size tool to help you convert between 4:3 slides and 16:9 slides.

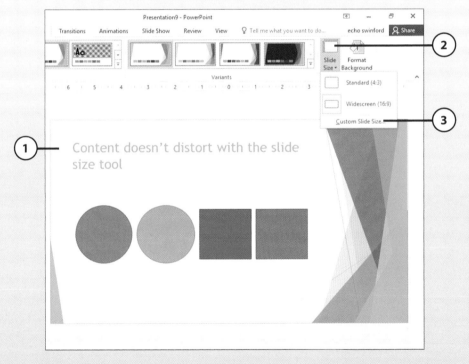

1. Create a new presentation. Add some circles and squares to it so you can easily see that the content is not distorted. See Chapter 3, "Creating and Working with Shapes," to learn how to create perfect circles and squares.

2. On the Design tab, click the Slide Size button and choose Standard (4:3).

3. Or to convert to a different size, choose Custom Slide Size.

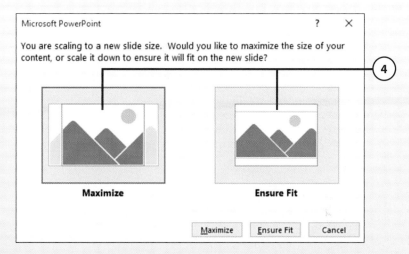

4. Choose whether to maximize your content or ensure that it fits. If you use the Maximize option, some objects might fall off the edges of the slide when you convert from 16:9 to 4:3. If you use Ensure Fit, everything will become slightly smaller to fit all contents onto the width of the new 4:3 slide.

Converting from 4:3 to 16:9

If you convert from 4:3 to 16:9, you won't be asked to maximize or ensure the fit because the 4:3 contents will fit on the 16:9 slide without being made smaller.

It's Not All Good

Dealing with Distorted Background Graphics

The Slide Size tool keeps the contents of your slide from distorting, but it may not be so kind to your background graphics.

If you are not using a stock Microsoft theme, your background graphics may be distorted when you use the Slide Size tool. The variants built into the Microsoft themes enable these seamless background transitions, but most corporate templates don't have these available.

If you resize your slides and the background graphics are distorted, there are a couple of things you can do:

- If you have a template that's the correct aspect ratio for the new slide size, open it and paste in the resized slides.

- If you have to rebuild the background graphics on your newly sized slides, open both the original presentation and the newly sized presentation in Slide Master view. Copy the background graphics from the old to the new and reposition them as necessary.

Another thing that can happen is a leftover variant from a stock Microsoft theme is reapplied when you resize your slides, and your background graphics disappear altogether. This happens when you've created a template based on one of the stock Microsoft themes but you've never actually saved it as a Template (.potx) file, which strips out the leftover variants. To resolve this, open the affected file (which probably has a .pptx extension) and save it as a PowerPoint Template (.potx). After you've stripped the variants in this manner, you can resave the file as a PowerPoint Presentation with a .pptx extension again.

Inserting Existing Slides

Most people seem to have hundreds, if not thousands, of slides hanging around that they'd like to be able to reuse. Knowing a few different techniques for using existing slides can help.

Copy and Paste Slides

The most straightforward way to reuse slides is to copy them from one presentation and paste them into another.

1. Open an existing presentation that includes the slides you want to copy. Call this the source presentation.

2. Open the presentation you want to add the existing slides to. Call this the destination presentation.

3. In the source presentation, select the slides you want to copy. You can select them in the Slides pane or in Slide Sorter view.

4. To select a range of slides, click the first slide thumbnail and then press Shift and click the last slide in the range. To select slides that are not next to each other, press Ctrl while clicking the thumbnails.

5. After the slides are selected, press Ctrl+C to copy, right-click and choose Copy, or click the Copy button on the Home tab.

6. Switch to the destination presentation where you want to paste the slides. You can paste the slides into the Slides pane or Slide Sorter view.

7. Press Ctrl+V to paste the slides. They will convert to the theme and colors of the destination presentation.

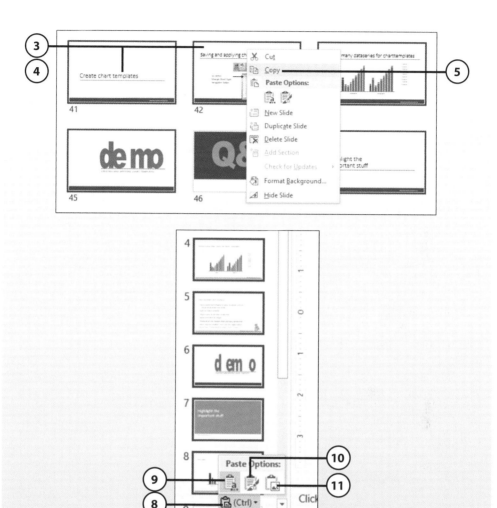

8. Right after you paste, look for the Paste Options button and click it. The Paste Options button appears immediately after you paste and disappears when you do something else—such as type text or move a slide.

9. Hover over each of the Paste Options to see a ScreenTip explaining what it does. The first option is Use Destination Theme, which is what PowerPoint just did when you pasted.

10. The second paste option is Keep Source Formatting. Click this to retain the theme from your source presentation.

11. The third paste option is Picture. This pastes the first selected slide as a picture on a slide in the destination presentation.

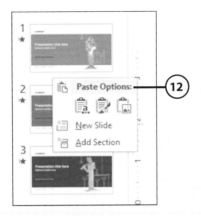

12. An alternative way to paste is to right-click in the Slides pane or in Slide Sorter view and click one of the Paste Options in the shortcut menu.

13. If any of your slides doesn't pick up the destination formatting as you expect, select it and then click the Layout button. Choose a different layout for the slide.

Destination Formatting Doesn't Apply

If your slide didn't pick up the destination formatting when you pasted it, you probably have an orphaned layout. This happens sometimes when the destination theme has different layouts than the source presentation and PowerPoint isn't sure what layout you want to use for the slide. Choose another layout for that slide or modify the graphics on the master layout so it matches the destination theme.

Sometimes the slide will pick up the destination background graphics, but the placeholders are in the wrong place or the formatting hasn't applied completely. This can also happen when you choose a new layout. To resolve it, click the Reset button (next to the New Slide button) to reset all the placeholders. Sometimes you'll need to click Reset twice to reapply all the formatting.

Reuse Slides

PowerPoint has a Reuse Slides tool you may find handy. With this option you don't need to open a separate copy of the source presentation.

1. Open a presentation you want to add existing slides to. This is the destination presentation.

2. Click the bottom of the New Slide button, and at the very bottom of that gallery, click Reuse Slides.

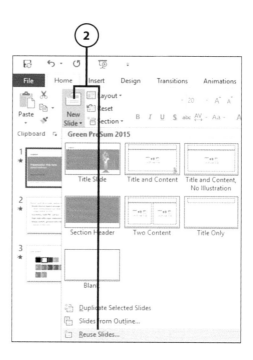

3. In the Reuse Slides pane, click the Browse button and select Browse File. (If your company uses a SharePoint Slide Library, you can choose Browse Slide Library.)

4. Find the presentation with the slides you want to reuse, select the file, and click Open. This is the source presentation. Hover over the slide thumbnails in the Reuse Slides pane to see larger previews.

5. Click a thumbnail to add the slide. Or right-click any thumbnail and select Insert All Slides if you want to insert all slides.

6. You can select Apply Theme to All Slides or Apply Theme to Selected Slides on the shortcut menu if you want to apply the source theme to the slides in the destination presentation.

7. Before inserting slides, check the Keep Source Formatting button if you want to keep the original formatting of the source slides when they're inserted.

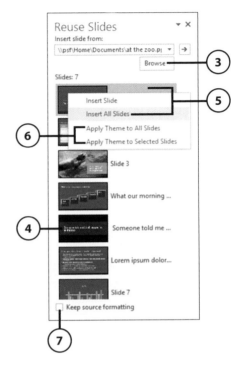

Resize Before Reuse

Whether you copy and paste slides or use the Reuse Slides pane, you'll have better results if you are working with files that are the same size. Inserting a 4:3 slide into a 16:9 presentation will distort the content. But you know that using the Slide Size tool prevents this distortion! So first use the Slide Size tool so both presentations are the same aspect ratio, and then combine the presentations.

>>>*Go Further*

BEST PRACTICES IN PRESENTATION DESIGN

Entire books could be—and have been—written about presentation design. If you're interested in taking your presentations to the next level, read *Presentation Zen* and *Presentation Zen Design* by Garr Reynolds, *slide:ology* and *Resonate* by Nancy Duarte, and *The Non-Designer's Presentation Book* by Robin Williams. These will help you focus on your content and introduce you to design principles that will serve your presentation well.

Saving Your Presentation

Of course you need to save your presentation now that you've at least gotten a good start on it. PowerPoint gives you what seems like dozens of formats to save as, but we're going to talk about the most common and basic ones here. Other options for saving and delivering are covered in Chapter 11, "Setting Up Your Slide Show."

If you've opened an existing presentation, you can press Ctrl+S or use File, Save to save. This resaves the file with the same name in its original location. If you're working with a brand-new presentation that has never been saved, clicking File, Save or pressing Ctrl+S will display the Save As screen instead. Either way, you should save your files periodically as you're working. PowerPoint does a good job of recovering files if Windows decides to reboot mid-project, but nothing beats having a recently saved file to return to just in case!

Save to OneDrive

PowerPoint's Save As screen defaults to OneDrive to encourage you to save there so your files are available on all your devices.

1. Open or create a presentation.

2. To save it, click File, Save As.

3. You'll notice that OneDrive, which is included as part of your Office 365 subscription, is the first option. It will already be selected (unless you have changed the default save setting in File, Options).

4. If you've been using OneDrive, folders you've created will be listed on the right. Click one to save the file in that folder.

5. The folder with your name followed by OneDrive (for example, Echo Swinford's OneDrive) is the root of your OneDrive account. You can save your file here, and it will be "loose"—that is, it won't be inside a folder, but it will be saved on OneDrive.

6. In the Save As dialog box, click inside the File Name box and rename your file.

7. Choose the type of file to save it as (Presentation, Template, Show, or another file type) from the Save As Type drop-down list.

8. Click Save to finish saving to OneDrive.

>>>Go Further

CREATE A ONEDRIVE FOLDER FROM POWERPOINT

If you need to create a new folder for your file on OneDrive, you can do that from within PowerPoint. On the Save As screen, click the root OneDrive folder. Then, in the Save As dialog box, right-click and choose New Folder. (On some systems you may need to choose New, then Folder from the flyout menu.) Name the new folder, press Enter, and then double-click the new folder and save your file inside.

Right-click and select New Folder

Save to Your Computer

You don't have to save to OneDrive; you can always opt to save the file directly to your hard drive instead.

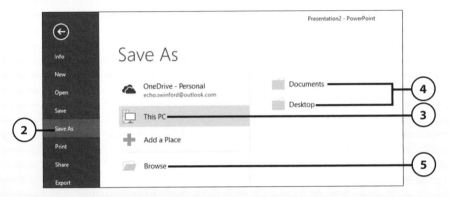

1. Open or create a presentation.

2. To save it, click File, Save As.

3. On the Save As screen, click This PC.

4. Click a folder on the right to save the file there.

5. Or click Browse to browse elsewhere on your hard drive.

6. In the Save As dialog box, click inside the File Name box and rename your file.

7. Choose the type of file to save it as (Presentation, Template, Show, or another file type) from the Save As Type drop-down list.

8. Click Save to finish saving to your hard drive.

Save as a Presentation or Show

Windows relies on the file type and extension to know what to do when you double-click a file in File Explorer. A PowerPoint Presentation file uses the extension .pptx, and it opens in Normal view to make it easy for you to edit. A PowerPoint Show file uses the extension .ppsx. It bypasses Normal view when double-clicked in File Explorer and opens directly in Slide Show view.

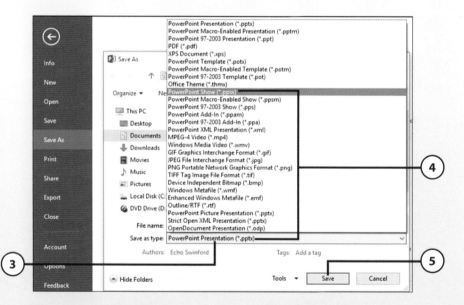

1. Open or create a presentation.

2. Click File, Save As. Choose to save to OneDrive or your computer.

3. Notice that the default setting is to save the file as a PowerPoint Presentation (.pptx).

4. Click the Save As Type drop-down and choose a different file type from the list.

5. Click Save to save the file.

Editing a PowerPoint Show

If you save your file as a PowerPoint Show (.ppsx), you can still edit it by open-
ing it from PowerPoint instead of double-clicking the filename in File Explorer.
Simply start PowerPoint and then choose File, Open and navigate to the
PowerPoint Show file.

>>>*Go Further*

SHOWING FILE EXTENSIONS

If you want to see file extensions (.pptx, .ppsx, and so on) in the Open
screen and Save As dialog box, you must turn them on in Windows. For
Windows 7, you can use the instructions in the first part of this blog post:
http://echosvoice.com/extract-pictures-video-and-audio-from-your-
presentations-in-3-easy-steps/. For Windows 8, 8.1, and 10, see the
instructions at http://www.file-extensions.org/article/show-and-hide-
file-extensions-in-windows-10.

Create and
duplicate
shapes

Format
shapes using
Quick Styles
and custom
formatting
tools

Rotate
objects

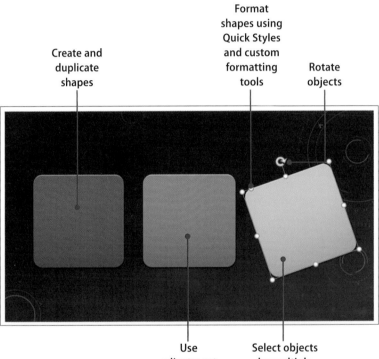

Use
adjustment
handles

Select objects
by multiple
methods

In this chapter, you will learn about inserting, formatting, and positioning shapes on slides. Specific topics in this chapter include the following:

→ Making and manipulating shapes
→ Formatting shapes
→ Formatting graphical text (WordArt)

Creating and Working with Shapes

One of the best things about PowerPoint is that it's actually a great drawing tool. You can choose from an extensive gallery of shapes, and there are tons of formatting options. PowerPoint also includes tools to help you position objects precisely so your graphical elements look exactly like you want them to.

Learning how to add, format, and position shapes is a good foundation for adding and formatting almost everything else in PowerPoint because most objects follow the same general process. If you run out of room on a slide while you're practicing the techniques in this chapter, just add a new one from the New Slide button on the Home tab or Insert tab. Choose the Title Only or Blank layout to give yourself maximum work space.

Making and Manipulating Shapes

The Shapes gallery probably seems like a pretty straightforward way to create shapes. Oh, but there's so much more! Many of the shapes have adjustment options you will want to take advantage of. You can even create your own shapes if PowerPoint doesn't have what you need.

Insert, Resize, and Rotate Shapes

Before you can format shapes, first you have to insert them onto a slide.

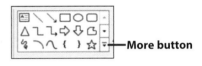

1. To create a shape, go to the Home tab or the Insert tab and click a shape in the Shapes gallery.

Expand the Gallery

Depending on your screen resolution, the Shapes gallery might already display some shapes on the Ribbon. Click the More button to expand the entire gallery.

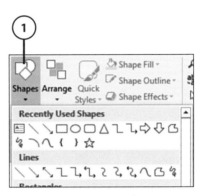

—More button

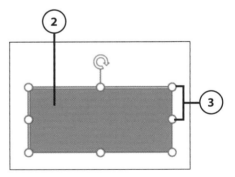

2. Click and drag on the slide to draw the shape. You can press Shift on your keyboard while you click and drag on the slide to create perfect circles (use the oval shape) and squares (use the rectangle shape).

3. Drag any selection handle to resize the shape. You can press Shift while dragging a corner handle to maintain the shape's aspect ratio. In other words, this keeps the shape's proportion intact.

Creating Quick 1" x 1" Shapes

Select a shape from the Shapes gallery and then just click the slide (and don't drag) to create a 1" x 1" shape. This is another great way to create perfect circles and squares.

4. Type the height in the Size group on the Drawing Tools Format tab and then press Enter.

5. Type the width in the Size group on the Drawing Tools Format tab and then press Enter.

6. Click the dialog box launcher in the Size group to open the Format Shape pane to the Size & Properties settings, where you can input specific values or percentages to size the shape.

7. Click the rotation handle and drag your mouse right or left to rotate a shape. You can press Shift while rotating if you want to constrain the rotation to 15-degree increments.

8. Or type the rotation value in the Format Shape pane. You can type a negative value if you want to rotate the shape counterclockwise.

9. Or use the Rotation tools on the Drawing Tools Format tab or in the Arrange tools on the Home tab to rotate or flip the shape.

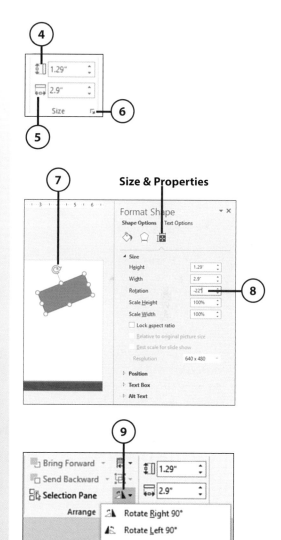

It's Not All Good

Sometimes when you rotate and flip shapes so they're perfectly positioned, the text inside them isn't oriented correctly. You can try changing the Text Direction setting in the Text Box section of the Format Shape pane, but usually it's easiest just to create a separate text box and drag it on top of the rotated shape.

Add Text and Text Boxes

You can add text to existing shapes or create a text box to hold text. The text boxes you add from the Shapes gallery are designed to hold short bits of text and don't really handle multiple levels of bulleted text well the way content placeholders do. Use them to label diagrams and to add text when formatting or positioning text in a shape is difficult.

1. To add text to an existing shape, select a shape such as a rectangle and start typing.

Just Start Typing!

Many people think that to add text to a shape, you must create a separate text box and drag it on top of the shape. The truth is, you can add text directly to shapes; you don't need extra text boxes.

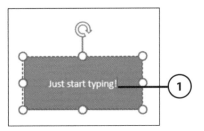

2. To insert a text box, open the Shapes gallery and click the Text Box shape.

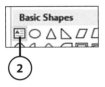

Buttons Everywhere

The Shapes gallery is available on the Home tab, on the Insert tab, and on various contextual tabs such as the Drawing Tools Format tab. You will also find a Text Box button directly on the Insert tab.

3. Click and drag on the slide to create a text box as wide as you need.

4. Type some text. If you don't type any text, the text box will disappear.

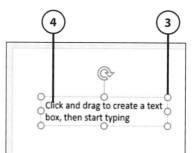

Shifting Shapes

Every time you use a shape, including the text box, it will move to the beginning of the Recently Used Shapes section at the top of the Shapes gallery. This makes it easy to find shapes you use frequently.

Duplicate Shapes

It's obviously faster to duplicate a shape than it is to re-create it. Here are a bunch of ways to duplicate shapes.

1. Click a shape to select it. Press Ctrl+D to duplicate the shape. Continue until you have as many copies as you want.

2. Click a shape to select it. Press Ctrl+C to copy the shape to the Clipboard. Then press Ctrl+V to paste it. Continue until you have as many copies as you want.

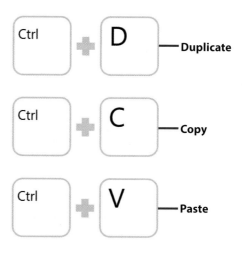

3. Right-click a shape and choose Copy and then right-click and choose the Use Destination Theme paste option. If you copied the shape from a different presentation, you'll also have a Keep Source Formatting paste option.

4. Select the shape. Click Copy and Paste on the Home tab.

5. Select the shape. Press Ctrl and drag the shape to create a copy. Let go of your mouse button before releasing the Ctrl key.

6. Select the shape. Press Ctrl and Shift while you drag the shape. This creates an aligned copy. Let go of your mouse button before releasing the Ctrl and Shift keys.

Select Objects and Shapes

Everyone has a favorite way to select shapes and other objects. Here are some of the options.

1. Click the edge of a shape to select it. Handles appear around the edge of the shape to indicate that it is selected.

2. Click inside a shape with text in it, and then press Esc on your keyboard to select the shape. You'll know when you have the shape selected because its edge will change from dashed to solid.

3. Click and drag over the shapes and objects you want to select. The entire object must be enclosed entirely within the marquee or it will not be selected.

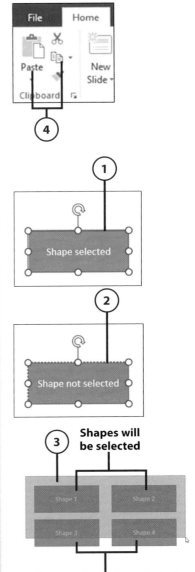

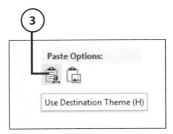

4. To select multiple shapes, select one shape and then press Shift on your keyboard while you click more shapes or objects.

5. Press Ctrl+A to select everything on the slide. To deselect some objects, press Shift while you click them.

Ctrl Can Be Shifty

It's common to press Ctrl while clicking to select multiple shapes. That's fine if it's what you're used to. However, pressing Ctrl while dragging an object is yet another way to create a copy. If you move the object the slightest little bit when you press Ctrl while clicking to select, you'll inadvertently end up with a copy. If you haven't already developed the Ctrl habit, now's a good time to develop the Shift habit instead.

Use the Selection Pane

The Selection pane is the best tool ever. It lists all the objects in your slide in order from top to bottom. Select an object in the Selection pane, and it's selected on the slide also, which is especially handy when one object is hiding behind others. You can even rename objects for easier identification.

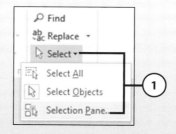

1. On the Home tab, click Select, Selection Pane.

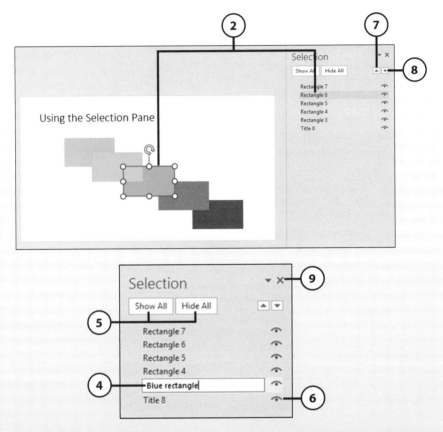

2. Click an object's name in the Selection pane, and the object is selected on the slide.

3. Press Ctrl and click object names to select multiple objects in the Selection pane.

4. Click an object to select it and then click again to rename it. Click away after you've typed the text.

5. Click Hide All to make all objects on the slide invisible. Click Show All to make all objects on the slide visible.

6. Click the eye icon beside an individual object to show or hide it.

7. Click the up arrow to move selected objects up a layer both in the pane and on the slide.

8. Click the down arrow to move selected objects down a layer both in the pane and on the slide.

9. Click the X to close the pane.

Think in Layers

Think of your slide as though it consists of layers. Each time you create or insert another object, it's automatically added to the top layer. The Selection pane lets you reorder the layers after you've added them.

Renaming objects in the Selection pane is useful if you plan to animate—especially if your slide is very complicated—because these object names also display in the Animation pane. It's a lot easier to distinguish Blue Circle from Red Circle than it is Circle 10 from Circle 14.

Control the Order of Shapes

In addition to reordering objects with the Selection pane, you can use the Order Objects tools to quickly move objects layer by layer or all at once to the back or front.

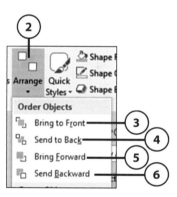

1. Select an object or objects.

2. On the Home tab, click Arrange and then click one of the Order Objects tools. These tools are also available on the Drawing Tools Format tab and the right-click menu.

3. Click Bring to Front to bring the selected object to the top layer.

4. Click Send to Back to send the selected object to the bottom layer.

5. Click Bring Forward to move the selected object up layer by layer.

6. Click Send Backward to move the selected object down layer by layer.

Tweak Shapes with Adjustment Handles

Use the yellow adjustment handles on a selected shape to make a rounded corner rectangle less rounded, give an arrowhead a different angle, or change a smile to a frown.

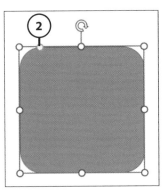

1. Open the Shapes gallery and create a Rounded Rectangle from the Rectangles section.

2. Click the adjustment handle and drag it slightly to the left.

3. Notice that the corners are less rounded after you've made the adjustment.

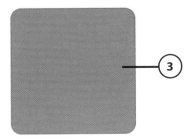

Multiple Handles

Some shapes have more than one adjustment handle. For example, a block arrow has two such handles: one for the arrowhead and one for the shaft.

It's Not All Good

Unfortunately, you cannot use the adjustment handles on more than one shape at a time. When you select multiple shapes, the adjustment handles disappear. If you know you'll need more than one adjusted shape, best practice is to create one and adjust it and then duplicate it. That's much easier than trying to adjust each shape and get them to match!

Change Shapes into Other Shapes

This is a handy trick to know when you need to do something like change the regular rectangles on a slide into rectangles with rounded corners or vice versa.

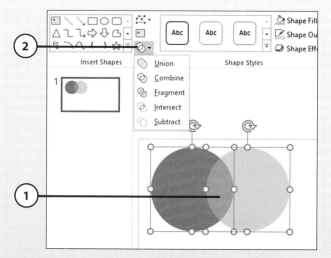

1. Create a shape and select it.
2. On the Drawing Tools Format tab, click the Edit Shape button and then point to Change Shape.
3. In the Change Shape gallery, click the shape you want to change the original into.

Save Time
You can select multiple shapes and use the Change Shape tool on all of them at once.

Create Your Own Shapes with Merge Shapes

Sometimes PowerPoint doesn't have the shape you need. For example, if you want to highlight the area between two overlapping circles, use Merge Shapes tools to create the shape in between.

1. Create and select at least two overlapping shapes on your slide.
2. On the Drawing Tools Format tab, click the Merge Shapes button.

Select Multiple Shapes to Use Merge Shapes

You must have more than one shape selected in order for the Merge Shapes tools to be available.

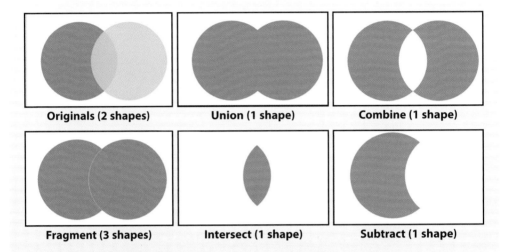

| Originals (2 shapes) | Union (1 shape) | Combine (1 shape) |
| Fragment (3 shapes) | Intersect (1 shape) | Subtract (1 shape) |

3. Click Union to turn the selected shapes into one shape.

4. Click Combine to turn the selected shapes into one shape, minus the overlapping parts.

5. Click Fragment to create separate shapes from the overlapping parts.

6. Click Intersect to create separate shapes from the overlapping parts and remove the parts that don't overlap.

7. Click Subtract to remove one shape and any overlapping parts from the other.

Tips for Merging Shapes

When you use the Merge Shapes tools, your original shapes will be converted to new shapes. Because of this, it's good to get into the habit of copying your original shapes or slide in case you need them again. You can always delete the copies later if you don't use them.

Also pay attention to which shape you select first. For example, when you use the Subtract tool, the first shape you select is the part that will remain; the second shape will be subtracted. If you don't get the result you want, press Ctrl+Z to undo, select the shapes in a different order, and try again.

>>>*Go Further*
TWEAK SHAPES WITH EDIT POINTS

You can manipulate your shapes even further using Edit Points, which is PowerPoint's answer to Bézier curves. To enable these, right-click a shape and choose Edit Points. Click and drag a point into position as needed. Right-click a point to change its behavior from smooth point to straight or corner point or even delete it altogether. Use the selection handles on a point to manipulate the segments between points. Right-click any of the segments to add a point or to make the segment itself straight or curved.

Edit Points works on most shapes but not on straight lines and connectors. If you know you'll need to start with a straight line for your shape, use the Freeform tool instead. Select the Freeform shape from the end of the Lines section of the Shapes gallery and then click once to create the start point and once to indicate the end point.

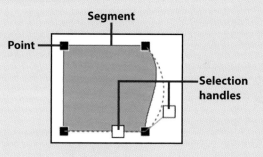

Formatting Shapes

Often, when you first create shapes and ad hoc text boxes, they're not formatted exactly as you want them to be. Luckily, PowerPoint gives you almost every type of formatting option imaginable. Just don't go too crazy—as with most things in PowerPoint, less is almost always more.

Apply One-Click Formatting with the Shape Styles Gallery

The Shape Styles gallery gives you various formatting options to apply with one click.

Shape Styles gallery

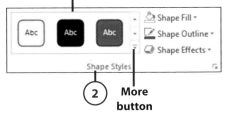

1. Create a shape on a slide and select it. The Drawing Tools Format tab becomes available.

2. On the Drawing Tools Format tab, scroll through the Shape Styles gallery or click the More button to expand the Shape Styles gallery so you can more easily see all the options.

3. Move your mouse pointer over the styles to see a Live Preview of what they'll look like on your shape. A checkerboard pattern in a style indicates no fill or a semi-transparent fill.

4. Click a style to apply it.

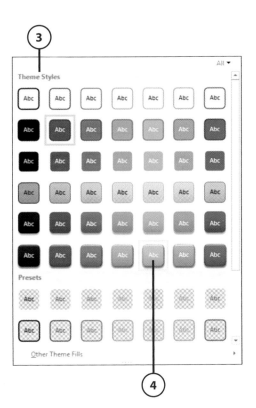

Text Boxes are Shapes, Too

You can apply formatting to text boxes just as you can to any shape. Add fills and outlines or even apply one of the shape styles. In addition, text boxes and text in shapes can be formatted using the same tools you use on text in placeholders, such as bold, italics, and so on. You can even add bullet points. Multiple levels of bullets are a real pain, though, and are usually better left to placeholders.

Manually Apply Solid Fill Colors

If you don't like the styles on the Shape Styles gallery, you can always apply formatting manually.

1. Create a shape and select it. The Drawing Tools Format tab becomes available.

2. On the Drawing Tools Format tab, click the Shape Fill button.

3. In the Shape Fill gallery, move your pointer over the different color chips to see what they'll look like when applied to your shape. Click one of the Theme Colors or Standard (off-theme) Colors to apply it.

4. Or click More Fill Colors.

5. Type your own RGB (Red, Green, and Blue) or HSL (Hue, Saturation, and Luminosity) values on the Custom tab.

6. Use the Transparency slider or input box at the bottom of the Colors dialog box to make the shape semitransparent.

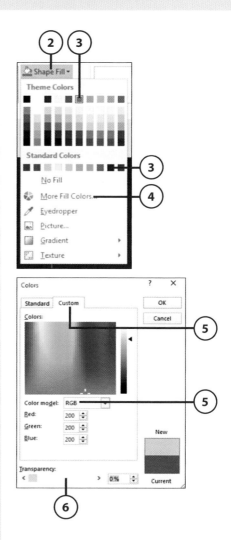

7. Click the Standard tab if you want to choose from the color honeycomb to fill your shape with a nonthemed color.

8. Click OK to apply your selection and close the dialog box.

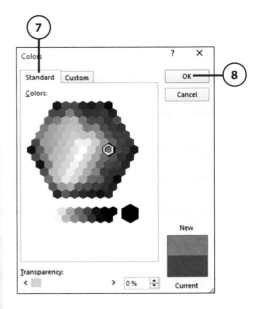

Recent Colors

After you head to More Fill Colors and create or choose a color there, it will show up in the Recent Colors section of the Shape Fill gallery. These colors are not theme colors, so they won't change when you change themes. After you've created more than 10 colors, the Recent Colors chips will disappear and be replaced with more recent Recent colors.

Apply Colors in the Format Shape Pane

Right-click a shape and choose Format Shape to open the Format Shape pane where you can apply colors and other settings. Click Shape Options and then click the Fill & Line button. Click the triangles next to the Fill and Line sections to expand them if necessary.

>>>Go Further

WHY ARE MY COLORS CHANGING?

Every PowerPoint file includes a set of theme colors. All the formatting galleries (Shape Styles as well as tables, charts, and SmartArt, to name a few) use these theme colors. You can also see them in the Shape Fill and Shape Outline color galleries.

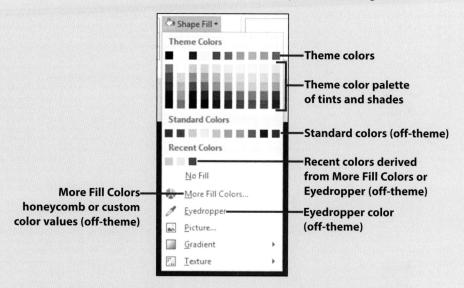

More Fill Colors — honeycomb or custom color values (off-theme)

— **Theme colors**

— **Theme color palette of tints and shades**

— **Standard colors (off-theme)**

— **Recent colors derived from More Fill Colors or Eyedropper (off-theme)**

— **Eyedropper color (off-theme)**

If you apply a theme color to an object and then apply a different PowerPoint theme or template to your presentation, the object's color will update to match the new theme colors. PowerPoint is just trying to help you create a cohesive look for your presentation content by applying theme colors specific to the new template.

But sometimes you don't want things to change color. For example, if you create red, yellow, and green circles to mimic a stoplight, it wouldn't be good if those changed to blue, purple, and orange when you applied a new template.

Never fear! In addition to the theme colors and palette of tints and shades, PowerPoint gives you colors that aren't tied to your theme. These are known as off-theme or absolute colors.

Colors you choose or create from Standard Colors and More Fill Colors, or apply with the Eyedropper tool, are all off-theme colors. When you use More Fill Colors or the Eyedropper, a new section called Recent Colors appears in the Shape Fill and Shape Outline galleries. These Recent Colors are also off-theme colors. If you apply them to an object, that color won't change when you apply a new template.

>>>Go Further

USING THE FORMAT SHAPE PANE

As with most things in PowerPoint, there are multiple ways to access the formatting tools. In addition to the various galleries on the Ribbon, you can usually click More Options at the bottom of any gallery to open the Format Shape pane. Another way to open that pane is to right-click a shape and choose Format Shape. Or you can click a dialog box launcher in the corner of many groups in the Ribbon.

Regardless of how you get to it, these tips should help you navigate the Format Shape pane.

Under the Shape Options heading, there are buttons for Fill & Line, Effects, and Size & Properties. As you'd expect, clicking the Fill & Line button takes you to options for shape fills and lines.

Click the Effects button and you'll find the settings for shadows, reflections, glows, soft edges, and 3-D format and rotation.

Click the Size & Properties button and you'll be able to specify the size and position of shapes. Because shapes can hold text, you can also set text options such as internal margins, vertical alignment, autofit, text wrap, and so on. You can add Alt Text here to describe the shape, which is necessary if you're creating accessible documents.

Click the Text Options heading to reveal buttons for Text Fill & Outline, Text Effects, and Text Box.

The Text Fill & Outline settings are almost identical to the Fill & Outline settings for shapes, but they apply to the text, not to the entire shape. It's the same with Text Effects—the shadows, reflections, glows, soft edges, and 3-D settings here apply to text, not to the entire shape.

The Text Box settings are the same as the Text Box settings for shapes. It's in both places just for convenience.

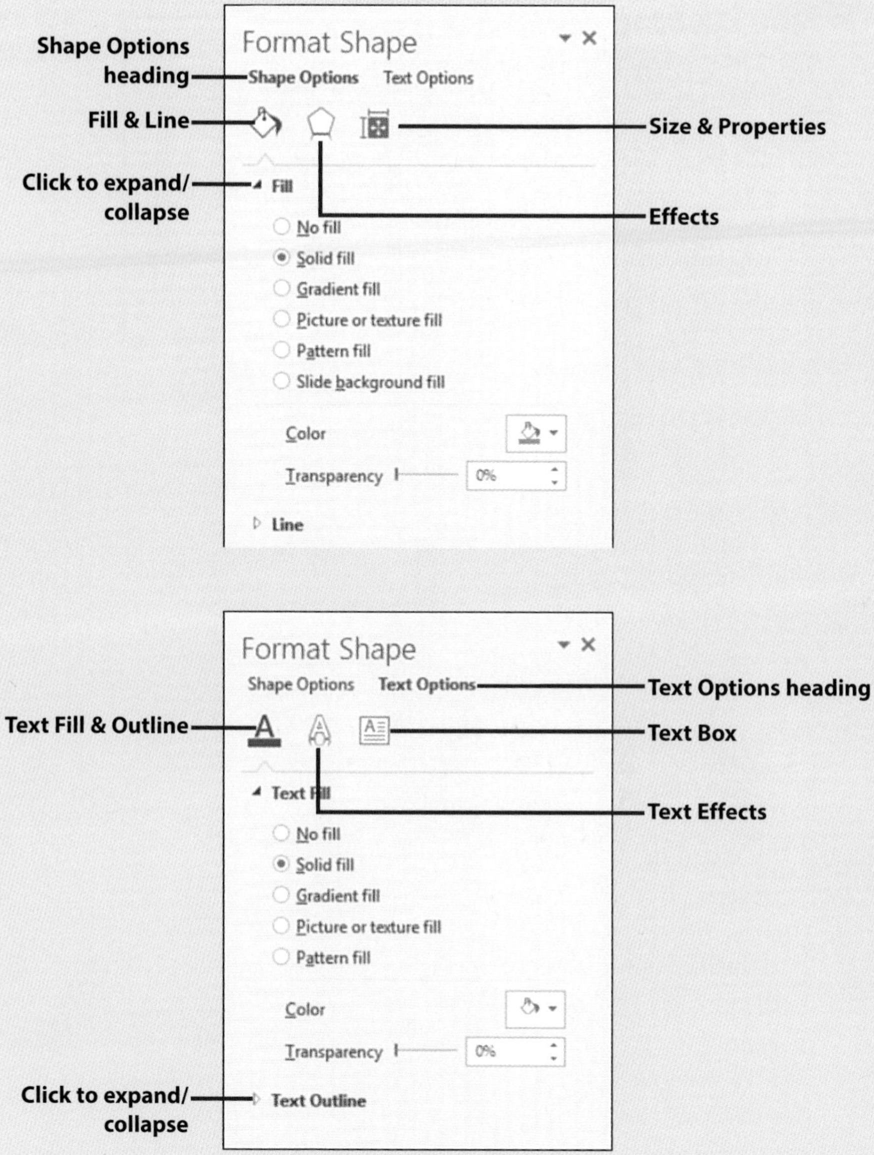

Shape Options heading

Fill & Line

Click to expand/ collapse

Size & Properties

Effects

Format Shape

Shape Options   Text Options

▲ Fill

○ No fill
◉ Solid fill
○ Gradient fill
○ Picture or texture fill
○ Pattern fill
○ Slide background fill

Color

Transparency   0%

▷ Line

Text Fill & Outline

Click to expand/ collapse

Text Options heading

Text Box

Text Effects

Format Shape

Shape Options   Text Options

▲ Text Fill

○ No fill
◉ Solid fill
○ Gradient fill
○ Picture or texture fill
○ Pattern fill

Color

Transparency   0%

▷ Text Outline

Use the Eyedropper to Apply Fill Color

The Eyedropper tool lets you pick up a color from another object on your screen and apply it to your shape.

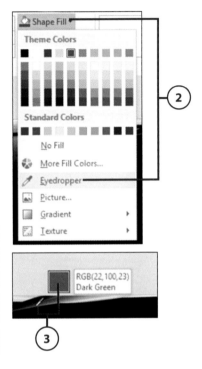

1. Create a shape and select it.

2. Click the Shape Fill button and then click Eyedropper. The pointer changes to an Eyedropper.

3. Move the Eyedropper pointer over other objects on your screen until the preview chip shows the color you want to apply. When you pause, a ScreenTip with the RGB values will also appear.

4. Click your mouse button to apply the color to the shape.

>>>Go Further

USE THE EYEDROPPER TO CHOOSE COLORS OUTSIDE POWERPOINT

It's a common misconception that you can't use the PowerPoint Eyedropper to choose colors from pictures or websites because the Eyedropper pointer disappears when you move it outside the slide workspace. Here's how to do it. Select a shape and click the Eyedropper tool as usual. After your pointer turns into the Eyedropper, simply press and hold the left mouse button. Now you can choose a color from anywhere on your screen—web pages, picture viewers, even email! Release the mouse button to apply the color to your selected shape.

Apply and Customize a Gradient Fill

Simple gradients are available with just a couple of clicks.

1. Select a shape. The Drawing Tools Format tab becomes available.

2. Click the Shape Fill button, and then point to Gradient to open the Gradient gallery.

3. Click a gradient preview to apply it.

4. If you want to apply a custom gradient, click Shape Fill and then point to Gradient again. Click More Gradients at the bottom of the Gradients gallery to open the Format Shape pane.

5. In the Format Shape pane, click Shape Options and then click the Fill & Line button. If the Fill options don't show, click the word Fill to expand the section.

6. Select Gradient fill if you didn't apply a gradient in the previous steps. Then click the Preset Gradients button and select an option to apply a stock gradient.

7. Use Type to change the gradient to Linear, Radial, Rectangular, or Path.

8. Change the direction of the gradient by selecting from the Direction options or inputting an Angle value.

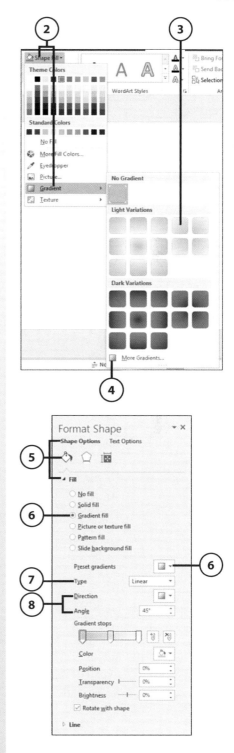

9. Click a Gradient stop and click the Color button to change its color.

10. Change the position of a Gradient stop by sliding it on the preview strip or changing the value in the Position input box.

11. Use the Transparency and Brightness sliders to change these settings.

12. Click a Gradient stop and then click the Remove Gradient Stop button to remove it. Click the gradient preview strip or the Add Gradient Stop button to add a Gradient stop.

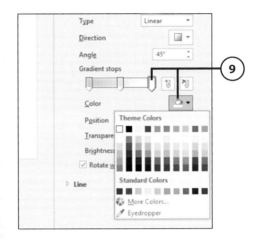

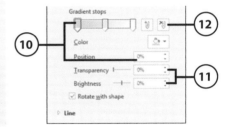

>>>Go Further

ABOUT CUSTOMIZING GRADIENTS

Each "stop" on a gradient indicates a color change. Add stops by clicking on the gradient preview in the Format Shape pane. Reposition stops by sliding the markers on the preview or by selecting a stop and changing its values in the Position box.

You can also change the transparency of any stop using the Transparency slider, which can be useful if you want your gradient to blend into the slide background.

In addition to recoloring and positioning each stop manually, you can choose from the preset gradients. Change from a straight linear to a radial or other gradient on the Type gallery, and change direction using the Direction and Angle options.

Add a Picture or Texture Fill

Of course you can crop pictures (see Chapter 5, "Working with Pictures," for specifics), but sometimes it's easier to make a series of pictures all the same size by filling shapes with them.

1. Insert a shape and select it.

2. On the Drawing Tools Format tab, choose Shape Fill, Picture.

3. Navigate to a picture on your hard drive or an online place and click Insert.

4. If the shape and the picture aren't the same aspect ratio, the picture might be distorted when it's inserted.

5. To resize the picture or correct any distortion, right-click the shape and choose Format Picture.

6. In the Format Picture pane, click Shape Options and then click the Fill & Line button. If necessary, click Fill to expand these tools.

7. Notice that the Picture or Texture Fill option is already selected.

8. Click the Tile Picture as Texture check box. This lets you resize the image within the shape frame.

9. Change Scale X and Scale Y values as necessary so the picture fits within the shape frame.

10. Use Offset X, Offset Y, and Alignment settings to position the picture within the shape frame.

11. To apply a texture fill to your shape, click the Texture button and select a texture in the gallery. Or choose Shape Fill on the Ribbon, point to Texture, and select from the Texture gallery.

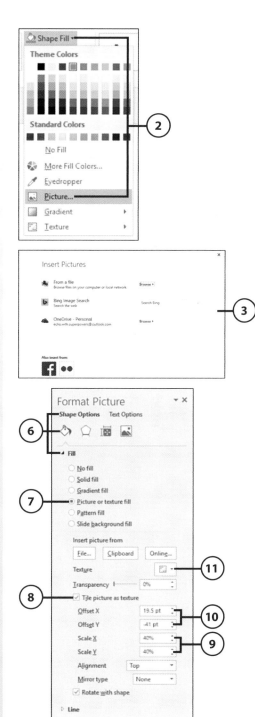

>>>Go Further

TIPS FOR ADJUSTING PICTURE AND TEXTURE FILLS

When you fill a shape with a picture, you'll have both Drawing Tools Format and Picture Tools Format tabs available on the Ribbon because you are, after all, working with both a shape and a picture.

- Keep the Scale X and Scale Y values the same so the aspect ratio of the picture is maintained.

- Your picture must be larger than the shape you're filling because you cannot scale a picture fill more than 100%.

- When you're adjusting the X and Y scales, don't use too small a percentage; otherwise, the image will begin to repeat inside the shape frame.

- Use Offset X and Offset Y to change the horizontal and vertical position of the picture within the frame.

- Start with Alignment settings to change the position of the picture within the shape frame by a large amount. Top left is the default position.

- PowerPoint's textures haven't been changed in at least 15 years, if ever. Most of them are horribly dated and best avoided. Consider applying artistic effects and colors from the Picture Tools Format tab (see Chapter 5) to give them new life.

- The Mirror Type setting in the Format Picture pane is used to smooth texture fills; it has no effect on picture fills.

Format Lines and Outlines

Lines, connectors, and shape outlines are formatted the same way.

1. Draw a line and select it. The Drawing Tools Format tab becomes available.

Straight Lines

Just as pressing Shift while drawing a shape constrains the height and width, pressing Shift while drawing a line lets you create a line that's perfectly vertical, horizontal, or angled at 45 degree increments.

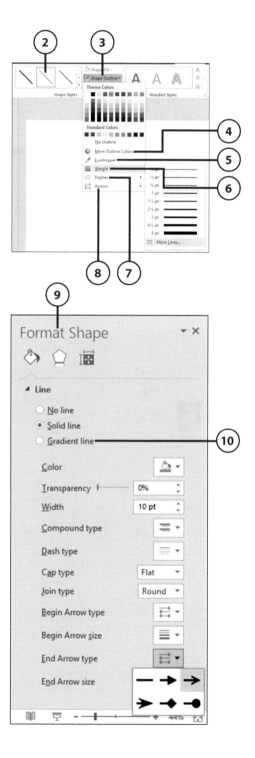

2. Apply a line style—which usually consists of a color, a thickness, and a shadow—from those available in the Shape Styles gallery.

3. Click Shape Outline and choose a color from the Theme Colors or Standard Colors palettes.

4. Click More Outline Colors to choose from the color honeycomb or input your own RGB or HSL values.

5. Click the Eyedropper to pick up and apply a color from elsewhere on the screen. (See the sidebar "Use the Eyedropper to Choose Colors Outside PowerPoint" to learn how to choose colors from outside the slide workspace.)

6. Click Weight and select one of the line weights to apply it.

7. Click Dashes to choose from dotted and dashed lines.

8. Click Arrows to choose different types of beginning and end points.

9. Right-click the line and choose Format Shape to open the pane where you can control all aspects of the line.

10. Choose Gradient Line in the Format Shape pane if you want to apply a gradient to your line or outline.

Shape Outlines Work Like Shape Fills

Most PowerPoint shapes will already have an outline when you draw them. To remove an outline, select the shape, click the Shape Outline button, and then click No Outline. If you need to add an outline to a shape, click the Shape Outline button and choose a theme color chip, select More Outline Colors, or use the Eyedropper. Finally, change the weight if necessary.

>>>Go Further
LINES AND CONNECTORS

In more recent versions of PowerPoint, lines act like connectors, which attach to shapes when the endpoint gets close to a shape's edge. This is great when you want to create a diagram with connections because a connected line will remain attached to the shapes and expand and contract as you move the shape around on the slide. If you've used connectors instead of straight lines or arrows, the connectors will bend as you move the shapes. You can adjust them with the yellow adjustment handles, but getting them in the right position can be a painstaking process—one that will almost always have to be repeated if you move the shape again.

When a line or connector is connected to a shape, the connected end will display as a green circle. (In previous versions this was a red circle.) If a line won't latch on where you want it to, you can add a point to the shape using Edit Points.

Add a Shadow

A shadow usually makes your shapes look more polished.

1. Create a shape and select it. The Drawing Tools Format tab becomes available.

2. Click Shape Effects and then point to Shadow. Click one of the shadow options to apply it.

3. To customize the shadow, right-click the shape and choose Format Shape. The Format Shape pane appears.

4. Click Shape Options, then the Effects button, and then click the word Shadow to expand the Shadow settings.

5. Change the shadow color using the Color button. (Shadows rarely have a color other than black or gray, so use colored shadows sparingly.)

6. Change the Transparency, Size, Blur, Angle, and Distance of the shadow as desired.

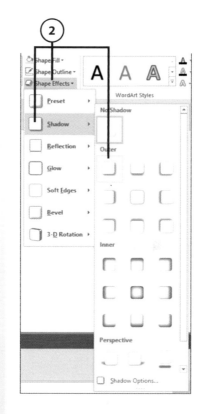

Start With a Preset Shadow

If you want a custom shadow, it's usually easiest to start with a preset shadow and then tweak it to your satisfaction.

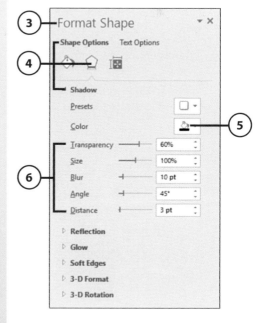

Add a Bevel

Many of the more intense styles in the Shape Styles galleries include bevels. You can add special effects such as bevels, reflections, and glows manually as well. Remember, though—less is more, so don't overdo it.

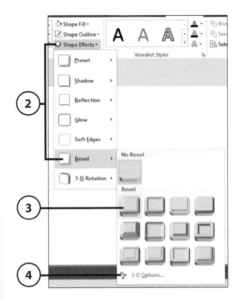

1. Create a shape and select it. The Drawing Tools Format tab becomes available.

2. Click Shape Effects and then point to Bevel.

3. Click a bevel to apply it.

4. To customize the bevel, select the shape and click Shape Effects, Bevel, 3-D Options. The Format Shape pane appears and opens to the 3-D Format section.

5. Type your own values for the top and bottom bevel settings, depth size and color, contour size and color, shape material, lighting type, and lighting angle.

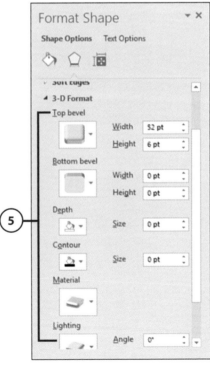

Apply 3-D Rotation

3-D Rotation settings let you add perspective to shapes. If your shape has text, make sure it's still easy to read after applying 3-D Rotation settings.

1. To apply 3-D rotation, click Shape Effects on the Drawing Tools Format tab and then point to 3-D Rotation. Or use the 3-D Rotation tools farther down in the Format Shape pane.

2. Click an option in the 3-D Rotation gallery to apply it.

3. Click Shape Effects on the Drawing Tools Format tab, point to 3-D Rotation, and then click 3-D Rotation Options to open the Format Shape pane.

4. Tweak the Perspective settings and the X-, Y-, or Z-axis Rotation options by inputting your own values.

5. Check the Keep Text Flat option if you don't want the text to be angled along with the shape.

6. Change the Distance from Ground setting. This change is easier to see if you've applied a shadow to your shape.

7. Click Reset in either the 3-D Format or the 3-D Rotation section to remove all 3-D settings that have been applied to the shape.

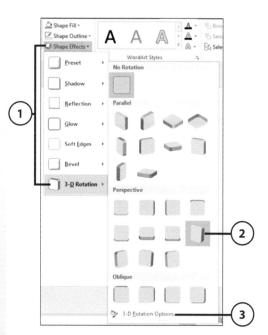

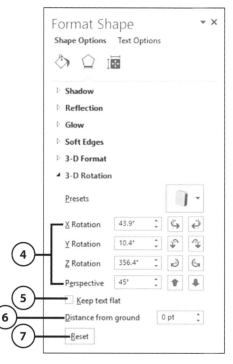

>>>Go Further

MORE SHAPE EFFECTS

You can apply additional shape effects such as Reflections, Glows, and Soft Edges. Applying them is the same as applying any other effect: Choose Shape Effects, point to the type of effect, and then click to apply one of the stock effects. Click Options at the bottom of any of the effects galleries to open the Format Shape pane, where you can tweak all the settings.

There is also a Shape Effects Preset gallery with combinations of various effects. For example, Preset 1 has a solid fill, a shadow, and a bevel that also gives the appearance of an outline; Preset 11 has a semitransparent fill along with a bevel and a perspective tilt.

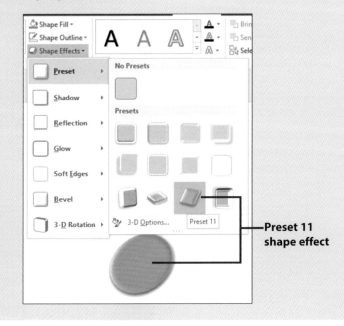

Preset 11
shape effect

Copy Formatting with Format Painter

The Format Painter lets you "paint" formatting from one object to another.

1. Create a shape with formatting you want to reuse and select it.

2. Click the Format Painter on the Home tab in the Clipboard group. This picks up the shape's formatting.

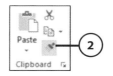

3. When you move the mouse pointer, you'll see it's turned into an arrow with a paintbrush. Click another shape to "paint" formatting onto it.

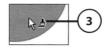

>>>Go Further

FORMAT PAINTER EVERYWHERE

If you want to use the Format Painter with an object on another slide, go right ahead! PowerPoint lets you use Format Painter on different slides and even on different presentations.

And here's a tip: If you have a bunch of objects you want to format, double-click the Format Painter to keep it active while you click them all. Press Esc on your keyboard or click the Format Painter again to deactivate.

There's also a shortcut to copy an object's formatting: Ctrl+Shift+C. To apply the formatting to another object, select it and press Ctrl+Shift+V. The beauty of using this shortcut is that the formatting stays in memory so you can do other things in between applying formatting to objects.

Set Default Shapes, Lines, and Text Boxes

If you get tired of formatting shapes manually, you can specify one as the default shape. Format a shape the way you want and then right-click it and choose Set as Default Shape. Now every time you create a shape, it will use that formatting. You can also specify a default line and text box the same way.

Formatting Graphical Text (WordArt)

Occasionally you need text to be more of a graphical element on your slide. The WordArt features let you make text that works more like an image. Use these stylistic features on bits of text that are prominent on the slide; as a general rule, don't use WordArt for typical body or title text.

Apply WordArt Formatting with One Click

Just as there's a styles gallery for shapes, there's also a styles gallery for WordArt. The text colors in the WordArt Style gallery are based on the presentation's theme colors.

1. Insert a text box and type some text. Select the border of the text box.

2. On the Drawing Tools Format tab, scroll through the WordArt Styles gallery or click the More button to expand it.

3. Select a WordArt style to apply it.

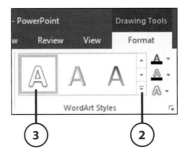

It's Not All Good

WordArt Styles

You should know that WordArt generally gets a bad rap, and some of it is truly deserved. Most of the available WordArt styles leave a lot to be desired, and there really aren't that many useful options. In fact, you really shouldn't use WordArt on small text because all the effects make small text very difficult to read.

The good thing is, you can always tweak the formatting after you've applied a WordArt style. For example, apply a WordArt style close to what you want and then change the fill color of the text using the Text tools in the WordArt Styles group. These tools—Text Fill, Text Outline, and Text Effects such as shadows and reflections—work just as they do for shapes.

Fill Text with a Picture

When you use WordArt, you should essentially think of your text as shapes because you can format your text just as you would a shape.

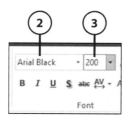

1. Insert a text box and type some text. Select the border of the text box.

2. Change the font to a heavy font such as Arial Black.

3. Increase the font size. For a size larger than 96 points, type a value in the Font Size box and press Enter.

4. Select the text box and fill the text with a picture by clicking Text Fill, Picture on the Drawing Tools Format tab. This opens the Insert Pictures dialog box.

5. Use the Insert Pictures dialog box to select a picture from your computer or online (see Chapter 5 for more details). Click Insert to fill your WordArt text with the picture.

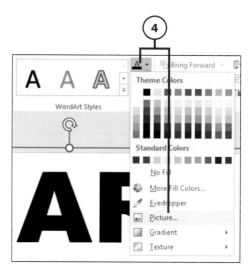

6. To transform your text into a true graphical object, which enables you to increase the height and width of the text to show off the image, click Text Effects and then point to Transform.

7. Select a transform from the gallery. Choose Square if you don't want to change the shape of the text.

8. Change the height or width of the transformed text using any of the selection handles. Remember that the yellow adjustment handle controls the slant of the text.

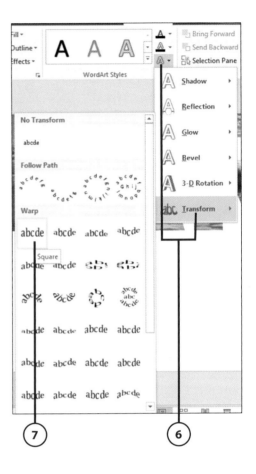

Text Transforms

Use the WordArt Text Effects, Transform options to create circular and semicircular text as well as other warped text forms.

>>>Go Further

MOVING PICTURES INSIDE SHAPES AND TEXT

Sometimes when you fill text with a picture, the picture isn't in exactly the right place. You can reposition these images by right-clicking the WordArt text and choosing Format Shape and then selecting Text Options, Text Fill & Outline.

From this point it's just like moving pictures inside a shape. This is the key: In the Text Fill section, select the Tile Picture as Texture check box so you can size and move the picture inside the WordArt. Make the picture smaller, if necessary, by specifying X and Y scale values. Don't make it too small, though, or the picture will start repeating inside the text!

You'll also want to ensure that the Scale X and Scale Y settings are equal values so your picture won't be distorted. The Alignment, Offset X, and Offset Y settings move the picture around inside the text.

Color Drawing
Guides

Align with
Smart Guides

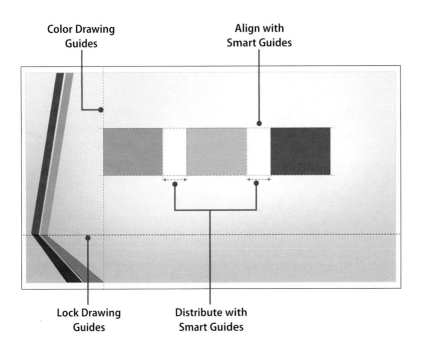

Lock Drawing
Guides

Distribute with
Smart Guides

In this chapter, you will learn about aligning and positioning objects on slides. Specific topics in this chapter include the following:

→ Using Smart Guides
→ Using Alignment tools
→ Using Dravwing Guides
→ Grouping for easier alignment

Aligning and Positioning Shapes

One hallmark of a professional presentation is that all elements on a slide are perfectly aligned. PowerPoint gives you a number of tools to help with this: Smart Guides, Drawing Guides, Alignment and Distribution tools, and a grid. You can use any one tool or a combination of all these tools plus grouping to align objects to each other and to the slide itself.

Using Smart Guides

Smart Guides are the dashed lines that appear when you move shapes and other objects around on a slide. Not only do they indicate alignment for any side of an object, but they also show when you have vertical and horizontal centers aligned as well as equal distribution between objects.

Align and Distribute with Smart Guides

Smart Guides have been improved in PowerPoint 2016 so they work with tables as well as all other objects on the slide.

1. Check to see that Smart Guides are turned on. Right-click an empty place on the slide, point to Grid and Guides, and then choose Smart Guides to select it if you don't already see a checkmark next to the command.

2. Select a shape on the slide and drag it near another shape. Let go of the shape when you see one or more orange dashed lines indicating that the edges are aligned.

3. Select a shape on the slide and drag it on top of another shape. Let go of the shape when you see the orange dashed lines indicating horizontal and vertical alignment.

4. Select a shape and drag it between other shapes. Let go when you see gray and orange dashed lines indicating equal distance between the shapes.

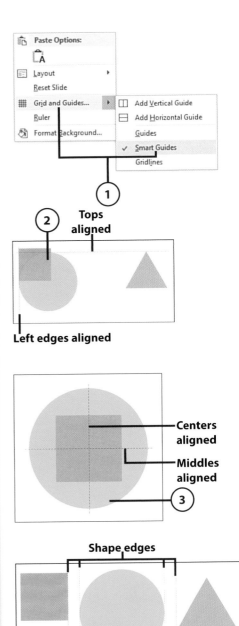

Using Alignment Tools

Especially when you have a lot of objects on your slide, it can be a little tricky to align them using the Smart Guides because so many appear as you move things around on the slide. Enter PowerPoint's alignment tools. These tools let you select objects and align them without having to drag things around manually.

Find the alignment tools on the Arrange button on the Home tab and in the Arrange group on various contextual tabs such as the Drawing Tools Format tab and the Picture Tools Format tab.

Align with Alignment Tools

The key to using the alignment tools is to understand that PowerPoint aligns to the object in the outermost position—the topmost, bottommost, leftmost, or rightmost outer edge. PowerPoint doesn't care which object you select first; it only cares which object is in the outermost position to serve as the point to align to.

1. Select multiple shapes on a slide.

2. In the Arrange tools, click Align and then click Align Top to align the objects to the top edge of the topmost shape. The top object will remain in place, and the other objects will move to align with it.

3. Click Align Left to align objects to the leftmost edge, Align Right to align to the rightmost edge, or Align Bottom to align to the bottommost edge.

4. Click Align Center to align selected objects to the center point and Align Middle to align to the middle point. PowerPoint splits the difference to find the center/middle of the selected objects.

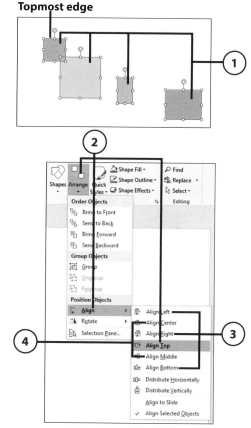

Topmost edge

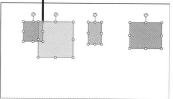

Shapes aligned to top

Distribute with Alignment Tools

Distribution means to equally space your objects. Using the alignment tools to distribute is almost identical to using them to align objects. The difference is that you set two parameters—the top and bottom or the left and right sides—to distribute everything else between.

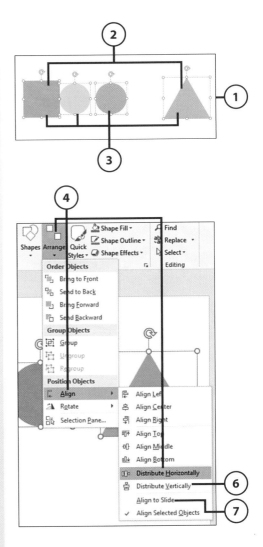

1. Draw at least three shapes on a slide. Align their tops or middles (refer to the preceding exercise).

2. Move one shape to the farthest left to specify the left distribution point. Move another to the farthest right to determine that distribution point.

3. Select all shapes.

4. In the Arrange tools, click Align, and then click Distribute Horizontally.

5. Notice that the left and right shapes stay in place, and the other shapes adjust between them so there is equal space between all the shapes. Continue to adjust the left and right objects and redistribute as needed.

6. In the Arrange tools, click Align and then click Distribute Vertically to distribute shapes between a top and bottom point.

7. In the Arrange tools, click Align and then click Align to Slide to make the edges of the slide serve as the top, bottom, left, and right parameters. Then click an Align or Distribute command to align or distribute the objects to the slide sides.

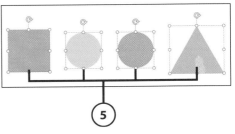

>>>Go Further
TIPS FOR ALIGNING

There are several tricks that come in handy when you are aligning and distributing shapes.

- When Align to Slide is activated and you choose Distribute Horizontally, selected objects are spread an equal distance across the slide.

- When you have only one object selected, Align to Slide is activated automatically. If you choose Align Center or Distribute Horizontally, the selected object or group aligns to the center of the slide.

- When Align to Slide is activated, choosing Align Middle or Distribute Vertically uses the whole slide—as though there's no area on the slide for a title. You can always use your keyboard arrows to nudge the objects up or down if necessary.

- Grouping can help with alignment. Group shapes together and then align the group to the slide.

- You can align only one direction at a time—horizontally or vertically. Think of it as aligning one row or column of objects at a time.

- A typical workflow is to align objects, then distribute them, and then group them together and distribute or center the group on the slide.

- Ctrl+Z is your friend. If you align objects and they don't do what you expect, undo the action by pressing Ctrl+Z. Then try again. Be sure to check that Align to Slide isn't activated by mistake; simply choose Arrange, Align, Align Selected Objects to turn off Align to Slide.

- With only one object (or group) selected, Align to Slide will be activated by default; any alignment or distribution you perform will use the slide for its parameters.

- When using Align Selected Objects, you must select more than one object to apply the alignment tools. You must have three or more objects selected for distribution tools to be activated.

Using Drawing Guides

PowerPoint has Drawing Guides in addition to Smart Guides. Drawing Guides are useful for indicating margins and safe areas on slides as well as serving as ad hoc alignment guides. They're also useful for aligning objects because you can drag objects to a guide and they'll snap into place.

Align Shapes Using Drawing Guides

In PowerPoint 2016, you can add Drawing Guides to the slide master, individual layouts, or to the slides themselves. Applying a color to the Drawing Guides can help establish a hierarchy of guides.

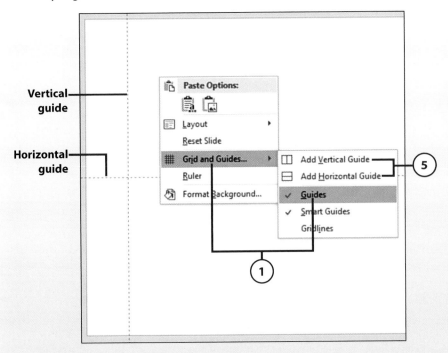

1. Turn on Guides by right-clicking the slide and pointing to Grid and Guides. Click Guides to toggle them on and off.

Where to Turn on Guides

In addition to right-clicking the slide and using the shortcut menu, you can also turn guides on and off by selecting the Guides check box on the View tab. The shortcut to toggle Guides on and off is Alt+F9.

2. Click and drag a guide to move it. Press Alt while dragging to move in smaller increments.

3. Drag a guide off any edge of the slide to delete it.

4. Press Ctrl while clicking and dragging a guide to create another guide. (Let go of the mouse before letting go of Ctrl.)

5. To add another guide, right-click an empty space on the slide, hover over Grid and Guides, and then click Add Vertical Guide or Add Horizontal Guide.

6. To change the color of a guide, right-click the guide, hover over Color, and then click to apply a color.

>>>Go Further

IT'S ALL GOOD! A GUIDE TO GUIDES

One complaint in previous versions of PowerPoint is that the Drawing Guides couldn't be locked down. As of PowerPoint 2013, guides added to the slide masters and layouts aren't selectable when you're working on the slides, so they won't get in your way and you won't move them by mistake.

Additionally, it's not a one-size-fits-all situation with the guides applying to every layout and slide. You can now set guides specific to individual layouts, which can be extremely helpful when you're working on different types of slides.

Of course, you can still create guides on the slides themselves, and these guides will display on every slide in the presentation. You can even assign different colors to the guides, which is a great way to tell locked guides on the layouts from ad hoc guides on the slides. When you switch to Master View and add a guide to the master or layouts, they'll be orange by default. Guides on the slides are gray by default.

We have so many guide options now that it's easy to end up with way too many guides everywhere! It might help you create a hierarchy of guides if you remember that any guide you apply to the slide master will also apply to every layout. First apply guides that should be on every layout, such as the centered horizontal and vertical guides, to the master. Or leave them off the master altogether. Then visit each layout and create guides to indicate the four sides of the content area. You probably won't need any guides on the Title Slide layout, for example, but you might want to mark a ¼" margin on all sides of the Blank layout. Then you can create temporary guides as needed to align objects as you're working on the slides.

>>>Go Further

WHAT ABOUT THE GRID?

Gridlines are yet another way to align objects in PowerPoint. To activate the grid, select the Gridlines check box on the View tab or right-click the slide, point to Grid and Guides, and select Gridlines.

The grid is like graph paper—it's a bunch of squares underlying your slide. In the Grid and Guides dialog box, you can specify the grid spacing—but it doesn't necessarily match the structure of your slide. It's definitely helpful if you're using PowerPoint for a floor plan, though! Right-click an empty space on the slide and click Grid and Guides to display the Grid and Guides dialog box.

Checking the Display Grid on Screen setting displays the visual grid on your slide, but you still have to select Snap Objects to Grid if you want your objects to lock into the grid. If you have selected Snap Objects to Grid and need to temporarily override that, press Alt while you drag objects on the slide.

Grouping Objects for Easier Alignment

Grouping makes disparate objects work together as one. Grouping is helpful when you want to center a drawing or diagram on the slide, but it's also useful when you need to resize a bunch of separate objects or animate them all at the same time.

Note that content in placeholders cannot be grouped. Also, animation applies to a group as a whole. Animation will be lost if you ungroup the group.

Group Shapes

If you've aligned or distributed some shapes and now you want to center the whole shebang on your slide, you don't have to start over.

1. Align and distribute the shapes. Select all the shapes.

2. Right-click the shapes and choose Group, Group to group the shapes. Group tools are also available from the Arrange button on the Home tab and the Arrange group on various contextual tabs.

3. Select the group and choose Arrange, Align, Align Center. The entire group is then centered on the slide.

Shortcut for Grouping

The shortcut to group selected objects is Ctrl+G. Ctrl+Shift+G ungroups them.

---

4. You can select and move or format individual objects in a group. Click to select the group and then click again on the object you want to select. The selected object's outline will be a solid line, and the outline of the group will be dashed.

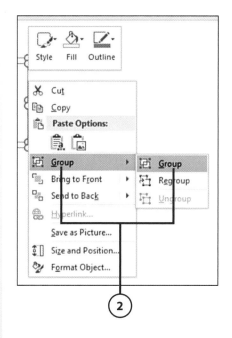

Selected shape   Group

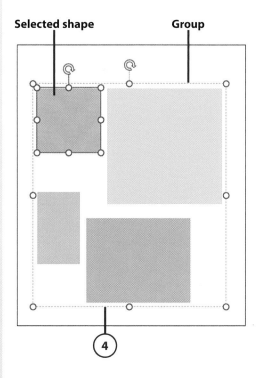

Correct and recolor
your pictures

Add borders and
shadows with one click

Crop and resize
pictures

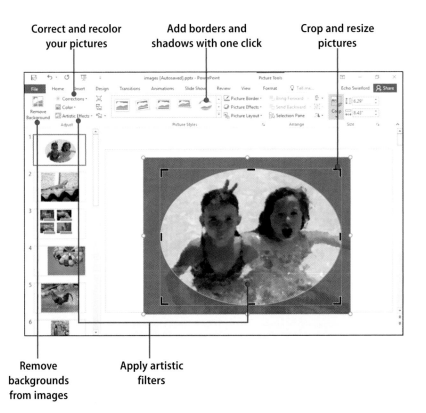

Remove
backgrounds
from images

Apply artistic
filters

In this chapter, you will learn about inserting and formatting pictures. Specific topics in this chapter include the following:

→ Inserting pictures
→ Cropping and resizing pictures
→ Formatting pictures
→ Compressing pictures
→ Creating a photo album

Working with Pictures

PowerPoint makes it easy to insert pictures both from your computer and from online locations. You can format inserted pictures in dozens of ways in PowerPoint. Apply a picture style to get a complete look with one click. Add a color tint to a series of random pictures to help them look more cohesive. Crop to fit your slide, drop out backgrounds, correct fuzziness—the list goes on and on....

Images can help tell your story and engage your audience, but you want to be careful when sourcing them. Make sure that the picture tells the story you're trying to tell and that it's appropriate for the audience.

Especially when searching online, you must be careful not to violate copyright laws. Just because an image is on the Web doesn't mean you have the right to use it in your presentation. Although PowerPoint searches by default for images available for use through Creative Commons licenses, in many cases, you're better off purchasing inexpensive royalty-free stock photos.

Inserting Pictures

There are quite a few ways to insert pictures onto a slide. You can use the picture tools on the Insert tab, you can use content placeholders, and you can use picture placeholders. We'll discuss all of these methods and more in this section.

Insert Pictures from Your Hard Drive

If you've already downloaded a picture to your hard drive, here's how to insert it.

1. Insert a new slide into your presentation. Choose a layout that uses a content or picture placeholder.

2. Click the Pictures icon in the placeholder. Alternatively, click the Pictures button on the Insert tab of the Ribbon.

3. Find the picture on your computer. Select it and click Insert.

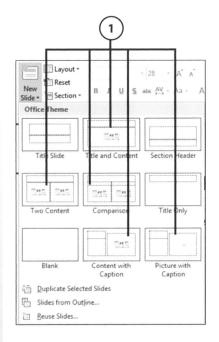

Choose the Correct Layout

When there is an empty content or picture placeholder on your slide, PowerPoint fills it with the picture even if you use the tools on the Ribbon to insert the image. If you don't want this to happen, choose a layout such as Title Only or Blank that doesn't have content or picture placeholders. Otherwise, you can temporarily fill the placeholder with text or other content—even just a space will work—and delete it after you've inserted the picture.

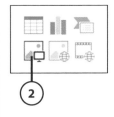

Insert Online Pictures

With Online Pictures, you can search for pictures online or insert them from OneDrive and other online storage.

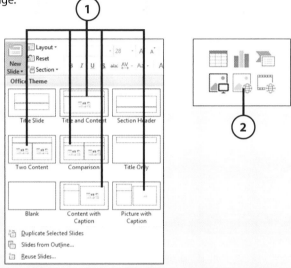

1. Insert a new slide into your presentation. Choose a layout that uses a content or picture placeholder.

2. Click the Online Pictures icon in the placeholder.

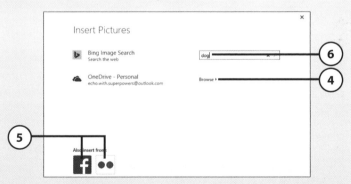

3. Alternatively, click the Online Pictures icon on the Insert tab of the Ribbon.

4. If the picture is stored on OneDrive, click the Browse button to see your files and folders on OneDrive.

5. If the picture is stored on Facebook or Flickr, click the icons at the bottom of the Insert Pictures dialog box to connect to your account.

6. If you don't already have an image, you can search for pictures using Bing Image Search. Enter the search terms and press Enter to begin.

Adding Places

If your images are stored in a location that isn't listed in the Insert Pictures dialog box, you may be able to add the location. To do so, click File, Account, Add a Service to see options for adding YouTube, LinkedIn, Twitter, and SharePoint accounts, among others.

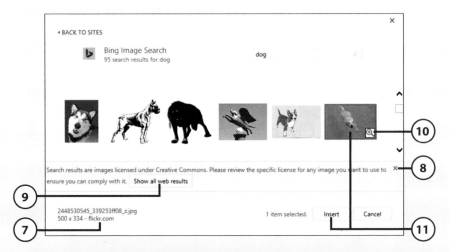

7. Note that the initial search results in images that are available to use under Creative Commons licensing, as explained in the informational banner. Specifics about the image appear in the lower-left corner of the Insert Pictures dialog box. Click that link to go to the image site and double-check for any license restrictions or attributions you must include when you use the image.

8. Click the X to minimize the informational banner about Creative Commons search results so you can see more thumbnails in the dialog box.

9. Clicking Show All Web Results removes the search filter that shows you only images licensed under Creative Commons. Be careful if you do this! You'll see more results, but you will need to check the copyright and any license restrictions for each image to ensure you're not using it illegally. In most cases, you should purchase the image in order to use it.

10. Hover over a thumbnail and click the magnification icon to see a larger thumbnail.

11. Click a thumbnail to select it and then click Insert to add it to your slide. Press Ctrl and click thumbnails to select multiple images or use Shift+click to select a contiguous range.

What Is Creative Commons?

Creative Commons gives photographers and other artists a free, standardized process to let the public use and share their creative work. There are many levels of Creative Commons licensing: Some levels require attribution, some allow only noncommercial work, and so on. To learn more about this, look up Creative Commons in your favorite search engine.

Insert Screen Captures

Use this feature when you want to include a screenshot in your presentation and don't have a screenshot utility handy.

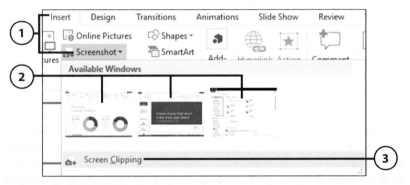

1. On the Insert tab, click Screenshot.

2. Other open applications appear in the Available Windows gallery. Click a thumbnail to add it to your slide.

3. Or click Screen Clipping to take a quick snapshot of part of the screen. PowerPoint automatically takes you to a view of the screen as it was just before you switched to PowerPoint and clicked Insert, Screenshot.

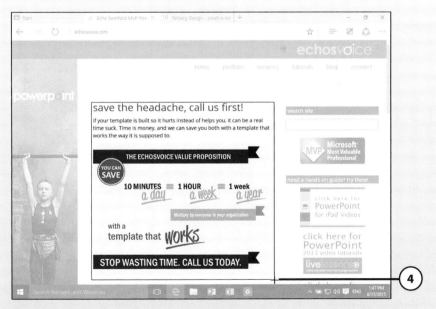

4. When the screen ghosts and your mouse pointer becomes a crosshair, click and drag to indicate the area of the screen to capture. When you release the mouse button, the screen grab will be inserted onto your slide.

Tips for Using Insert Screenshot

If a window or an application is minimized, it won't appear in the Available Windows gallery. Use the buttons on the Windows taskbar to switch to the application, size and position its window, and then immediately switch to PowerPoint and click Insert, Screenshot.

If the window or application still doesn't appear in the Available Windows gallery, use Screen Clipping to snag it. Use the same process to size the window; then click the button on the Windows taskbar to move back to PowerPoint and click Insert, Screenshot, Screen Clipping.

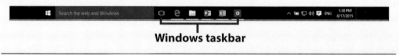

Windows taskbar

Turn Pictures into SmartArt

Some SmartArt graphics have picture placeholders that you can click to add images from your hard drive or online storage locations. (You'll learn about this topic in Chapter 6, "Creating Diagrams and Tables.") If you already have pictures inserted onto your slide, though, use the following technique to turn them into a SmartArt graphic.

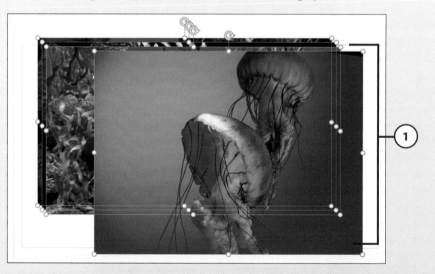

1. Select the picture(s) on the slide. The Picture Tools Format tab will become available.

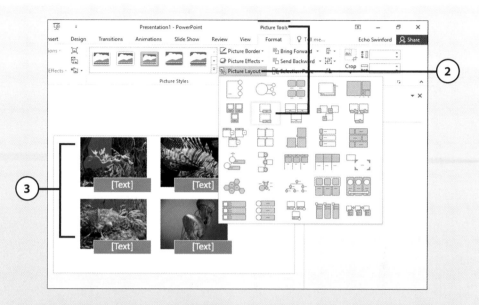

2. On the Picture Tools Format tab, click Picture Layout and then choose a SmartArt layout from the gallery. Remember that you can point to different selections in the gallery to preview the effect on the slide before you click to apply a SmartArt layout.

3. Complete the SmartArt diagram by adding text, changing colors, or even changing to a different Picture diagram layout on the SmartArt Tools Design and Format contextual tabs that appear when you select the SmartArt graphic you just created. To learn more about formatting SmartArt graphics, see Chapter 6.

Cropping and Resizing Pictures

It's important to learn to crop and resize pictures properly rather than simply stretching them to fit into a space. Not only does this avoid the warped "funhouse mirror" images that result from stretching, but a good crop will often increase the drama factor of your image and make it stand out that much more. You can also crop pictures into shapes such as an oval or a rounded rectangle.

Resize Pictures

Always resize pictures proportionately; otherwise, people and objects
will look too wide or too narrow.

1. Insert a picture onto a slide and
   select it. Click and drag a corner
   handle of the image to resize
   smaller or larger.

Press Shift to Maintain Proportions

Press Shift while you drag a corner
handle to prevent stretching and
keep your picture in proportion.

2. Don't drag from any of the side
   handles; this will distort the picture even if you do press Shift!

Fitting a Square Peg into a Round Hole

If your picture isn't sized right for
the space it should go into, then
you'll need to crop it. You may want
to use the Crop to Aspect Ratio
tools, which are covered later in this
section, to make this job easier.

3. If your picture is distorted, click
   Reset Picture on the Picture Tools
   Format tab, and then click Reset
   Picture & Size. The Reset Picture
   option above it removes artistic
   effects and other formatting
   options, but it doesn't restore the
   proportion.

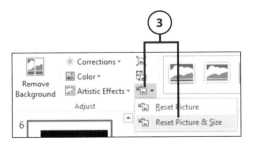

Resizing by the Numbers

If you know the width or height you want the image to be, input one of those values on the Size group of the Picture Tools Format tab and press Enter. Your picture should resize proportionately.

If it doesn't, right-click the picture and choose Format Picture. In the Format Picture pane under Size & Properties, click Size to expand those options. Make sure Scale Height and Scale Width are the same value, and then click Lock aspect ratio to keep everything in proportion when you resize.

Crop Pictures

Use PowerPoint's crop tools to get rid of parts of pictures and help them better fit into their designated space. Insert a picture onto a slide to get started.

1. Select the picture and click the Crop button on the Picture Tools Format tab.

2. Crop handles will appear on the sides and corners of the image, indicating that you're ready to crop.

3. Move your mouse pointer toward a crop handle. When it turns into a black crop tool, click and drag the crop mark to crop the picture.

4. Notice that cropped areas of the picture will become semitranspar-ent so you can easily see what you're cropping out and what you're leaving in.

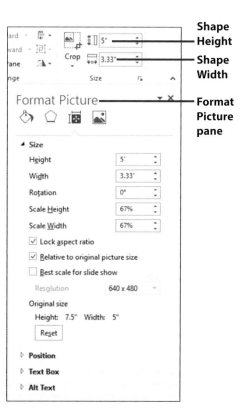

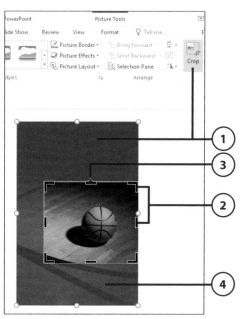

5. After you've positioned the crop handles, you may want to resize the picture inside the crop frame. To do this, click and drag one of the round corner handles. If necessary, press Shift to keep the picture from distorting.

6. To reposition the picture inside the crop frame, click anywhere on the picture. When the cursor becomes a four-headed arrow, drag it into position.

7. When you're finished, click away from the picture, press Esc on your keyboard, or click the Crop button on the Ribbon to apply the crop.

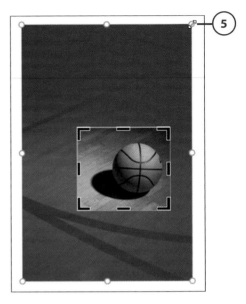

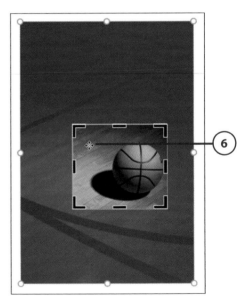

>>>Go Further

CROPPING BY THE NUMBERS

If you need finer control than the crop handles can give you, or if you want to further refine a rough crop you did with them, use the Crop settings in the Format Picture pane.

Right-click the picture and choose Format Picture (to open the formatting pane), and then click the Picture icon. Click Crop to expand those settings.

Format Picture

Picture

▷ Picture Corrections
▷ Picture Color
▲ Crop

Picture position

Width	4.45"
Height	6.67"
Offset X	-0.45"
Offset Y	-0.2"

Crop position

Width	3.45"
Height	3.31"
Left	3.9"
Top	2.31"

When you're cropping by the numbers, it helps to think of the crop as a frame sitting on top of the picture. You can adjust either the picture or the crop frame itself.

Picture Position Width and Height settings indicate the size of the original picture. You probably don't want to change either value here because the aspect ratio isn't locked the way it can be in the Size & Position settings. If you change one value, the other one won't automatically change proportionately, and your picture will become distorted.

The Picture Position Offset X and Y settings indicate how far off-center the picture is inside the crop frame. For example, if Offset X and Offset Y are both zero, the picture is exactly centered inside the crop frame. Changing these settings moves the picture inside the frame.

The Crop Position Width and Height settings indicate the size of the crop frame, which is also the size of the cropped picture. Changing these settings changes the size of the frame. If you make either one too big, it may be larger than your picture, in which case it will look like the picture is cut off. If this happens, you can always resize the picture inside the crop. See step 5 in this exercise for the easiest way to accomplish this task.

The Crop Position Left and Top settings indicate the position of the crop frame on the slide. Input 0 for Crop Position Left, and the crop frame will be flush with the left edge of the slide. Add a 0 for Crop Position Top, and the crop frame is flush with the top edge of the slide.

Crop to Aspect Ratio

Crop to Aspect Ratio is the fastest way to create pictures that will perfectly fit your slide. To begin, insert a picture onto your slide and select it.

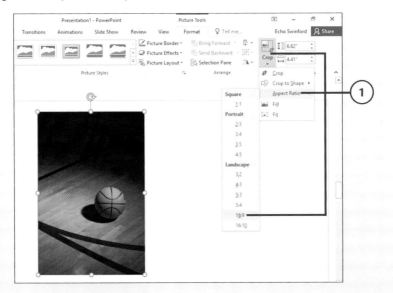

1. On the Picture Tools Format tab, click the Crop button arrow, point to Aspect Ratio, and then choose 16:9.

What Are All These Aspect Ratios?

The aspect ratios listed in the Crop to Aspect Ratio settings are typical slide and picture proportions. To crop a picture so it fills a widescreen slide, choose 16:9. To fill a 10" x 7.5" slide, which was the default in PowerPoint 2010 and prior versions, select the 4:3 aspect ratio. For a perfect square, click 1:1.

2. Crop marks will appear so you can see how the picture will be cropped in order to fit the desired aspect ratio. Resize and reposition the picture inside the crop frame if necessary. See steps 5 and 6 in the previous exercise for instructions.

3. Click the Crop button again when you're finished cropping.

4. If necessary, select the picture again to resize it. On the Picture Tools Format tab, input 7.5 as the Height value and press Enter. Assuming you cropped to the 16:9 aspect ratio, the width will automatically change to 13.33". If you cropped to the 4:3 aspect ratio, the width would automatically change to 10".

5. Drag the picture into place to cover the slide or use the Align tools to position it.

Crop to Shape

You can fill a shape with a picture, but sometimes it's easier to crop the picture into a shape. To begin, insert a picture onto your slide and select it.

1. On the Picture Tools Format tab, click the Crop button arrow, and then point to Crop to Shape.

2. Select a shape from the shape gallery that appears. The picture will be cropped to the selected shape.

3. If necessary, select the picture again and click the top of the Crop button so you can resize and position the picture within the shaped crop frame. Use the instructions in steps 5 and 6 of the Crop Pictures exercise.

4. Apply more formatting as desired, for example, soft edges or artistic filters.

How Can I Crop a Picture into a Circle?

To crop a picture into a perfect circle, first use Crop to Aspect Ratio and choose Square, 1:1. Then use Crop to Shape and choose the oval. An oval with a 1:1 aspect ratio is a circle.

>>>Go Further
WHAT ARE CROP TO FILL AND CROP TO FIT?

At the bottom of the Crop button menu are options for Fill and Fit. You can use these with pictures inserted into picture placeholders, such as the one on the Picture with Caption layout. Insert a picture on this layout and you'll see that it fills the placeholder and crops the excess areas of the picture that don't fit. Use Crop, Fit to show the entire picture in the picture placeholder area. Use Crop, Fill to go back to filling the placeholder.

Formatting Pictures

Because pictures are treated mostly as shapes on a slide, you can use many of the same formatting options on them as you can on shapes. For example, you can add a border to your picture and change its color and width. Or you can add a reflection, a shadow, or soft edges by selecting these options from the Picture Effects galleries—just as you would select them from the Drawing Effects galleries to apply them to a shape.

Since you already know how to apply those effects, in this section we'll concentrate on the additional options that PowerPoint reserves strictly for pictures. Adjusting brightness, contrast, and sharpness may not completely save a really bad picture, but it might make the difference between one that's usable and one that's not. Artistic effects make your picture look like a sketch or painting, which may add some interest to your presentation. And recoloring pictures is an easy way to help make them feel as though they go together. Unleash your inner artist!

Apply Formatting with Picture Styles

Picture styles provide combinations of shapes, borders, and shadows to apply to your pictures with one click.

1. Insert a picture onto your slide and select it.

2. On the Picture Tools Format tab, click the More button to expand the Picture Styles gallery.

3. Click a style from the Picture Styles gallery to apply it.

4. To resize or reposition the picture within the Picture Styles frame, click the Crop button and follow the instructions in steps 5 and 6 of the Crop Pictures exercise.

5. To remove the Picture Style formatting, click the Reset Picture button on the Picture Tools Format tab.

Remove Picture Backgrounds

Removing the background of an image lets the slide background appear instead. For example, if your slide has a dark background, you might want to remove a white background from a corporate logo image.

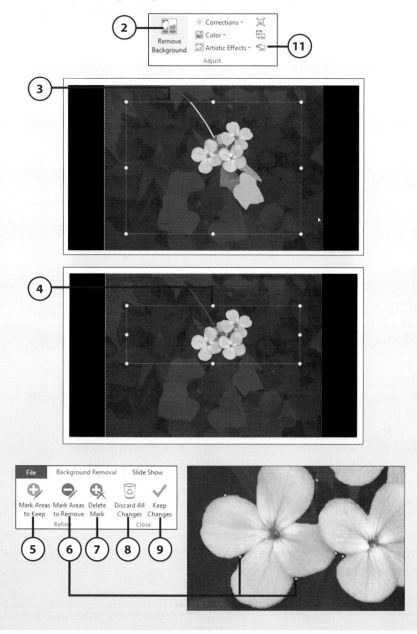

1. Insert a picture onto your slide and select it.

2. On the Picture Tools Format tab, click the Remove Background button.

3. Notice that parts of your image will be colored magenta. The magenta parts of the picture will be removed.

4. The internal frame gives PowerPoint a general guess as to what you want to keep. Dragging the handles to resize and position that frame may help PowerPoint select more appropriate areas to discard. It doesn't hurt to try, anyway!

5. If parts of the picture you want to keep are colored magenta, click the Mark Areas to Keep button, and then click and drag on that area in the picture so it becomes colored again. Zoom in if necessary, and use as many "keep marks" as you need. "Keep" marks appear with a + symbol.

6. If parts of the picture you want to be discarded are not colored magenta, click the Mark Areas to Remove button, and then click and drag on those areas in the picture. Zoom in if necessary, and use as many "remove marks" as you need. "Remove" marks appear with a – symbol.

7. Click Delete Mark and then click on a mark to remove it.

8. Click Discard All Changes to start over.

9. Click away from the picture to deselect it or click the Keep Changes button when you're finished.

Refining the Image

If a lot of empty space is left around the edges of the image when you're finished, you can crop the picture. Use the instructions in the Crop Pictures exercise.

10. Apply effects such as color or artistic filters if you want.

11. To remove all changes to the picture, click the Reset Picture button on the Picture Tools Format tab.

It's Not All Good

The Remove Background tool can be super finicky. Sometimes when you add a Keep or Remove mark or resize the internal frame, another area of the image reverses itself and either becomes visible or turns magenta (indicating it will be discarded). The only thing you can do to help this is to pay attention. If you know which mark is causing it to happen, you can delete that mark and add another in a slightly different place or at a slightly different length.

If you're having trouble getting into the nooks and crannies of a picture, try using the Picture Effects to add a 1- or 2.5-point soft edge. Sometimes just softening the edges that little bit is enough to make it work even if you've left tiny bits of the background or ragged edges, as you can see in the picture here.

Apply Picture Corrections

Tweaking brightness and contrast are pretty standard image correction procedures, as is sharpening a slightly blurry image.

Brightness and contrast generally work together. Brightness refers to the overall lightness or darkness of a picture, and contrast refers to the difference in brightness between objects or areas in the image. Together, brightness and contrast can improve pictures that are a little too dark or light.

Sharpen and soften controls are more straightforward. Sharpen helps refine edges of objects in the image to enhance the details. Soften blurs edges of objects and contrasting regions to make the photo less detailed. Sharpen can help correct a slightly blurry image, but it's not a miracle tool!

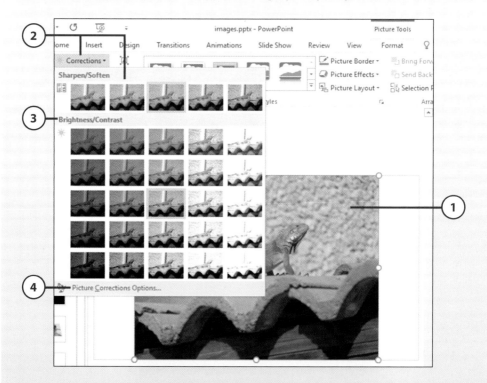

1. Insert a picture onto your slide and select it.

2. On the Picture Tools Format tab click Corrections and then hover over the Sharpen/Soften options. You will see a Live Preview of what that setting would look like if applied to your image. Click a thumbnail to apply that setting.

3. In the same Corrections gallery, hover over the Brightness/Contrast thumbnails. You will see a Live Preview of what that setting would look like if applied to your image. Click a thumbnail to apply that setting.

4. To further refine any of these settings, click Picture Corrections Options at the bottom of the Corrections gallery. This opens the Format Picture pane.

5. In the Format Picture pane, adjust the sharpness by moving the slider or typing in a specific value. You can also access the same options that were available in the Corrections gallery by clicking the Presets button.

6. Also in the Format Picture pane, you can adjust the Brightness and Contrast settings separately. Move the sliders or input your own values for each. Select from the same options that were available in the Corrections gallery by clicking the Presets button.

7. Click Reset to remove all Picture Corrections changes.

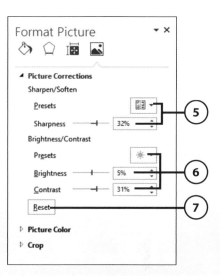

Recolor and Color Correct a Picture

PowerPoint has quite a few color options and corrections for images, including color saturation, color tone, and various recolor settings.

Use a Light Hand with Color Correction Tools

Saturation refers to the intensity of color. Highly saturated images have overly bright colors, which usually don't project well. Just remember that a little saturation goes a long way and don't overdo it.

The same goes for color tone, which refers to color temperature. A lower temperature value produces cool tones. With too low a temperature, the picture may look overly blue. Likewise, higher temperature values produce warm tones, which potentially make a picture look too yellow. As with saturation, a little tonal correction can go a long way.

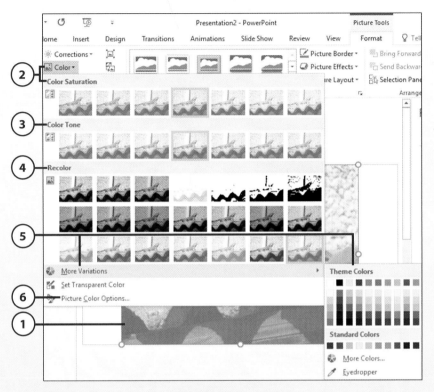

1. Insert a picture onto your slide and select it.

2. On the Picture Tools Format tab click Color and then hover over the Color Saturation options. You will see a Live Preview of what that setting would look like if applied to your image. Click a thumbnail to apply that setting.

3. In the same Color gallery, hover over the Color Tone thumbnails. You will see a Live Preview of what that setting would look like if applied to your image. Click a thumbnail to apply that setting.

4. Hover over the various Recolor thumbnails to see how they affect your picture if applied. Your options on the top row include grayscale, sepia, washout, and various percentages of black and white. You also have dark and light duotone recolor options based on your theme colors.

5. Click More Variations at the bottom of the Color gallery to access the complete theme color palette, to mix your own color in the More Colors gallery, or to use the Eyedropper tool to match a color anywhere on your screen.

What Is Set Transparent Color?

You may have noticed the Set Transparent Color option near the bottom of the Color gallery. Select this tool and then click your image. All pixels that are the same as the clicked color will become transparent. Sounds great, right? The drawback is this tool makes only one specific color transparent, but most photographs use a mix of many colors to create a color. For example, a white area on a picture may consist of pixels that are many shades of white, even though it looks like one color of white to your eye.

The point is, if you click the Set Transparent Color tool and then click your photo to make that color transparent, don't be surprised if the results aren't what you expect. Sometimes you'll get lucky, but if you don't, try using the Remove Picture Background tool instead.

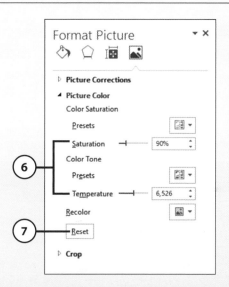

6. Click Picture Color Options to open the Format Picture pane, where you can enter your own color saturation and tone values. Access the same settings that were available from the Ribbon by clicking the Presets buttons.

7. Click Reset to remove all color saturation, tone, and recolor settings that have been applied.

Apply Artistic Effects

Artistic effects apply filters to the image to make it look more like a sketch or painting.

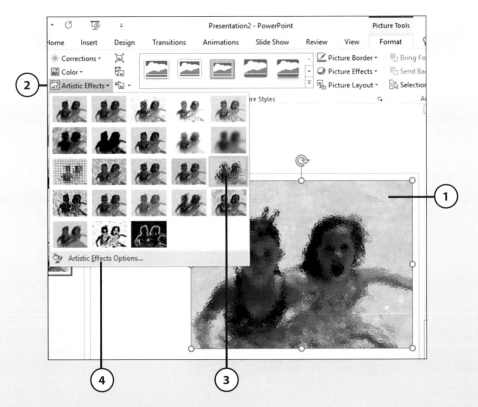

1. Insert a picture onto your slide and select it.

2. On the Picture Tools Format tab, click Artistic Effects.

3. Hover over the thumbnails to see how the effect will affect your image when applied. Click a thumbnail to apply it.

4. To further refine the effect you've applied, click Artistic Effects Options. This opens the Format Picture pane.

5. If necessary, in the Effects section of the Format Picture pane, click Artistic Effects to expand those options.

6. Use the sliders or input your own values for the settings applicable to that artistic effect.

7. Access the Artistic Effects gallery from the Artistic Effects button. Unfortunately, you won't see a Live Preview when you access the gallery here. Click any thumbnail to apply the effect.

8. Click the Reset button to remove the artistic effects and settings that have been applied.

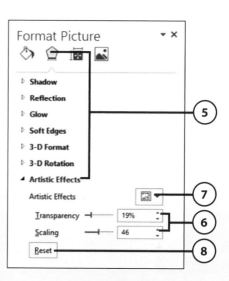

Artistic Effects Can Affect File Size

Artistic effects can greatly impact your file size. This is because PowerPoint practices what is known as "nondestructive editing." In other words, you can reset your picture at any time to remove the artistic filters and restore your original image. This requires that PowerPoint keep your original image as well as a copy of it with the filter applied, all of which contributes to a larger file size. In fact, picture compression doesn't usually work on images that have artistic effects applied, and although it's counterintuitive, using picture compression often increases the file size when artistic effects are in play!

Swap One Picture for Another

Sometimes it's helpful to substitute one picture for another. That's what the Change Picture command is for.

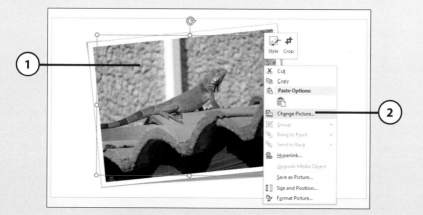

1. Insert a picture onto your slide and select it. On the Picture Tools Format tab, apply a style from the Picture Styles gallery.

2. Right-click the picture and choose Change Picture. You can also click the Change Picture button on the Picture Tools Format tab.

③ ──────── Insert Pictures   ×

      From a file   Browse ▸
      Browse files on your computer or local network

      Bing Image Search   Search Bing
      Search the web

      OneDrive - Personal   Browse ▸
      echo.with.superpowers@outlook.com

      Also insert from:

3. The Insert Pictures dialog box that opens combines options to add pictures from your hard drive or from an online search or storage location. Choose a new picture and click Insert.

Tips for Using Change Picture

One of the benefits of using Change Picture is not having to reformat everything when you want to swap one image for another. But not all picture formatting remains when you use Change Picture.

Styles applied from the Picture Styles gallery remain. So do picture borders and Picture Effects settings such as shadows, reflections, glows, soft edges, bevels, and 3-D rotation—basically anything you see and apply in the Picture Styles group on the Picture Tools Format tab of the Ribbon.

Settings applied from the Adjust group are removed when you use Change Picture. These include remove background, brightness/contrast and sharpen/soften settings, color corrections and recoloring, and artistic effects. If you need to change a picture that has these settings applied, you'll generally be better off inserting the new picture as usual and then using Format Painter on the Home tab to "paint" the formatting from the old to the new image.

Also, don't use Change Picture on pictures you inserted in placeholders because strange things can happen to the size of the picture, and it may not fill the space as it should. Instead, delete the picture to get back to the empty placeholder and then click the icon in the placeholder to add the new picture as usual.

>>>Go Further

PICTURES IN CONTENT PLACEHOLDERS
VERSUS PICTURE PLACEHOLDERS

PowerPoint has two kinds of placeholders that let you add pictures, and they work differently.

A content placeholder lets you add seven types of content: text, tables, charts, SmartArt graphics, pictures (from your hard drive), online pictures, and video. Most of the default layouts include content placeholders.

A picture placeholder lets you add only a picture. The default Picture with Caption layout uses a picture placeholder. You may have custom layouts that use them as well.

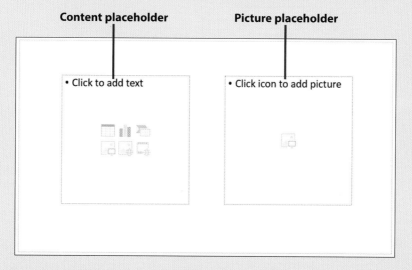

Content placeholder　　　　**Picture placeholder**

The biggest difference between these is how they behave when you insert a picture, whether it's an online picture or one from your hard drive. When you insert a picture into a content placeholder, the entire picture is inserted and fitted into the placeholder as best it can. For example, if you have a square content placeholder and you insert a horizontal picture in it, the picture will fit the width of the placeholder and leave the top and bottom areas blank. Likewise, if you add a more vertical picture to a square content placeholder, the picture fits to the vertical size of the placeholder and you have blank areas on either side.

When you insert a picture into a picture placeholder, the picture is cropped, and the entire placeholder area is filled. If you don't like the way PowerPoint crops your pictures in a picture placeholder, click the Crop button and reposition the picture within the crop frame as you learned earlier in this chapter. Or you can use Crop, Fit, and the picture will fit inside the picture placeholder just as it does with a content placeholder. Use Crop, Fill to go back to filling the entire placeholder area.

Content placeholder   **Picture placeholder**

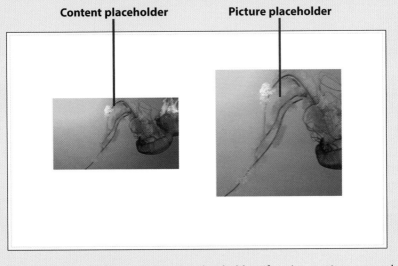

For you template builders, use picture placeholders if you're creating custom layouts for a photo collage or a full-screen picture, for example. This way, inserted images fill the entire space regardless of the size or orientation of the picture itself. It's generally less work for your users.

By the way, picture placeholders have only one Pictures icon, which inserts pictures from your hard drive. To insert an online picture, go to the Insert tab and choose Online Pictures while you're on any slide with an empty picture placeholder. This way you bypass the picture icon, and the online picture will automatically fill the placeholder. Inserted pictures will also automatically fill any empty content placeholders, but it's not as critical with them since they have icons for both pictures and online pictures.

Compressing Pictures

With today's cameras and phones that take mega-megapixel pictures, it's easy to end up with huge files. When this happens, you might consider using the Compress Pictures feature to bring them to a more manageable size.

You should know a few things about picture compression. First is that it's on by default. Yes, PowerPoint automatically compresses your pictures when you save your file. It uses a target pixels-per-inch resolution of 220, which gives an adequate balance of quality versus file size for most uses. Second is that you can still use Compress Pictures to compress more. Third is that after PowerPoint has compressed your images, it won't compress them again at a higher resolution because that would cause your pictures to look really bad.

Compress Pictures to Reduce File Size

Apply picture compression according to how you intend to use your file. For example, if you need to email it, you might want to apply maximum compression.

1. Select a picture on a slide. Ideally, use a presentation that includes a number of pictures.

2. Click the Compress Pictures button on the Picture Tools Format tab. This opens the Compress Pictures dialog box.

3. To apply compression to all images in the file, uncheck Apply Only to This Picture.

4. Uncheck Delete Cropped Areas of Pictures if you want to leave the cropped areas available.

5. Select the target output resolution, which will depend on how you intend to use the file. Select E-mail (96 ppi) for maximum compression. Use Web (150 ppi) if you plan to post your presentation online or project it. Choose Print (220 ppi) if you intend to print. The HD option (330 ppi) is now available for high-definition displays.

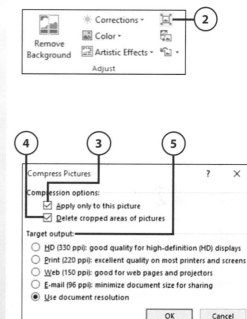

Some Options Aren't Available

If the picture has already been compressed, higher-resolution compression options may not be available. For example, if you've saved the file and left PowerPoint's default 220 ppi compression setting selected, you won't be able to compress the image again using 330 ppi (HD).

Many images you download from the Web will already be fairly compressed, so many of the higher-resolution compression options may not be available for them. Also, although PowerPoint will let you specify compression settings for CMYK images, they won't actually compress at all.

The option to Use Document Resolution refers to the resolution specified on the Slide Show tab in the Set Up Slide Show settings. Usually this resolution is the same as your computer screen, unless you consciously changed it.

It's Not All Good

Change or Disable Automatic Compression

You can change the automatic picture compression setting for any open file by going to File, Options, Advanced. In the Image Size and Quality settings, opt to discard editing data such as cropped areas that are used to restore an image to its original state, turn off compression altogether, or choose a different target resolution setting. (The 330 ppi option is new in PowerPoint 2016.)

The biggest drawback here is you must remember to do this for every file. If you're willing to edit your registry (or know someone who's willing to do it for you), you can turn off automatic image compression for all PowerPoint files. To learn how, see the instructions at http://www.pptfaq.com/FAQ00862_PowerPoint_2007_and_2010_make_pictures_blurry-_loses_GIF_animation.htm. (Substitute 16.0 for 12.0 in the registry key listed.)

After disabling image compression this way, you'll have to use Compress Pictures any time you want to compress the file. But at least that way you, not PowerPoint, choose when and how much it happens.

Creating a Photo Album

If you have a bunch of pictures you want to pull together for a presentation, a quick way is to create a photo album. Unfortunately, the Photo Album feature is pretty old and doesn't give you a way to insert online pictures. Download pictures from your online storage or set up a synced folder on your hard drive so you can access all the images you want to include.

Create a Photo Album

Turn your pictures into a photo album, fast.

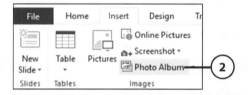

1. Go to File, New and start a new presentation based on the Blank Presentation theme.

2. On the Insert tab, click Photo Album. This opens the Photo Album dialog box.

3. Click the File/Disk button to insert pictures from your hard drive. Select pictures you want to include and click Insert to add them to the picture list. You can press Ctrl while clicking to select multiple individual pictures. To select a range of pictures, press Shift and click the first and last pictures in the range.

4. Click New Text Box to create a slide with a text box you can type in later. This is useful to create sections throughout your photo album.

5. You can change the picture layout to multiple pictures or multiple pictures plus slide title. The default photo album uses a Fit to Slide Picture Layout, which fills each slide with a picture.

6. When the pictures don't encompass the entire slide, you'll be able to change the Frame shape to apply settings such as rounded rectangles or soft edges. The preview thumbnail will give you an idea of what the slide will look like.

7. Reorder or remove pictures using the buttons below the picture list. Be sure to check the box beside the pictures to make these tools available.

8. Use the buttons below the picture preview to adjust brightness and contrast or rotate a picture.

9. Turn on Captions below all pictures to automatically add the filename below each image.

10. Choose a theme at the bottom of the dialog box if you want. You'll have a better selection of themes to choose from if you skip applying a theme here and do it afterward from the Design tab.

11. After you're finished with all the settings and picture touch-ups, click Create to make your photo album!

12. Other steps to complete your photo album might include adding any necessary text, applying automatic transitions (Chapter 8, "Adding Animations and Transitions"), and setting the presentation to loop (Chapter 11, "Setting Up Your Slide Show").

13. To add pictures to or otherwise edit your photo album later, go to the Insert tab and click the arrow next to the Photo Album button, and then choose Edit Photo Album.

Use Table Styles and other options for quick formatting.

Learn to create, format, and edit SmartArt graphics.

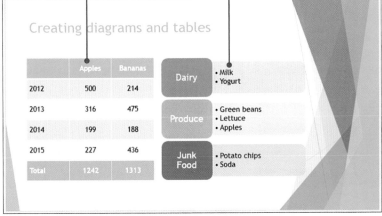

In this chapter, you will learn about creating SmartArt diagrams and tables. Specific topics in this chapter include the following:

→ Creating SmartArt graphics
→ Formatting SmartArt graphics
→ Working with tables
→ Formatting a table

Creating Diagrams and Tables

Diagrams and tables can be very efficient ways to present information in PowerPoint. The nice thing about them is they are visual formats that can help organize your data—which is perfect for a presentation.

Best practice when using both diagrams and tables is to streamline your text. Even though the information is organized, that still doesn't mean you get to put every word on the slide!

Creating SmartArt Graphics

When using SmartArt, pay attention to the type of diagram you're using. Choose one that's appropriate for the information you're trying to convey. Otherwise, you run the risk of confusing the audience rather than helping them understand.

Insert a SmartArt Graphic

Starting a SmartArt diagram (properly known as a SmartArt graphic) is pretty straight-forward. You can insert a SmartArt diagram from an icon in a content placeholder or by clicking the SmartArt button on the Insert tab.

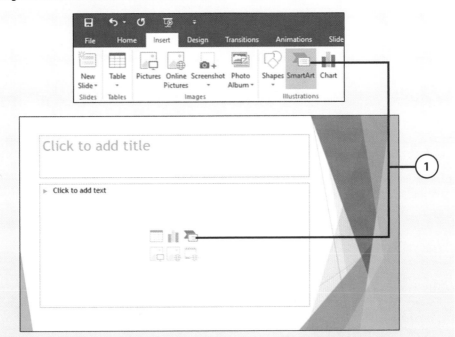

1. Click the SmartArt button on the Insert tab or in a content placeholder to open the Choose a SmartArt Graphic dialog box, where you choose a SmartArt graphic.

Switching the Slide Layout

If you need to change the slide layout to one with a content placeholder, use the Layout button on the Home tab.

2. Jump to a specific category of diagram on the left pane in the dialog box.

3. Click a specific diagram in the middle area to see its preview and description on the right.

4. Click OK to create the diagram.

Change to a Different Diagram

If you decide you want to change the type of diagram you're using, you don't have to start all over. Select the current diagram and then choose a different layout from the gallery on the SmartArt Tools Design tab.

The gallery will show other SmartArt graphics in the current category you're working with. If you don't see the diagram you want, click the More button to expand the gallery and then choose More Layouts from the bottom of the gallery to see all the categories and diagrams.

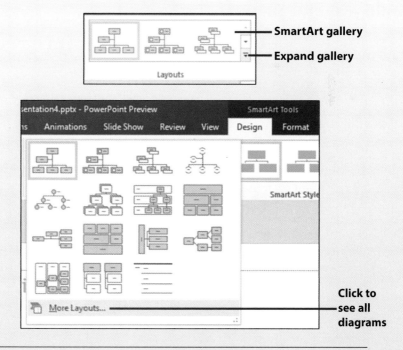

>>>Go Further
WHICH DIAGRAM DO I CHOOSE?

When you select a diagram in the Choose a SmartArt Graphic dialog box, a description of the diagram appears on the right. This can be helpful if you're not sure your content is exactly right for the diagram. In addition, you may see information about how much text the diagram can handle. For example, Vertical Bullet List tells you it works well for lists with long headings or top-level information. The Increasing Arrows Process tells you it's limited to five Level 1 items and that Level 2 can contain large amounts of text.

The Picture tab on the left of the dialog box simply displays all the diagrams that can use pictures in one category. These diagrams are repeated in their respective category tabs as well. The Office.com category shows diagrams that are downloaded upon insertion, so you must be signed in and have an Internet connection to add them.

Add Text and Shapes

When you're working with text in a SmartArt diagram, it may help to think about which "level" the text represents. You can promote and demote text in a SmartArt diagram just as you can with bulleted text lists.

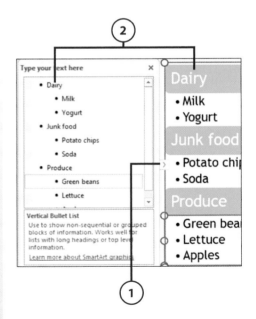

1. When you first insert a SmartArt diagram, the text pane will display to the left of the diagram. If it's not displayed, use the Text Pane button on the SmartArt Tools Design tab or click the small button with the chevron to toggle it on.

2. Type text in the pane, and it will appear in the diagram; type text in a shape in the diagram, and it will appear in the text pane.

Where to Type Text

You can type text into the text pane, or you might find it easier to type directly into the SmartArt diagram. When you're working in the text pane, the location you've selected is outlined in yellow. If you're typing in the diagram, the selected area is outlined in gray in the task pane.

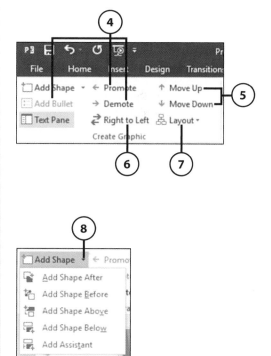

3. Press Enter to create a new line of text. You can then press Tab to create second-level text or Shift+Tab to promote second-level text to first-level text.

4. Click the Add Bullet and the Promote and Demote buttons on the SmartArt Tools Design tab to add text and increase or decrease its level, as necessary. Depending on the shape or text you have selected, one or more of these might be unavailable.

5. Click the Move Up and Move Down buttons as needed to reorder shapes or text in the pane.

6. Click the Right to Left button if you want to change the direction of a diagram. For example, this would change the arrow in a Continuous Block Process diagram from right to left.

7. Click the Layout button if you want to change the way the branches hang on an organization chart.

8. Click the Add Shape button arrow and select an option if you want to add a shape to a diagram.

>>>*Go Further*

OTHER OPTIONS BUTTONS

The Add Shape button on the SmartArt Tools Design tab might come in handy if you're having trouble inserting a shape manually. Not all options are available on all diagrams; they'll be grayed out if you can't use them on the current diagram. If you're interested in exactly what each option does, experiment with the options in an organization chart because org charts can use all of the options, including Layout, Right to Left, and every Add Shape option. You can find organization charts in the Hierarchy category of SmartArt diagrams.

Convert Text to SmartArt

So you've already typed your text as a bulleted list, and now you want to give it a little oomph. It's a piece of cake to change that text box into a SmartArt graphic.

1. Type text in a text box or placeholder.

2. Right-click in the placeholder and choose Convert to SmartArt.

3. Select a diagram from the flyout gallery or click More SmartArt Graphics at the bottom to open the complete diagram gallery.

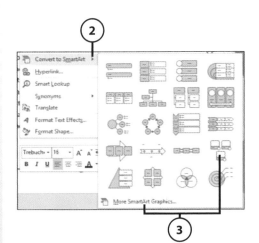

Convert Diagrams Back to Text

You can convert text to a SmartArt graphic, but what about the other way around? Of course you can change a diagram back into text!

To do so, click in a SmartArt diagram and choose Convert, Convert to Text on the SmartArt Tools Design tab.

Create a Picture Diagram

A lot of the SmartArt diagrams have placeholders to make it easy for you to include pictures.

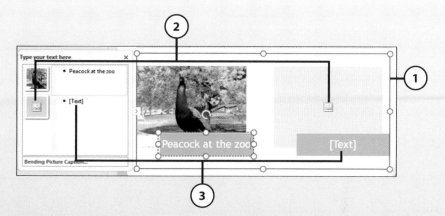

1. Insert a SmartArt graphic and choose one of the Picture diagrams.

2. Click the icon in a picture placeholder to insert a picture from your computer, from your OneDrive, from a Bing search, or from other places you've connected to (like Facebook or Flickr).

3. Click in a text placeholder to add text as usual.

Formatting SmartArt Graphics

SmartArt graphics can be formatted manually, but why not save time by using the various preset options? They're available on the SmartArt Tools Design tab and on the right-click (shortcut) menu.

Change Diagram Colors

When you insert a SmartArt diagram, it uses your theme's Accent 1 color by default. If you'd rather choose a different Accent color or see more colorful options, use the Change Colors button.

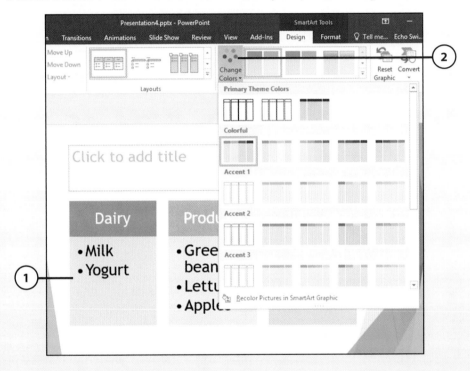

1. Insert a SmartArt diagram.

2. On the SmartArt Tools Design tab, click the Change Colors button and click an option to apply it.

Recolor Pictures in SmartArt

If your diagram includes pictures, you might want to experiment with the Recolor Pictures in SmartArt Graphic setting at the bottom of the Change Colors gallery.

>>>Go Further

USE SHAPE FORMATTING ON SMARTART GRAPHICS

At the heart of it, SmartArt graphics are really just shapes. If you prefer to use the same styles that are available in the Shape Quick Styles gallery, head to the SmartArt Tools Format tab, which is almost identical to the Drawing Tools Format tab.

An even faster way to access the Shape Quick Styles gallery and the Fill and Line tools is to click inside the SmartArt diagram and select one or more shapes. Then right-click the shape and choose your weapon.

It's Not All Good

The colors in the SmartArt Change Colors gallery are based on the accent colors in your theme colors. That's good. What's not so good is that the Colorful options usually start with the Accent 2 color instead of Accent 1.

The other thing that's not so good is the lighter tints used in many of the diagrams. Luckily, SmartArt graphics can be recolored manually, so you're not stuck with them. You might want to manually apply a light gray color from the SmartArt Tools Format tab as a replacement for some of those tints.

Change Diagram Styles

SmartArt styles included in the Best Match for Document section of the SmartArt Styles gallery are based on effects provided by your theme; those in the 3-D section are not.

1. Insert a SmartArt diagram.

2. Click the More button on the SmartArt Tools Design tab to expand the Styles gallery.

Reset Graphic button

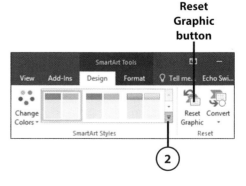

3. Click a style to apply it.

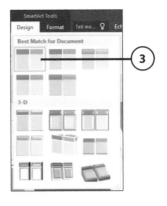

Reset Is Your Friend

If you completely mess up your diagram formatting and want to start over, click the Reset Graphic button on the SmartArt Tools Design tab. If you need to reset a single shape, right-click the shape and choose Reset Shape.

3-D Doesn't Apply

If you choose one of the styles in the 3-D section of the SmartArt Styles gallery, and the diagram doesn't change, make sure you haven't selected Edit in 2-D on the SmartArt Tools Format tab. This setting helps you edit text and resize shapes in a 3-D diagram by temporarily making it 2-D.

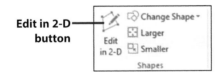

It's Not All Good

Most of the styles in the 3-D section of the SmartArt Styles gallery are poorly designed. The extra formatting and odd angles often detract from your content rather than enhancing it. Use these sparingly and make sure the text in your diagram can still be read easily.

Format Fonts in Diagrams

Fonts in a SmartArt graphic resize automatically as you type. This is definitely convenient, but if you've streamlined your content as you should, it can result in some really clunky text.

1. Insert a SmartArt diagram and add text. Note that the text is very large relative to the size of the shapes, but it resizes as you type more text in a shape.

2. Select text and use the Font tools on the Home tab to change text size and apply other formatting such as bold or italics.

3. Or you can select text in the diagram and format it with the tools on the Mini Toolbar that appears.

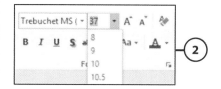

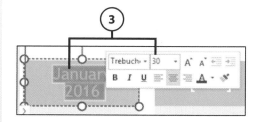

Formatting Text Is Formatting Text

You can use any of the typical text formatting tools on text in a SmartArt graphic. Either select text directly or select one or more shapes and apply the formatting you want. Of course, if you select the entire diagram, the formatting will apply to all fonts in the diagram.

After you manually format text in a SmartArt graphic, it loses its "smartness" and won't automatically resize any longer. If you continue to add or remove shapes, you may need to manually resize the text again.

Working with Tables

Tables are a great way to organize information into a visual format, but the tendency is to include way too much text. One trick for streamlining text in a table is to remove redundant text—or move it into the first column or header row.

Create Tables

As with pretty much everything else in PowerPoint, you can create a table from the Ribbon or use the icon in the content placeholders.

1. Click the Table button on the Insert tab to see a list of table creation options.

2. Move your mouse pointer over the grid to indicate how many rows and columns you want in your table. Click to insert the table.

3. Or click Insert Table, type the number of columns and rows in the Insert Table dialog box, and press Enter.

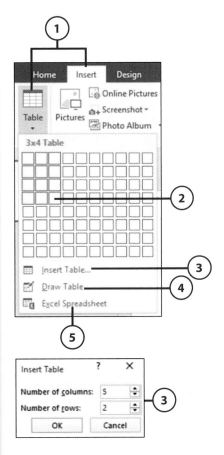

Inserting a Table

When you create a table using the grid or the Insert Table option, the table will be inserted into any empty content placeholder on the slide. If you don't have any empty content placeholders, the table will be inserted onto the middle of the slide.

4. Or click Draw Table and drag a rectangle on the slide to create a one-cell table in which you must manually draw rows and columns. This command is fine to use with existing tables, but it is not a good way to create a new table.

5. Or click Excel Spreadsheet to insert an embedded Excel spreadsheet. This method enables you to use Excel's formatting tools.

6. Or click the Table icon in a content placeholder. If you need to change the slide layout to one with a content placeholder, use the Layout button on the Home tab.

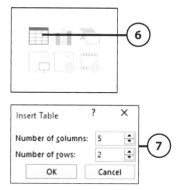

7. When you click the Table icon, the Insert Table dialog box opens. Type the number of columns and rows you want and press Enter.

Move Around in a Table

You'll generally use the keyboard when you're navigating a table.

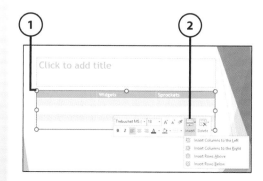

1. Click in a table cell and start typing to add text. Then use any of the following actions to move within the table:

- To move to the next cell on the right, press Tab. To move to the next cell on the left, press Shift+Tab.

- Pressing Tab at the end of a row moves you to the beginning of the next row.

- Pressing Tab in the last cell of the table adds a new row.

- To move to the next row down, press the down arrow on your keyboard. Press the up arrow to move up a row. The left and right arrows will move you left and right.

2. Right-click inside a table cell and choose Insert or Delete from the Mini Toolbar and make a selection to add or remove rows or columns. These Insert and Delete options are also available on the Table Tools Layout tab.

3. Select multiple cells by clicking and dragging your mouse pointer across cells.

4. Select columns by clicking and dragging your mouse pointer. Or you can move the pointer above or below a column until it turns into a black arrow and click to select the column. You can also click and drag this pointer to select multiple columns. Similarly, hover to the left or right of the table to select rows.

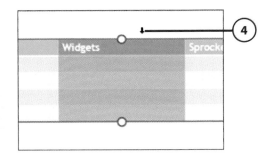

5. If you're having trouble selecting a row, column, or the table itself, use the Select tool on the Table Tools Layout tab.

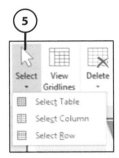

Resize Tables, Rows, and Columns

Tables can be a little tricky to size. The best practice is to size the whole table first and then resize individual columns and rows as necessary.

1. Click and drag any outside edge of a table to resize it.

2. Use the Table Size tools on the Table Tools Layout tab to resize the entire table by the numbers. Press Enter after you type a height or width.

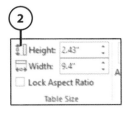

3. Hover near cell borders with your mouse until the pointer changes to a double-headed arrow. Click and drag to manually resize a column or a single row.

4. With your double-headed pointer on the right-hand border of a column, double-click to resize. The column will become as wide as the longest text in it.

5. To shorten a line of text within a table cell, press Shift+Enter where you want the line to break.

6. Use the Cell Size tools on the Table Tools Layout tab to resize selected cells. Press Enter after you type a row height or column width.

7. Click the Distribute Rows button to make selected rows the same height.

8. Click the Distribute Columns button to make selected columns the same height.

Formatting a Table

The best practice for table formatting is to keep it clean and simple and let the content shine. Anything that makes the text difficult to read is a no-no. Toning down the shading and removing borders, or at least making them not so obvious, can work wonders.

Apply Table Quick Styles

Table quick styles are great for fast formatting, but you may want to tweak some of the settings afterward.

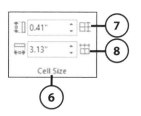

1. Select your table. Click the More button on the Table Quick Styles gallery to expand it.

2. Click a table thumbnail to apply the style.

3. Or click Clear Table to remove all formatting and revert to black text with black borders and no cell fills.

4. Click the options on the Table Tools Design tab for Header Row, Total Row, Banded Rows, and so on, to toggle them on and off. If the table style you chose doesn't have fill shading, the banding settings may turn border lines on and off.

It's Not All Good

Although the table quick styles are a handy way to format your table all at once, they are often a better starting point than ending point. Unfortunately, many of the table styles have a lot of distracting elements.

Especially when you're working on a slide with a light background, be wary of the styles labeled Dark and Best Match for Document. These often incorporate gradients and heavy shading that can detract from your content. Remember, you want the content to shine, not the table itself.

Also think about shading—the fill colors in some cells. It's good to have a light touch here and stick with gray shading if you can. Sometimes the fastest way to format a table with gray shading is to choose one of the options from the first column in the Table Quick Styles gallery and then manually change the heading color to Accent 1.

Format Table Shading

Adding or changing cell shading is similar to applying a fill to a shape.

1. Select the cells you want to apply shading to. Usually you'll select an entire row or column.

2. Click the Shading button on the Table Tools Design tab and choose the color to fill the cells with. On a slide with a white background, using white and light gray or two shades of light gray usually works well because it's neutral and will not fight with the content.

3. Click another row or column and click the Shading button or press Ctrl+Y to repeat adding that same fill color to the new row.

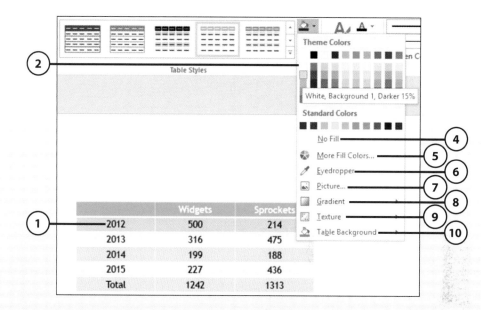

4. Click No Fill if you want to remove existing shading.

5. Use More Fill Colors to input RGB values or choose from the color honeycomb.

Highlight a Cell

Use a darker or brighter cell color fill and change the font to white to help highlight a cell or cells.

6. Use the Eyedropper to choose and apply a fill color.

7. Use the Picture option to fill each selected cell with a picture. If you want to use one picture to fill the whole table, choose Table Background and then Picture.

8. Use the Gradient option to fill selected cells with a gradient. To customize the gradient, choose More Gradients at the bottom of the Gradient gallery flyout.

9. Use the Texture button to fill selected cells with a texture.

10. Use the Table Background option to specify a fill for the table as a whole. Note that you may not be able to see table background formatting if you've applied a fill to the cells.

Adding Your Own Shading

If you plan to apply your own shading, it's usually easiest to start with a style that doesn't have any shading, such as Light Style 2.

Light Style 2

Format Table Borders

If your table has shading, you may not need borders. Or you may want to remove or lighten borders to let the content "breathe."

1. Select the cells you want to apply a border to. Usually you'll select the entire table, at least to start.

Selection Matters

When you're working with table borders, pay attention to what cells you've selected because borders are applied to the selection overall, not necessarily to individual cells.

For example, if you've selected a group of cells three columns wide by three rows deep and you apply a top border, it will be applied only to the first row of selected cells; a top border will not be applied to every selected row.

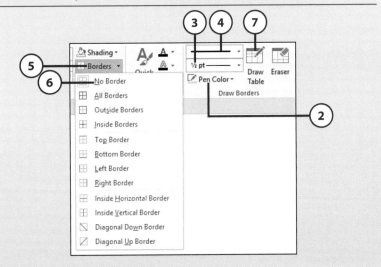

2. Use the Pen Color button to specify the border color.

3. Use the Pen Weight button to specify the border thickness.

4. Use the Pen Style button to specify dashed or solid borders.

5. Click the arrow beside the Borders button to open the Borders gallery. Click a border option to apply to the selected cells. Repeat with other border options (top, bottom, left, right, and so on).

6. Choose No Border if you want to remove all the borders from the table or selected cells.

Inside Borders

The Inside Horizontal and Vertical borders are useful when you have an entire table selected. Use these to add borders between all the internal cells. You will still need to apply top and bottom borders to the selection, but it's a lot faster than applying a top or bottom border to every row.

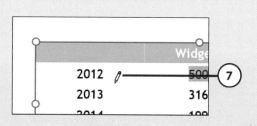

7. Alternatively, click on the Draw Table button, and your pointer will turn into a pencil. Click on appropriate cells in the table to apply borders.

>>>*Go Further*

DEALING WITH TABLE BORDERS

Table borders are one of the most poorly designed and fiddly features in PowerPoint. Generally, when you select a table or cells and then click the Borders gallery, you will have no idea which borders have actually been applied.

If you choose No Border, all borders on the selected cells will be removed. If you need to add some back after that (for example, you wanted to keep the top and bottom borders but not the left and right borders), it will be difficult for you to match the borders that are already there. This is because the table border tools don't reflect the current settings the way typical shapes and lines do.

If you're using the Borders gallery, you may want to start by selecting the table and clicking No Border to remove all borders from the table. Then specify the border formatting and add back what you need. Depending on which border you want and the particular cells you have selected, you may need to click the border tool to turn on a border, turn it off, and then turn it back on again to get it right.

Probably the easiest way to apply border formatting is to use the Draw Table button. Specify pen color, thickness, and style, and then click the Draw Table tool and click on each border you want to format. Don't click the Eraser button! This doesn't remove the border formatting; it removes the actual border between cells and merges them.

Format Text in a Table

Format table text just as you would any other text.

1. Select cells or specific text and right-click to access text formatting tools on the Mini Toolbar and the shortcut menu. Or you can use the text formatting tools on the Home tab if desired.

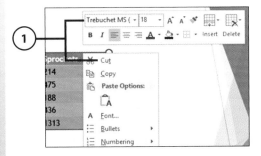

2. In the WordArt Styles group on the Table Tools Design tab, click Quick Styles to access WordArt text styles.

3. Click Text Fill, Text Outline, or Text Effects to apply any of these styles.

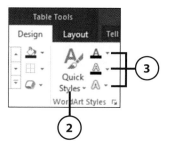

WordArt and Tables Don't Mix

Rarely should you use any WordArt (other than text fill color) in table text.

4. Select the table and click Center Vertically on the Table Tools Layout tab so the text isn't so top-heavy in the cells.

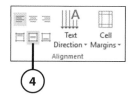

>>>Go Further

SPLITTING AND MERGING CELLS

You can split and merge cells using the tools on the Table Tools Layout tab. For the Merge Cells tool to become available, you must select more than one cell.

When you click the Split Cells button, you'll be prompted to specify how many rows and columns to split the cell into.

Usually you'll want to size your table and most cells before merging and splitting because resizing can be a hassle afterward. But you can leave borders alone, at least until after you've finished merging, because borders are removed when you merge cells.

Create charts and leverage styles for fast formatting

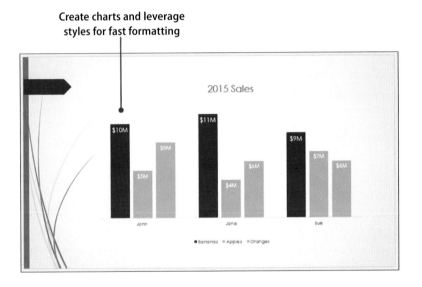

In this chapter, you will learn about creating and formatting charts. Specific topics in this chapter include the following:

→ Creating charts in PowerPoint
→ Formatting charts
→ Using the data tools
→ Inserting charts from Excel

Creating and Formatting Charts

A lot of people are intimidated when they have to create charts, but there's really no reason to be. PowerPoint especially makes it really easy. In fact, when you create a chart in PowerPoint, you get a set of dummy data and a sample chart! This lets you see what the chart looks like and can be handy so you know where to input your own data on the data grid.

Charts can be a fantastic way to display data. The trick is to keep them extremely clean so the data can shine. Don't clutter them up with tons of text and gridlines and tick marks if you don't have to.

Creating Charts in PowerPoint

Sooner or later you'll need to create a chart of some type in PowerPoint. The most common types are line charts, column charts, and pie charts. Line charts are helpful when you need to visualize a trend in data over time. Column charts are better to compare values between groups or to track changes over time at a specific point in time (such as year-end data).

Pie charts compare parts of a whole. If your pie chart has more than about five slices, you should consider using a table or a column chart instead. If small differences between specific data points is important, use a table instead.

Regardless of the type of chart you're using, best practice is to avoid 3-D charts. The angles used with 3-D distort the charts, which almost always results in misleading data.

Insert a Chart

You can insert a chart by clicking an icon in a content placeholder or by clicking the Chart button on the Insert tab.

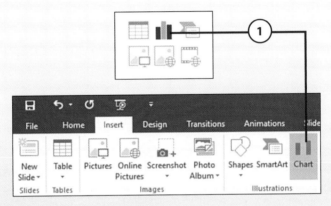

1. Click the Insert Chart icon in a content placeholder or the Chart button on the Insert tab. The Insert Chart dialog box appears.

Switching the Slide Layout

If you need to change the slide layout to one with a content placeholder, use the Layout button on the Home tab.

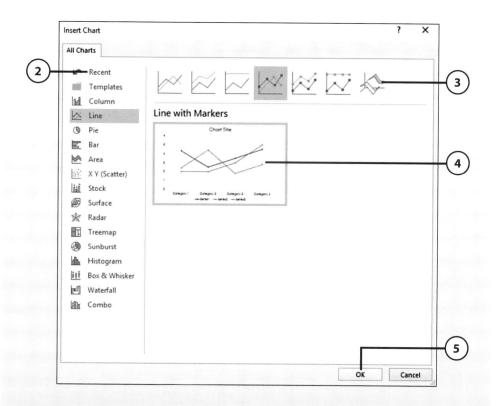

2. Select a category of chart from the column on the left.

3. Choose from a subset of chart type options for each category. For example, if you choose the Line category on the left, you'll have options for Line, 100% Stacked Line, Line with Markers, and more across the top.

4. Hover over the chart preview for a closer look.

5. Click OK to create the chart.

This Chart Is No Dummy

PowerPoint charts are automatically created with dummy data so you can see what the chart will look like in general. The chart's data grid, also known as a datasheet, should also appear automatically when the chart is created.

>>>Go Further

NEW CHART TYPES

Five new chart types have been added to Office 2016: Treemaps, Sunbursts, Histograms, Box and Whisker, and Waterfall charts.

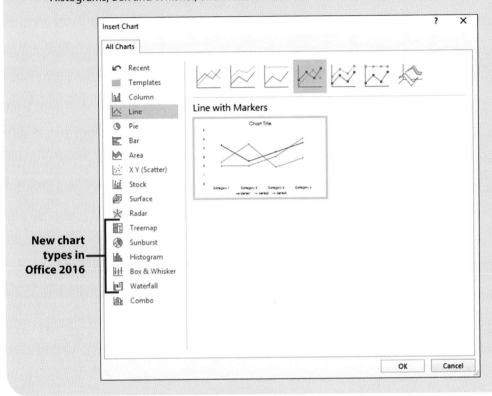

New chart types in Office 2016

Add or Change Chart Data

At some point you'll need to change PowerPoint's dummy chart data into your actual data.

1. If the data grid isn't open, click the Edit Data button on the Chart Tools Design tab or right-click the chart on the slide and choose Edit Data.

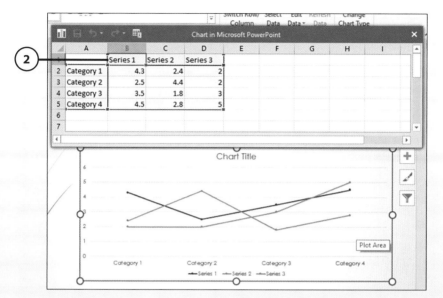

2. Click in a cell and type your own category, series, and data information. The chart will update as you type.

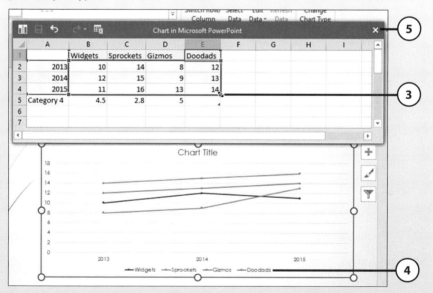

3. Hover over the blue selection handle in the corner until your pointer becomes a two-headed diagonal arrow. Click and drag to the right or down to add series or categories; click and drag left or up to omit series or categories.

4. Notice that the chart updates to accommodate more or fewer series and categories.

5. Click the X in the upper-right corner of the data grid to close it.

Close the Data Grid

If you try to insert or edit another chart without closing the data grid from a previous chart, you should see an informational box that tells you to close the first data grid. However, sometimes PowerPoint gets confused and doesn't cooperate. You might see incorrect information in the data grid, or you might hear a sound when you try to insert another chart. To avoid oddities like this, get into the habit of closing the data grid before moving on to the next chart.

>>>Go Further

BUT WHAT IF I NEED EXCEL?

Clicking Edit Data opens the basic data grid that lets you input data without the Excel interface being in your face. If you actually need to use any of the tools Excel makes available, click the Edit Data in Microsoft Excel icon at the top of the data grid or click the bottom of the Edit Data button and choose Edit Data in Excel. This lets you use Excel's data-crunching tools with your PowerPoint chart.

Note that if you choose this option to edit data in Excel, your chart and its data do not become a standalone Excel file; the chart and data grid are still embedded in the PowerPoint presentation and do not exist as separate files. You can tell this by looking at the top of the datasheet when you use Edit Data in Excel: You will see the green interface with Excel buttons, and you will also see the words Chart in Microsoft PowerPoint—Excel at the top. This tells you specifically that the chart (and this data) lives in PowerPoint, not in Excel.

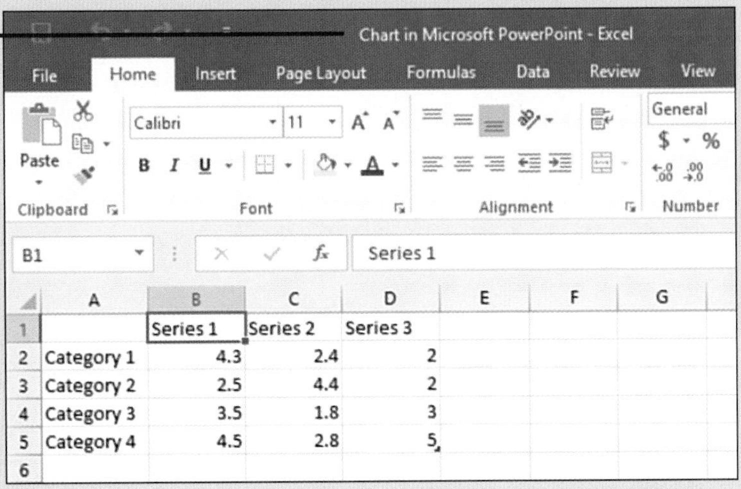

If you prefer, you can create your chart in Excel and paste it into PowerPoint so the data actually lives in a separate file. See "Inserting Charts from Excel," later in this chapter, to learn how.

Change the Chart Type

Changed your mind? You can change the type of chart you're working with very easily.

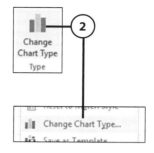

1. Insert a chart and select it.

2. Choose Change Chart Type on the Chart Tools Design tab. Or right-click the chart and choose Change Chart Type. The Change Chart Type dialog box appears.

3. Select another chart type.

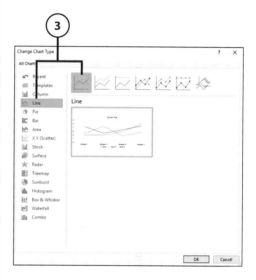

Select the Entire Chart

When you decide to change chart types, be sure you've selected the chart or the plot area, not a data point or series within the chart. If you have only a series selected, only that series will be changed into the different chart type.

This can actually be helpful at times. For example, if you've already created a column chart and need to change one series into a line, you can select that series and then choose Change Chart Type. This will open the Combo settings in the Change Chart Type dialog box, where you can turn that series into a line and even tie it to a second axis.

Create a Combination Chart

The Combo chart category makes it easy to create Column + Line charts or plot a data series on a second axis. Other chart type combinations are also available.

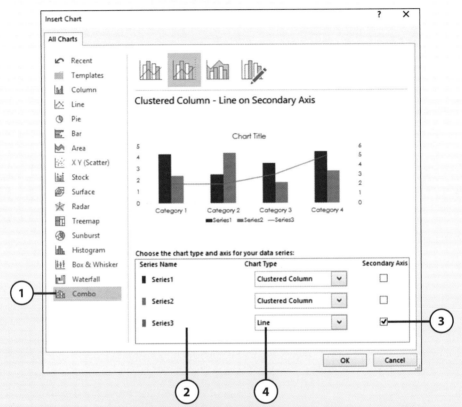

1. Click the Insert Chart button and choose Combo from the chart categories in the Insert Chart dialog box.

2. Or, using an existing column chart, right-click one series and choose Change Chart Type. The Insert Chart dialog box opens with the Combo chart type selected and the data series settings displayed.

3. Select the Secondary Axis check box to plot any series on a different axis.

4. To change any series, click the Chart Type menu and choose a different chart type.

Column + Line = Combo

Column + Line charts are the most common type of combination chart. Occasionally you may want to use an area chart (or one of the other chart type options in the menu) instead of a line, but that's pretty rare.

Formatting Charts

There are so many options for formatting charts that it can be a little overwhelming. Don't let it be! Charts are just like most other shapes and text in PowerPoint.

It's important to keep your charts clean so the data really stands out. Remove anything that's repetitive or simply not necessary. For example, if you have labels on all your data, do you really need that value axis?

Apply Quick Styles and Layouts

PowerPoint gives you a number of built-in formatting styles and layouts to make things easy and quick.

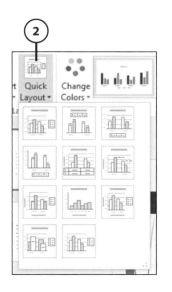

1. Insert a chart and select it.

2. Click Quick Layout and choose a chart layout from the Quick Layout gallery on the Chart Tools Design tab.

3. Choose a style from the Chart Styles gallery on the Chart Tools Design tab.

Save Time with Chart Styles and Layouts

You can use quick layouts and chart styles together or separately. In general, think of the quick layouts as the basis for what elements will actually be displayed and where. Think of chart styles as font formatting and fill effects. Colors are based on the theme.

If one of the layouts or styles is close to what you want but not exact, apply it and then format the rest manually as needed. It'll still get you where you want to go faster than formatting everything by hand.

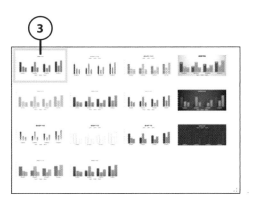

>>>Go Further
FORMATTING CHART TEXT

Format text in a chart just as you would any other text. Mostly you'll use the tools on the Home tab to increase or decrease font sizes or change colors.

Some bits of text in a chart can't be separated. For example, if you choose one of the labels along the horizontal axis, they're all selected. You can't format one bit of axis text without the rest. If you must format them differently, remove the axis labels and replace them all with text boxes so you can format the individual label the way you want. Don't try to cover one label with a text box, though—you'll never get it to line up with the rest of the labels. You can, however, format individual data labels if you want.

If you've selected a chart style that formats the chart or axis titles with all caps, you can use the Change Case button on the Home tab to change that back to Capitalize Every Word or another setting you prefer. Change Case doesn't work on axis labels or legend text, which use the exact text you input in the data grid.

Change Chart Colors

By default, chart colors are based on the theme colors used in your presentation. You can manually format colors, or you can use the built-in color sets.

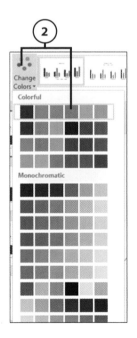

1. Insert a chart and select it.

2. Click the Change Colors button on the Chart Tools Design tab and click a color set. These colors apply to the entire chart.

Where Do the Colors Come From?

The Colorful sets are based on the accent colors from your theme, arranged in different orders. The Monochromatic sets are also based on your theme's accent colors. These same color sets (and the chart styles) are also available from the icons that appear to the right of a chart when you select it. Click the Chart Styles icon (the paintbrush) and then click Color and select a color set.

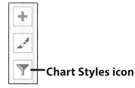

Chart Styles icon

Shades of Gray

Usually the monochromatic color set named Color 11 consists of shades of gray. This can be really helpful! Try applying it to your chart, and then select one data series or data point and change it to a brighter color. This is a great way to highlight data.

3. Click a data point once to select an entire data series.

4. Click the data point again if you want to select only that data point.

5. Use the Shape Fill or Shape Styles tools on the Chart Tools Format tab to apply a different fill color to the selected data series or point.

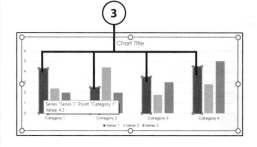

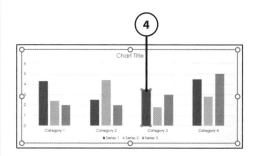

>>>*Go Further*

MANUALLY FORMATTING CHARTS

Charts can be formatted just as shapes can. There are a gazillion ways to manually format a selected data series:

- Use the Fill, Outline, and Effects tools on the Chart Tools Format tab.

- Use the Shape Styles gallery on the Chart Tools Format tab.

- Use the Fill and Outline tools on the Mini Toolbar that appears when you right-click a data series or data point.

- Right-click a data series and choose Format Data Series. Then click the Fill & Line icon or the Effects icon.

>>>*Go Further*

USE THE FORMAT DATA SERIES PANE

Different charts include different elements to format. To get to the nitty-gritty formatting options for these, either right-click and choose Format Data Series to open the Format Data Series pane or click the Shape Styles dialog box launcher on the Chart Tools Format tab.

If you're working with a line chart, for example, you'll have options for both Line and Marker under the Fill & Line (paint bucket) options in the Format Data Series pane. Line refers to the lines used for the data, and Marker refers to the little circles or squares that mark the individual data points. You can change the markers by selecting the Built-In option and then choosing the Type and Size. There are also Fill and Border options specific to the markers.

Format Data Series pane for a line chart

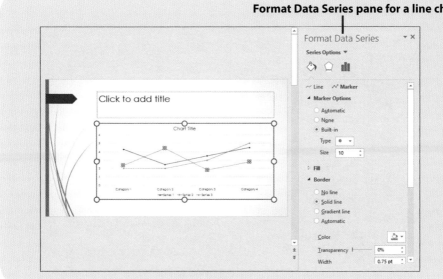

Add and Remove Elements

The Chart Elements icon that appears when you select a chart (the + symbol) is the most straightforward way to control what appears on your chart.

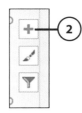

1. Insert a chart and select it.

2. Click the Chart Elements icon that appears when you select the chart.

3. In the Chart Elements gallery, select the objects you want to appear in the chart.

4. Deselect the check boxes for elements that shouldn't appear in the chart.

5. Click the arrow to the right of any element to see a flyout with additional options. Some elements, such as axes and legends, let you specify their position from the flyout.

6. Click More Options at the bottom of any flyout to open the Format pane, where you can access all settings related to that element.

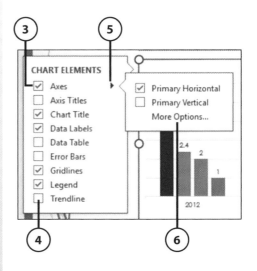

7. Notice the additional settings that are available in the Format pane (in this example, the Format Axis pane).

8. To format a different chart element, select it from the Options drop-down list in the Format pane.

Selecting Chart Elements

There's also a list of all the chart elements on the Chart Tools Format tab (in the Current Selection group). Remember that you can always close the Format pane and use the Chart Elements icon to get started again, too.

Position and Format Data Labels

You can position all the data labels in your chart with just a couple of clicks. If you want to turn one into a callout to help that data stand out, that's just a couple more clicks.

1. Insert a chart and select it.

2. Click the Chart Elements icon and select the Data Labels check box if it's not already selected. Click the arrow to open its flyout.

3. Select one of the position options. Inside End is often a good option for column charts.

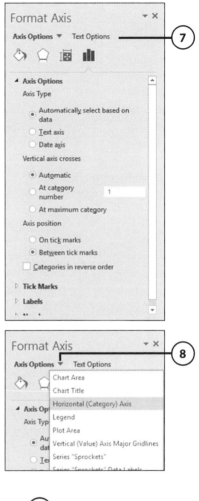

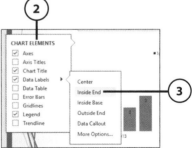

4. Click once on a data label to select all data labels in that series. Then click Data Labels, Data Callout on the Chart Elements flyout.

5. Click More Options.

6. In the Format Data Labels pane, deselect the Category Name check box so that only the data value shows in the callout.

7. Use the other formatting tools in the Format Data Labels pane, on the Chart Tools Format tab, or on the shortcut menu to remove the border or change the fill color of the data labels. Use the text tools on the Home tab to format the font.

Drag Labels to Move Them

If you need to further position a data label or callout—for example, you might need to move it up so it doesn't overlap with nearby data— just click again to select the individual label and drag it into place.

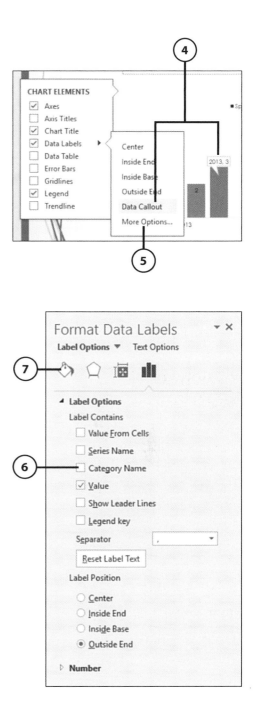

Format Numbers

Use number formatting to change the numbers in chart elements such as axes and data labels to currency, percentages, and so on. You also can specify how many decimal places you want to see.

1. Insert a chart.

2. Double-click the axis to open the Format Axis pane. You can also right-click the axis or use the Chart Elements icon and select Axes, More Options.

3. Open the Number section at the bottom of the Axis Options pane and select a number category such as Currency.

4. Decimal places will default to 2. Change this to 0. You usually don't need decimal places on a chart axis or data labels.

5. Change the money symbol if necessary.

6. Choose a format for negative numbers. If you don't have any negative numbers, don't worry about this.

7. Select the Linked to Source check box if you want the number on the chart to use the number formatting from the data grid.

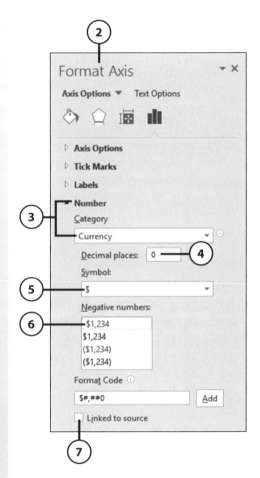

Apply Number Formatting Everywhere

You can apply number formatting to axes, data labels, and any other numbers in a chart. You can also apply number formatting to the numbers in the data grid.

>>>Go Further

WHAT'S A FORMAT CODE?

You may have noticed the Format Code option in the number formatting settings. Format codes tell PowerPoint and Excel how to display the numbers. You'll see a format code appear after you select a number category. The code usually looks something like this: #,##0.00.

One cool way to use a format code is to add text after numbers in data labels without changing the data itself. For example, you might want a data label to read $10M instead of $10. To do that, you'd add "M" after the digits in the Format Code area.

To learn more about number format codes, search online for *number format code Excel*.

Change the Value Axis Scale

The value axis on most charts depends on your data—it changes as your data changes so nothing gets cut off. This is usually great, but what if you want a specific axis range, like from 0 to 100, no matter what the data is? In that case, you have to set up a fixed axis scale.

1. Insert a column or line chart.

2. Double-click the axis to open the Format Axis pane.

3. In the Axis Options section of the Format Axis pane, change the Maximum Bounds value to 100 and then press Tab to see the change reflected in the chart.

4. In the Minimum Bounds box, change the value to 0 and press Tab. Chances are good that the default 0 setting wouldn't change when you change your chart data, but why take chances?

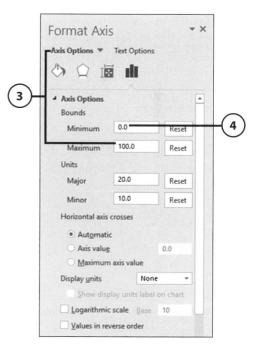

5. Click the Reset button next to Minimum or Maximum if you want to revert to an automatically scaled axis.

6. Change the Major Units value to specify which value axis labels appear. If you set these to 20, the value axis labels will be 20, 40, 60, 80, 100, and so on.

7. Change the Minor Units value to specify where the minor gridlines appear if you display them.

Format Axis

Axis Options ▼   Text Options

◢ Axis Options
  Bounds
    Minimum   0.0   Reset
    Maximum   100.0   Reset
  Units
    Major   20.0   Reset
    Minor   10.0   Reset
  Horizontal axis crosses
    ● Automatic
    ○ Axis value   0.0
    ○ Maximum axis value
  Display units   None
    ☐ Show display units label on chart
  ☐ Logarithmic scale Base 10
  ☐ Values in reverse order

Using the Data Tools

When you're charting in PowerPoint, chances are you don't need to do a ton of data crunching. After all, you can always open the data grid in Excel if you need that kind of power.

PowerPoint does give you some tools to help with selecting data and specifying what exactly will be plotted. These tools are handy when you need to reorder data in your chart but don't want to change the info on your data grid.

Hide and Unhide Data

You can hide data on the datasheet so that it won't plot on the chart.

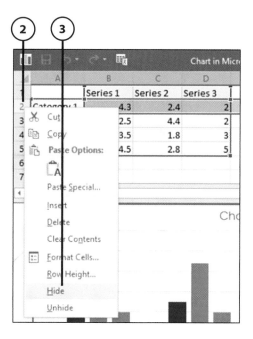

1. Insert a chart or select an existing chart and choose Edit Data, if necessary, to display the datasheet.

2. In the datasheet, click the row number or column letter for the data you want to hide. The row or column is selected.

3. Right-click the selection and choose Hide to hide the data.

Hidden Data Isn't Invisible

You will see a marker between the rows or columns in the datasheet to indicate there's hidden data.

---

4. Select the two rows or columns on either side of the hidden data and then right-click the selection and choose Unhide.

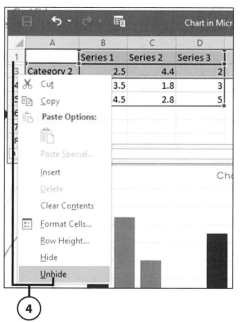

Use the Chart Filters Icon

The Chart Filters icon gives you a quick way to omit data from displaying on your chart without changing your data grid.

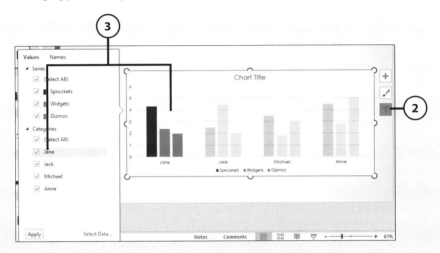

1. Insert a chart and select it.

2. Click the Chart Filters icon (funnel icon) that appears when you select the chart.

3. Hover over any series or category in the filters gallery, and it will be highlighted in the chart. This visual preview helps you easily make the connection between a series or category and its data points.

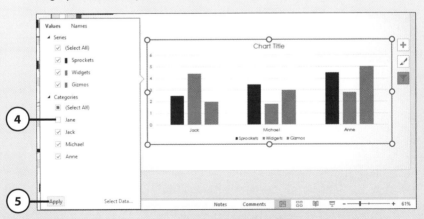

4. Deselect a series or category to omit that data from the chart. Select a series or category to include it. The data grid will remain unchanged.

5. Click Apply to apply the filter.

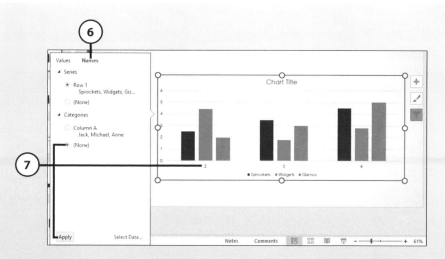

6. Click Names at the top of the Chart Filters gallery to see the series and category labels.

7. Click None and then click Apply to change the labels to generic numbers. This can be useful if you want to anonymize the labels in the chart without actually removing the information from your data grid.

>>>Go Further

USING THE SELECT DATA SOURCE DIALOG BOX

The Select Data Source dialog box is where you can reorder data series on your chart or select a different data range altogether. You can also tell PowerPoint to use different cells in the data grid for axis and data labels. There are two ways to access the Select Data Source dialog box:

- Click the Select Data button on the Chart Tools Design tab.
- Click the Chart Filters icon and then click Select Data in the filters gallery.

When you open the Select Data Source dialog box, the chart's data grid will open as well.

At the top of the dialog box, you'll see a chart data range. This tells you the location of the charted data. (Search online for *cell references Excel* if you'd like to learn how PowerPoint and Excel interpret the numbers and symbols used in a data range.)

Reorder series   **Collapse Dialog button**

Select Data Source	?	X

Chart data range: =Sheet1!$A$1:$D$5

Switch Row/Column

Legend Entries (Series)

Add   Edit   Remove ▲ ▼

☑ Sprockets
☑ Widgets
☑ Gizmos

Horizontal (Category) Axis Labels

Edit

☑ Jane
☑ Jack
☑ Michael
☑ Anne

Hidden and Empty Cells   OK   Cancel

To change the data range, select the text in the Chart Data Range box and then click the Collapse Dialog button to the right. This collapses the dialog box so you can more easily access the data grid. Click and drag in the data grid to select a new data range and then click the Collapse Dialog button again to restore the dialog box.

Click the Edit button above the list of Horizontal (Category) Axis Labels to open the Axis Labels dialog box, where you can indicate a new range of cells to use for the axis labels. You can type the cell addresses of a new range directly in the input area, or you can use the Collapse Dialog button and select the range directly in the data grid.

The Edit button above the Legend Entries (Series) list lets you change the label and data range for the individual series. Select one in the list and then click Edit to select a new set of cells in the data grid.

Click Remove to omit a series from the chart but leave the data intact on the data grid. Use the arrows to reorder the series on the chart, again without changing the data itself. Use Add to add a new series and its data.

Sometimes your data grid is set up the opposite of what you want it to be, which makes the chart "backward." Click Switch Row/Column to automatically plot the rows and columns on opposite axes.

Click Hidden and Empty Cells to tell PowerPoint what to do with blank cells. You can opt to leave gaps or plot the missing data as though it were a 0. With line charts you'll also have the option to connect the surrounding data points so there's no gap in the line, which is known as interpolation.

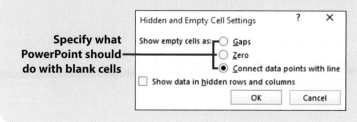

Specify what PowerPoint should do with blank cells

Inserting Charts from Excel

We've been working with charts created in PowerPoint, but it's also very common to create charts in Excel and then insert them into PowerPoint.

Be aware of where the chart data actually lives. If you create your chart in PowerPoint, the data lives in PowerPoint.

If you create your chart in Excel and paste it onto a slide, by default it is linked to the Excel file. This means the data lives in Excel. You can format the chart on your slide, but in order to edit the data, you must have access to the linked Excel file. If you send this presentation to someone outside your organization (who doesn't have access to the Excel file), that person won't be able to see the chart's underlying data.

If you create your chart in Excel and opt to embed when you paste the chart into PowerPoint, the entire workbook will be copied into the presentation. This means the data lives in PowerPoint and you will perform any edits in PowerPoint, not in a separate Excel file. Note that the entire workbook is embedded in the PowerPoint file, not just the data specifically relevant to the chart.

When you're creating charts in Excel, you can use the same colors, fonts, and effects as your PowerPoint charts. Head to the Page Layout tab in Excel and apply the same theme you're using in PowerPoint.

Link and Embed Excel Charts

When you copy a chart in Excel and then right-click a slide, you'll have a number of options available in the dynamic Paste Options list. Hover over each option to see a preview thumbnail and a ScreenTip describing the behavior.

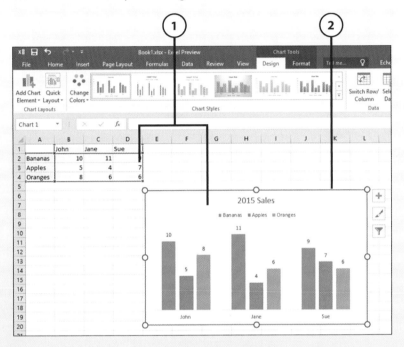

1. Create a chart in Excel. Save the Excel workbook before proceeding further; otherwise, the Paste Options in PowerPoint may be different.

2. Select the chart in Excel. Press Ctrl+C to copy it.

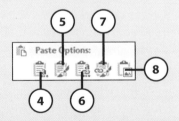

3. Right-click a PowerPoint slide and hover over each of the dynamic Paste Options.

4. Choose Use Destination Theme & Embed Workbook. This option applies the PowerPoint theme formatting to the chart and embeds the entire workbook into your PowerPoint file. The data lives in PowerPoint.

5. Or choose Keep Source Formatting & Embed Workbook. This option leaves the chart with its Excel formatting and embeds the entire workbook into your PowerPoint file. The data lives in PowerPoint.

6. Or choose Use Destination Theme & Link Data. This is the default behavior if you use Ctrl+V to paste the chart. It applies the PowerPoint theme formatting to the chart and links to the Excel workbook for the data. The data lives in Excel.

7. Or choose Keep Source Formatting & Link Data. This option leaves the chart with its Excel formatting and links to the Excel workbook for the data. The data lives in Excel.

8. Or choose Picture. This pastes the chart as a picture. You won't be able to edit either the formatting or the data.

Edit Linked Excel Chart Data in PowerPoint

If you linked your chart's data from Excel, you can edit it from within PowerPoint if the Excel file is available. Any changes you make in the datasheet will be saved to the Excel file.

1. Create a chart in Excel and save the Excel workbook. Copy the chart in Excel.

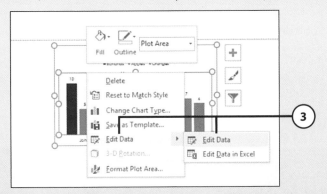

2. Right-click a PowerPoint slide and choose Use Destination Theme & Link Data (the middle Paste Options icon). This creates a link between your Excel file and your PowerPoint file.

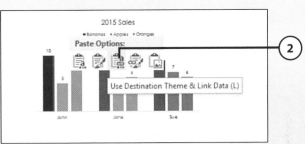

3. Close Excel. Save the PowerPoint file, and then right-click the chart in PowerPoint and choose Edit Data.

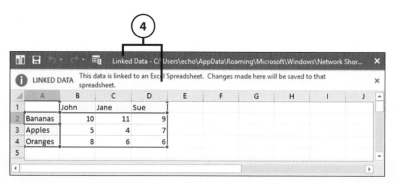

4. The spreadsheet will appear and you will be able to edit the data. The data grid tells you specifically that the data comes from a linked Excel spreadsheet and reminds you that changes will be saved to that spreadsheet. It even gives you the path to the file!

Editing Linked Charts

If you attempt to edit data on a linked chart and the Excel file isn't available, you will see a message telling you the linked file is not available. The message directs you to the Edit Links to Files option so you can reestablish the link if you have access to the Excel file. If you don't have access to it, you won't be able to reestablish the link.

Information   ✕

The linked file is not available. To edit the link, click the File tab. Click the Info tab, and then under Related Documents, click Edit Links to Files.

                                              OK

This is also how it works if you send the PowerPoint file to someone outside your organization and they don't have access to the linked Excel file.

Note that you can turn on data labels or the data table and see the basic data used to plot the chart, but you won't be able to see any of the underlying data from the inaccessible Excel spreadsheet. Remember that even though you can't edit the data, you can still change formatting such as colors and font sizes.

Edit Linked Excel Chart Data in Excel

You can always edit your linked chart and data in Excel and then update it in your presentation. Here's how.

1. Add a linked Excel chart to your presentation. To do so, follow steps 1 and 2 in the preceding exercise. Save the PowerPoint file.

2. Change some of the data in your Excel file. The chart will update in Excel. Save the Excel file.

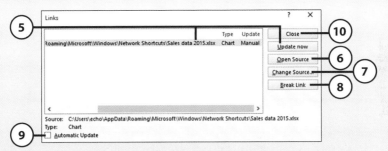

3. In PowerPoint, click the File tab and then click Info.

4. Click Edit Links to Files.

5. In the Links dialog box, select a linked chart. Click Update Now to update it.

6. Click Open Source if you want to open the linked Excel file.

7. Click Change Source if you want to select a different Excel file to link to. This can be a bit difficult to do, especially if your data doesn't use the same data range in both Excel workbooks.

8. Click Break Link to break the link to the Excel file. After breaking the link, when you right-click the chart and choose Edit Data, you will receive a message saying that the Excel file is not available.

9. Select Automatic Update to automatically update the selected chart. After this, when you open the PowerPoint file, you'll be prompted to update links. Any charts that have been set to Automatic Update will update at that time.

10. Click Close when you're finished editing the links.

Animate text and objects

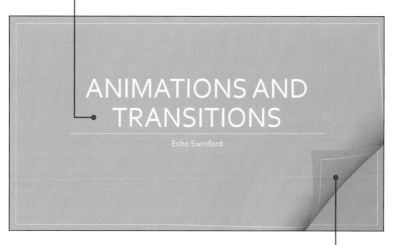

ANIMATIONS AND TRANSITIONS

Echo Swinford

Apply transitions to move from one slide to the next

In this chapter, you will learn about animations and transitions. Specific topics in this chapter include the following:

→ Applying transitions
→ Understanding animation basics
→ Fine-tuning animations

Adding Animations and Transitions

PowerPoint's animation tools are very powerful, but they get a bad rap because they're often overused and misused. You don't have to animate every object on every slide, nor do you have to animate every bit of bulleted text. Rarely are letters falling from the sky either appropriate or interesting! In fact, gratuitous, boring, cheesy animation can undermine your credibility.

Good animation always has a purpose, is consistent with the rest of the presentation, and doesn't overwhelm your message. Be thoughtful when you're adding it. Make sure your animation isn't just extraneous stuff flying around on the slide and that it explains or clarifies a concept, adds emphasis, or helps transition from one thing to another.

Applying Transitions

Animations are applied to objects on a slide, whereas transitions move you from one slide to another. It can be tempting to use all the different transitions in one presentation, but resist! You want the audience paying attention to you, not thinking about which transition they'll see next.

If you want to add variety, apply a more dramatic transition to the title slide and any section-break slides. Slides with full-page photos are also good candidates for more dynamic transitions. The best practice for the bulk of the slides, though, is to stick with one simple transition such as Fade or Wipe.

Add Transitions to Slides

You can use the tools on the Ribbon to apply a transition to selected slides or to all the slides.

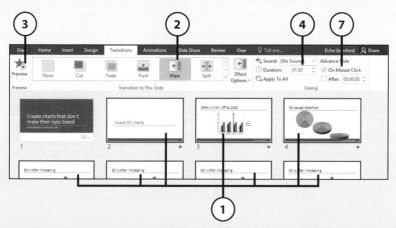

1. In the Slides pane or in Slide Sorter view, select the slide or slides you want to apply a transition to.

Selecting Multiple Slides

To select multiple slides, click the first slide you want to include. Then press Shift and click the last slide in the group to select all slides in between; press Ctrl and click each additional slide to select noncontiguous slides.

2. In the Transition to This Slide gallery on the Transitions tab, select a transition. The transition will be applied to all selected slides.

3. If the transition preview is slowing you down, click the red square on the Preview icon to stop it. Click the green arrow to run the preview.

4. Change the Duration for the transition, if desired. Duration is the time it takes for the transition to complete.

About Duration

A duration of 2.50 is two-and-a-half seconds. Each click of the spinner arrows increases or decreases the transition duration by .25 seconds, but you can type an increment between .01 (one-hundredth of a second) and 59 seconds.

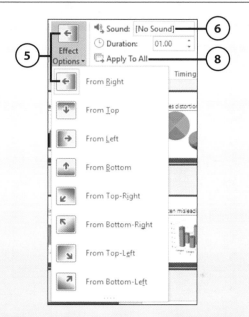

5. To change direction and other transition settings, click the Effect Options button and select an effect from the list.

6. To add a stock sound or a custom sound to the transition, click the Sound drop-down list and make a selection. Transition sounds can be annoying to your audience, so use with extreme caution.

Using Custom Sounds

If you want to add your own sound to a transition, select the Other Sounds option in the Sound drop-down list and then navigate to the location of the sound file. Only .WAV files can be used as transition sounds.

7. Choose to advance the slide when you click the mouse or automatically after a specific amount of time. (See the next section for specifics about automatic timing.)

8. If you want to apply these transition settings to all slides in the presentation (not just the selected slides), click Apply to All.

Advance Slide Using More Than Just a Mouse Click

Even though the setting is called Advance Slide On Mouse Click, it really means "advance any way PowerPoint lets me advance." When you're in Slide Show view, you can advance to the next animation or slide by clicking the mouse; by pressing the up or right arrow, the N key, the spacebar, Enter, or Page Down buttons on the keyboard; by clicking the right arrow on the pop-up toolbar that appears in the lower-left corner of the slide; or by right-clicking on the slide and choosing Next.

>>>*Go Further*

CHECK OUT THE TRANSITIONS

As with all other galleries on the Ribbon, you can click the More button to expand the Transition to This Slide gallery.

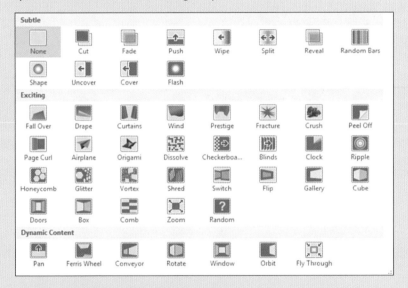

Transitions are divided into three categories: Subtle, Exciting, and Dynamic Content. Subtle transitions are simple, just like you'd expect. These are good transitions to use for all body slides because they won't upstage your content.

Exciting transitions add a bit more oomph to a presentation, but they can quickly become overwhelming when used on every slide. Reserve Exciting transitions for title slides and section headers, and you won't go wrong.

Dynamic Content transitions make it look like your content is moving on and off the screen independently from the slide background.

Advance Slides Automatically

By default, a slide transitions to the next one when you click the mouse in Slide Show view, but you can also set slides to transition automatically after a certain amount of time. You'll need to do this when you create self-running presentations or save your presentation as a video.

1. In the Slides pane or in Slide Sorter view, select the slide or slides you want to apply an automatic transition to.

2. Click a transition in the Transition to This Slide gallery on the Transitions tab to apply it to the selected slides.

3. In the Timing group, select the Advance Slide After check box and set a time after which you want the slide to transition to the next one.

4. Uncheck On Mouse Click to force the slide to advance only after the time has elapsed. Leave On Mouse Click selected if you want to have the option to click to move forward before the time is up.

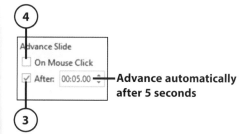

Advance automatically after 5 seconds

About Automatic Timing

The After timing, which you may want to think of as the "Advance slide after this much time" setting, is indicated in minutes and seconds. 23:59.59 (a hundredth of a second shy of 24 minutes) is the longest automatic timing you can apply.

You can apply a different After time to each slide if you want.

Understanding Animation Basics

PowerPoint has four main types of animation: Entrance, which brings objects onto the slide; Exit, which removes objects from the slide; Emphasis, which highlights objects; and Motion Path, which moves objects from one place to another on the slide.

Coupling these with the capability to start an animation with a mouse click, at the same time as the previous animation, or after the previous animation gives you endless possibilities. Talented animators are able to create amazing animations in PowerPoint leveraging these simple tools.

Add Animation and Specify When It Plays

An entrance animation is very simple to set up.

1. Insert a shape or picture onto your slide and select it.

2. Click an animation in the gallery on the Animations tab to apply it to the shape. You can click the More button to expand the gallery or scroll row by row to see more animation options such as Exits and Motion Paths.

3. Click More Entrance Effects, More Emphasis Effects, More Exit Effects, or More Motion Paths at the bottom of the Animation gallery to choose from a complete set of animation options for each category.

4. Select one of the effects in the resulting dialog box and click OK.

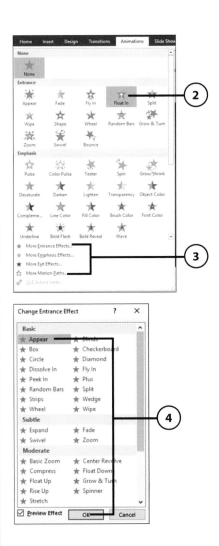

5. Click Effect Options to change direction and other settings, if available. If your shape includes text, you may see sequence options for text as well.

6. Choose the Start setting On Click if you want the animation to start when you click the mouse button in Slide Show view.

7. Or choose With Previous to start the animation at the same time as the previous animation.

8. Or choose After Previous to start the animation after the prior animation is complete.

9. Change the Duration if you prefer that the animation take more or less time to complete than the default.

10. Add a delay to the animation if desired.

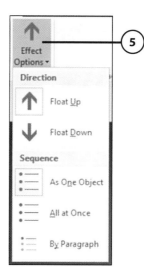

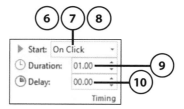

About Duration and Delay

Duration and Delay are both displayed in seconds. Note that 59.00 (59 seconds) is the longest you can input for both, and .01 (one-hundredth of a second) is the shortest.

Duration indicates how long it takes to complete the animation. Delay adds a delay to the animation start. For example, if you input Delay 1.50 for an animation that starts On Click, when you click the mouse in Slide Show view, PowerPoint then waits one-and-a-half seconds before it actually begins animating the object.

Getting Rid of Animations

Remove animations from a selected object by selecting None in the Animation gallery. Alternatively, click the arrow to the right of the animation in the Animation Pane and select Remove.

Add a Second Animation to an Object

Often you'll need to add two animations to an object. For example, you want it to animate onto the slide (entrance animation) and then later exit the slide.

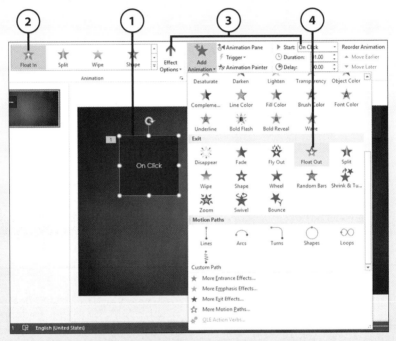

1. Insert a shape or picture onto your slide and select it.

2. Apply the first animation, for example, an Entrance animation, from either the Animation gallery or the Add Animation gallery on the Animations tab.

3. Set the Effect Options, Start, Duration, and Delay as desired.

4. Apply the second animation, for example, an Exit animation, by choosing from the Add Animation gallery.

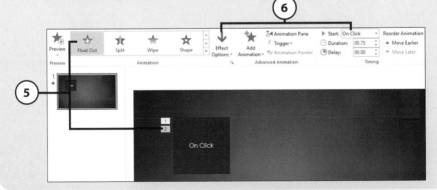

5. Click the animation indicator next to the object. The selected animation name will display in the Animation gallery.

6. Set the Effect Options, Start, Duration, and Delay for the second animation, as desired.

What the Animation Indicators Tell You

When the Animations tab is active, animations on that slide are indicated as numbers next to the objects they're applied to. Each numbered animation indicator represents an On Click animation. With Previous and After Previous animations are represented by stacked indicators. The numbers themselves represent the order in which the animations will occur.

It's Not All Good

The Animations tab of the Ribbon is one of the most horribly designed interfaces in PowerPoint. It's fine if you just need to apply one animation, but if you need more, it's confusing to have to remember to insert only one animation from the Animation gallery on the left and insert everything else from the Add Animation gallery on the right—especially since the galleries are otherwise identical! You may find it easiest to get in to the habit of adding all animations using the Add Animation gallery and ignore the Animation gallery unless you want to change an existing animation to a different one.

If you do use the Animation gallery to change an animation effect, be sure you've selected the animation by clicking the animation indicator next to the object or by selecting the animation in the Animation Pane. If you select the object and then choose another animation from the Animation gallery, it will replace all existing animations with the new choice.

Add Animation to Text

Usually one of the first things people want to animate is bulleted text. Here's how.

1. Enter text into a content placeholder. Then either select the placeholder or click so your cursor is inside the placeholder.

Pay Attention to What You've Selected

If you actually select text in the placeholder, the animation will be applied only to those lines of text.

2. Click an animation in the Add Animation gallery to apply it. By default, the text will be animated By Paragraph. This means that the top-level bullet and its associated sub-bullets will animate in at the same time.

3. Click the Effect Options button and select an effect to change how the text is animated.

4. Click the Animation Pane button to open the Animation Pane and see the details of the animation settings.

5. Click the chevron in the Animation Pane to expand or collapse the text animation.

6. Select an animation in the pane and use the Timing tools on the Animations tab to change any of its settings: Start, Duration, Delay, and so on.

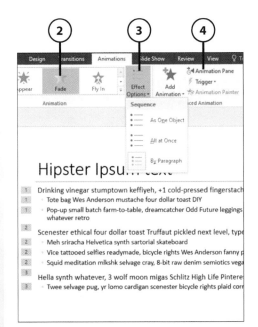

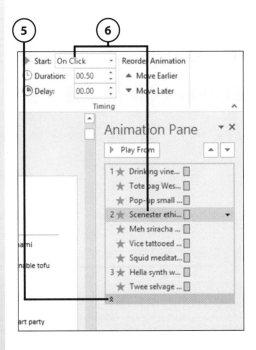

>>>Go Further

ABOUT ANIMATION INDICATORS AND TEXT

The animation indicators next to lines of text show you how it's animated. With the By Paragraph setting, text with the same indicator number will be animated in response to the same mouse click. (Use the Animation Pane to break this down further if you want.) The As One Object setting animates the entire text box as though it's one solid block of text. The All at Once setting animates all lines of text at once, which is essentially the same as As One Object when used on a text placeholder.

If you're using a shape with text typed in it, As One Object treats the text and shape as a combined object with the same animation. All at Once animates the shape and its text at the same time but allows you to apply different animation effects to the shape and its text.

Add Emphasis Animation

Emphasis animation highlights an object or text. Some typical emphasis actions include making the object larger and changing its color.

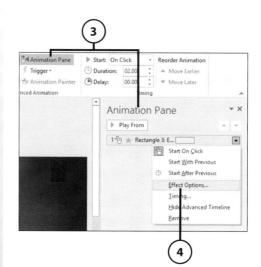

1. Insert a shape or another object on the slide and select it.

2. In the Add Animation gallery on the Animations tab, choose an Emphasis animation such as Grow/Shrink.

3. Click the Animation Pane button to open the Animation Pane.

4. Right-click the animation in the pane and choose Effect Options.

5. In the Effect Options dialog box, choose your settings. For example, with Grow/Shrink, click Size. Choose any of the stock options or type your own percentage into the Custom box. Press Tab after you input so the value sticks.

6. Choose Auto-reverse if you want the shape to revert to its original size. In other words, it will grow to the specified size and then automatically shrink back to normal. Click OK.

7. Change Start, Duration, and Delay settings as desired.

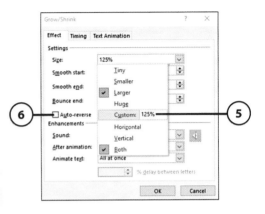

Create a Motion Path Animation

Motion paths move objects on the slide in Slide Show view.

1. Insert a shape or another object to animate. Select it.

2. In the Add Animation gallery on the Animations tab, scroll to the bottom and choose a Motion Path animation.

3. The motion path animation is applied. Notice that its start point is in the middle of the shape, indicated with a green circle or arrow. A ghosted shape shows you where the animation ends.

4. Click Effect Options on the Animations tab and choose a direction for the path.

5. Click the red circle or arrow indicating the end point of the path and drag it to the desired position.

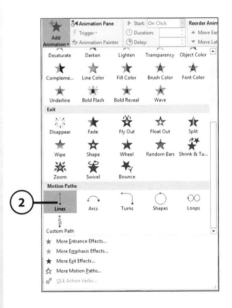

Animated shape   Motion path   Ghosted shape (end position)

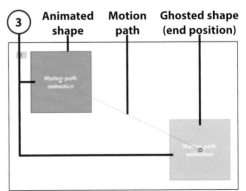

>>>Go Further

TIPS FOR WORKING WITH MOTION PATH ANIMATIONS

Motion path animations can be extremely powerful, and they have some settings that aren't immediately apparent. Following are some tips for working with motion path animations.

- When you've selected a motion path by clicking it, the ghosted shape displays, showing where the animated shape will end up.

- The Reverse Path Direction option swaps the start and end points of the motion path. You can access it by right-clicking the path or by clicking the Effect Options button.

- Motion paths are unlocked by default. This means that when you move the shape around on the slide, the motion path moves with it. A locked motion path stays in place even if you move the shape.

- You can use Edit Points to refine your motion paths. Right-click and choose Edit Points to begin. (See Chapter 3, "Creating and Working with Shapes," for specifics about using Edit Points.)

- Edit Points aren't available on Motion Path Lines. If you know you'll want to use Edit Points on your path, choose Custom Path when you apply the Motion Path animation and draw the path by clicking for each point. You can then use Edit Points to refine the path.

Add a Trigger Animation

Trigger animations are super helpful when you create games and self-running presentations. If you want to click an object and have another object animate, trigger animations are at your service.

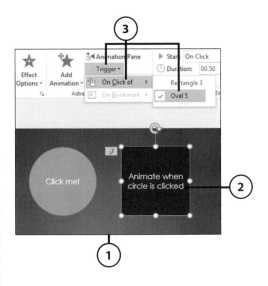

1. Insert two objects on your slide, for example, a square and a circle.

2. Apply an animation to the object that should animate. It can be any type of animation—entrance, exit, emphasis, or motion path.

3. Set the trigger, which is the object you'll click to initiate the animation. Select the animated object and on the Animations tab click Trigger, On Click Of, and then select the trigger.

Trigger Indicators

Objects that will be animated by a trigger are represented with a lightning bolt on the animation indicator. The trigger doesn't have to animate—it can, but it doesn't have to.

4. Open the Selection Pane from the Drawing Tools Format tab if you want to rename objects to make it easier to select the correct trigger in the Trigger On Click Of list.

5. In the Animation Pane, the object that's animated is located directly below its trigger.

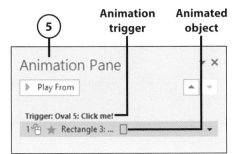

Fine-Tuning Animations

PowerPoint gives you a lot of options and flexibility to tweak all kinds of settings for animations. You can attach sounds to animations, set animations to repeat, and smooth the beginning and end of motion paths. Most of these more advanced settings are accessed from the Animation Pane. The available options depend on the type of object you're animating.

Set Duration and Delay in the Animation Pane Timeline

The timeline in the Animation Pane is invaluable for visualizing how your animation works in real time. Sometimes it's easier to drag animations around on the timeline to set their duration and delay than it is to input numbers into those fields on the Animations tab.

1. Insert at least two shapes or other objects and add animations to them.

2. Click Animation Pane on the Animations tab to open the Animation Pane. You should see blocks of color indicating the animation occurrences. Green is an entrance animation, yellow is emphasis, red is exit, and motion paths are blue.

3. If you don't see the colored timeline, right-click any animation and choose Show Advanced Timeline.

4. To change the duration of an animation, hover with your mouse pointer over the end of an animation bar on the timeline. When the pointer turns into a two-headed arrow, drag the end of the bar right or left to increase or decrease the duration.

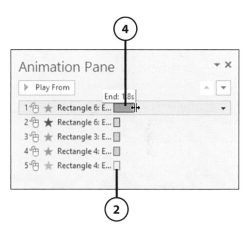

Rename Objects for Easier Animation

Don't forget that you can rename objects in the Selection Pane, which you can open from the Drawing Tools Format or Home tab. Those new names will also appear in the Animation Pane, which may make life easier as you animate.

5. Click the first animation, press Shift, and then click the last animation in the pane to select them all. Right-click the selection and choose Start With Previous so that all animations begin automatically when you transition to this slide.

6. To add a delay to an animation, point to the middle of an animation bar on the timeline. When the pointer turns into a two-headed arrow, drag the bar into position. When you let go of the mouse button, you'll see the new Delay setting on the Animations tab.

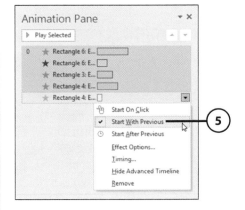

How to Exceed the 59-second Limit

You can drag on the timeline to exceed the 59.00-second limit on Duration and Delay settings.

7. To reorder any of the animations, drag and drop them in the Animation Pane. You can also use the arrows in the top-right corner of the pane or on the Animations tab.

8. Click the Play From button on the Animation Pane to preview your animation. It will begin with the animation you've selected, which is handy for long, complicated sequences. You can also use the Preview button on the Animations tab to preview the entire animation sequence.

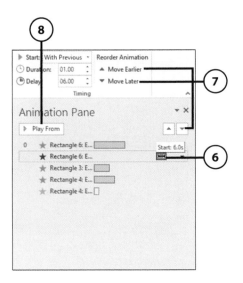

Repeat an Animation

Most, if not all, animations have Timing settings that allow you to repeat the animation.

Repeating animation

1. Insert a shape. Apply an Emphasis effect such as Pulse.

2. In the Animation Pane, right-click the emphasis and choose Timing.

3. Change the Delay if desired. The Delay setting delays the start of the animation as a whole; it doesn't delay each repeating occurrence of the animation.

4. Change the Duration if desired. Duration applies to each occurrence of the animation, not the entire sequence.

5. Choose a stock option or type your own value in the Repeat box. If you type your own, press Tab so your value sticks.

6. Or select Until Next Click to repeat the animation until you click the mouse again.

7. Or select Until End of Slide to continue the animation until you move to the next slide.

8. Click OK to apply the settings.

It's Not All Good

One fairly common request is to fade an object in and out of a slide continuously until the next slide displays. Unfortunately, you cannot repeat a sequence of animations this way in PowerPoint.

To do something like this, you'd have to create the object, apply the Fade Entrance and Fade Exit animations to it, and then duplicate the shape multiple times—more than enough to last you through the end of the slide.

If you put in enough copies to last until the end, you should finish speaking before the animations complete. In this situation, you'll have to click an extra time: Click once to stop the animations and then click again to transition to the next slide.

There are a couple of ways you could accomplish this same effect, but using many duplicates is the most straightforward approach.

Reuse an Animation

The Animation Painter lets you "paint" animation settings from one object to another. It's a huge time saver!

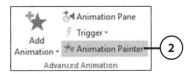

1. Insert two shapes on a slide. Apply animation to one of the shapes.

2. Select the animated shape and then click Animation Painter on the Animations tab.

3. Hover over the other object you want to apply the animation settings to. When your pointer changes to an arrow with a paintbrush, click the object.

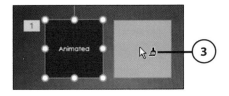

Animation Painter Tricks

You can apply the Animation Painter to an object on another slide. Click Animation Painter as usual, click the appropriate slide thumbnail in the Slides pane, and then click the object to apply animation settings to.

Double-click the Animation Painter to make it "sticky" so that you can apply animation settings to multiple objects. Click Animation Painter again or press Esc to get out of Animation Painter mode.

Animate a Chart or SmartArt Graphic

Animation effect options come in handy when you want to animate certain objects like charts and SmartArt graphics.

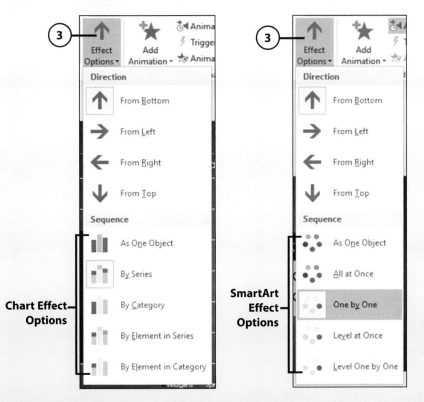

1. Insert a chart or SmartArt graphic on a slide and select it.

2. Apply an animation from the Add Animation gallery. Wipe is often a good choice for charts.

3. Click Effect Options to change the direction and sequence of the animation as desired. You'll see similar choices in the Effect Options for both charts and SmartArt graphics.

Animating Charts

If you use a Wipe animation, the default is to wipe from the bottom. This is perfect for column charts, but it looks pretty silly on line charts. Use the Effect Options to specify wipe From Left for most line charts.

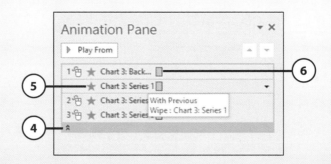

4. Open the Animation Pane and click the chevron to expand the chart series.

5. Select the second animation in the list and change its Start setting to With Previous so that it animates along with the chart background.

6. Or, if you want to remove the chart background animation altogether, right-click it in the Animation Pane and choose Remove.

Chart Background Animation

Another way to remove the chart background animation is to double-click it in the Animation Pane to open the settings dialog box, choose the Chart Animation tab, and uncheck Start Animation by Drawing the Chart Background. This isn't always the best idea, though. If you remove chart background animation, the empty chart structure sits there until the data animates in, and that can sometimes look a bit strange. Usually it's better to animate the chart background at the same time as or just before the first data animation.

It's Not All Good

Unfortunately, you cannot animate tables in PowerPoint. Well, you can animate tables, but only as a whole. You cannot animate tables by row or by column.

Probably the easiest way to fake animating a table is to place shapes on top of the table to cover it and then apply exit animations to the shapes to remove them and reveal the table.

Using a background-filled shape often makes this seamless. Right-click the shape and choose Format Shape. Choose Slide Background Fill to fill the shape with whatever image or gradient is being used in the slide background. You'll be able to move the shape around on the slide and it will be filled with that portion of the background so that it blends seamlessly. Of course, if you're using a solid-colored background, you can simply use a solid-filled shape as well.

>>>Go Further

CREATING A "BUILD"

Way back in the early days of PowerPoint, animations were called "builds," and you'll occasionally hear that term in use today. Usually it refers to an animation sequence that adds objects or text one after the other—it "builds" the slide.

Especially if you have a complicated diagram, it can be easier and quicker to use a series of slides for this type of animation than it is to actually animate all the pieces. It's also great if you need to print; with an animated slide all you can print is the final state of the slide.

Best practice for this process is to be subtractive. Start with the final slide, duplicate it, and remove pieces you don't need for the preceding step. Then duplicate that slide and remove more pieces. Repeat until you've created a slide for each step. If you start with the first slide, duplicate it, and add elements, inevitably somewhere along the line you'll need to change something—and that means you'll have to change it on all the previous slides as well. That usually turns into a huge time commitment and never seems to end up perfect, so objects are slightly off and jump around as you move from slide to slide.

After you've finished creating all the slides for the build, add a Fade transition to the slides, and it will look as though the pieces are fading in each time you click. Nobody will even know you didn't actually bother to animate all that!

Add audio and video
to your presentation

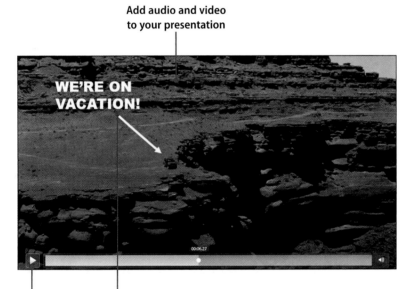

WE'RE ON
VACATION!

00:06.27

Set your media   Sync animations
start options   to your media

In this chapter, you will learn about using multimedia in your presentation. Specific topics in this chapter include the following:

→ Inserting audio and video
→ Editing and formatting audio and video
→ Setting up audio and video playback
→ Making your media more portable

Using Multimedia

If a picture is worth a thousand words, a video must be worth a million. And the perfect audio or video clip can be priceless.

Multimedia, which refers to both audio and video, can be powerful in your presentation. It's often extremely engaging. But as with anything, if it's overdone it can be off-putting to your audience. Similarly, low-resolution video and poor-quality audio are rarely worth the trouble.

If you need good multimedia to use in your presentations, search online for royalty-free music and royalty-free video. Royalty free doesn't mean zero cost, but it does mean you'll be able to purchase quality media files at a reasonable price.

Inserting Audio and Video

There are many kinds of video files floating around, and knowing which format to use can be confusing. PowerPoint 2016 is happiest with .MP4 video files, which are also known as MPEG-4 videos. For audio files, Microsoft recommends .M4A files.

The format that gives you the best compatibility overall is .MP4 encoded with H.264 video and AAC audio. If you don't know exactly what that means, don't worry—the person creating the media file usually will. Just look for .MP4 video files and .M4A audio files, and if you have a choice of codec opt for H.264 and AAC.

Insert Video or Audio from Your Hard Drive

When you insert a media file from your hard drive into PowerPoint 2016, it is automatically embedded in your PowerPoint file. You don't have to send the video or audio in addition to the PowerPoint file because the media file is already in the presentation.

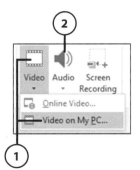

1. On the Insert tab, choose Video, then Video on My PC.

2. Or to insert audio, on the Insert tab, choose Audio, then Audio on My PC.

3. Navigate to the video or audio, select it, and click Insert.

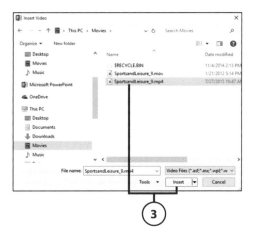

About .WMV and .MOV Videos

If you know that your presentation will be played only on PCs and never on Macs, you can stick with .WMV video files. Likewise, if you know that your presentation will be played mostly on Macs or on PCs with the latest QuickTime player installed, then you can use .MOV video files. Here's a word of caution, though: PCs running 64-bit Windows won't have the latest QuickTime player because there is no QuickTime player for 64-bit Windows.

>>>Go Further

TO LINK OR NOT TO LINK

In the not-so-distant past when you inserted video and most audio into your presentation, PowerPoint didn't embed the media file. Instead, it created a link to the video or audio. This meant the PowerPoint file wasn't self-contained and you had to remember to include the media file if you moved your presentation to another computer or sent it to someone.

Linking to video especially can be good because embedding it often creates very large PowerPoint files. The drawback is that these types of links can be fragile, and PowerPoint easily loses track of them. If you're going to link to a video, you should put a copy of the video file in the same folder with your presentation before inserting. You'll also want to make sure to send the video along when you send the presentation to someone because it's not included in the PowerPoint file. The same technique also applies for audio.

To create a link to the media instead of embedding it, choose Insert, Video/Audio on My PC, and then click the arrow on the Insert button and choose Link to File.

Insert Online Video

The important thing to know about inserting most online video is that you're actually creating a link to the video. This means you must have a solid, fast, reliable Internet connection during your presentation in order to play the video.

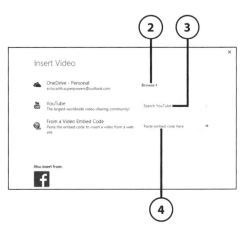

1. On the Insert tab, choose Video, Online Video.

2. Click Browse to navigate to a video on OneDrive, and then click Insert to add it to your slide. Because OneDrive is for your own files, this video will actually be embedded in your presentation.

3. Or enter a search term to look for a video on YouTube, select the video, and then click Insert to add a linked video to your slide.

4. Or paste an embed code from a video site into the box and press Enter to add a linked video to your slide.

It's Not All Good

> **IMPORTANT!**
>
> YouTube videos and embed codes are linked to your presentation. (Using an embed code means you're embedding a link to a media file.) If you don't have an Internet connection during your presentation, you'll see an image of the video but it won't play.
>
> You'll also want to note that Google sometimes changes YouTube's embed code structure, which can break the links to videos in your presentations. This is a risk you run when using online video.

Record Your Own Audio

PowerPoint enables you to record your own audio into a presentation.

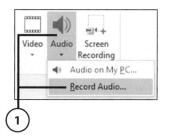

1. On the Insert tab, choose Audio, Record Audio. The Record Sound dialog box displays.

2. Rename the sound if you want. This name will show up in the Selection and Animation Panes.

3. Click Record (the red circle) to begin recording.

4. Click Stop (the blue square) to stop recording.

5. Click Play (the green triangle) to play the recording so you can review it.

6. Click OK to add the recorded sound to your slide, where you can edit it as with any other sound. (See "Editing and Formatting Audio and Video" later in this chapter for audio editing instructions.)

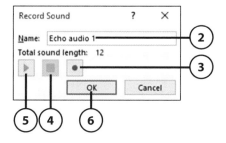

Where's the Pause Button?

There is no pause button in the Record Sound dialog box. If you stop a recording and then click the red circle again, you'll overwrite your original recording.

Record a Video of Your Screen

You can use PowerPoint to record video for anything that appears on your screen.

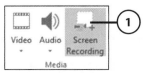

1. On the Insert tab, choose Screen Recording. A menu bar with recording tools appears at the top of your screen.

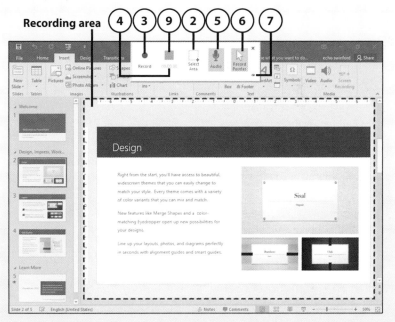

2. Click Select Area and then click and drag on the screen to indicate the area to record. A thick red dotted line outlines the area you selected. If you make a mistake and need to reselect, click the Select Area button again.

3. Click the red Record button to begin recording. The Record button changes to a Pause button while you are recording so you can stop and start as necessary.

4. Notice that the recording time is indicated below the Stop button.

5. Click the Audio button to turn off audio recording. This button is on by default and is highlighted when audio is recording.

6. Click the Record Pointer button if you don't want the mouse pointer to show in your recording. This button is on by default and is highlighted when the pointer is being recorded.

7. The menu bar will disappear when you move your mouse away from it. Moving your mouse toward the top of the screen will reveal the menu bar again. Click the

thumbtack icon to "pin" it in place. The menu bar will be recorded if it's pinned within the recording area.

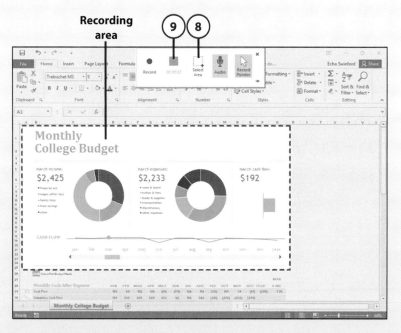

8. Press Alt+Tab or use your Windows taskbar to switch to a different program and select the recording area there.

Record Any Screen

You're not limited to recording your PowerPoint screen; you can switch to any other program. Whatever appears in the recording area will be recorded.

9. When you finish recording, click the Stop button on the menu bar. Or use the Windows Key+Shift+Q to stop the recording. The resulting video will be inserted onto your slide, where you can edit it just as you would any other video.

Editing and Formatting Audio and Video

You can spend a lot of money on software to edit audio and video files. Luckily, PowerPoint has tools for basic editing. They're not a substitute for professional media editing software, but they're perfect for trimming a bit of time from the beginning and end of clips and fading them onto and off of your slide.

Additionally, many of the tools you'd use on pictures in PowerPoint can Le used on your videos as well: recoloring; adjusting brightness and contrast; and adding borders, shadows, reflections, and other effects. You can also apply styles and play video within a shape. With all these options at your fingertips, your media will be the star of the show.

Trim Time from Audio and Video

One of the most basic edits you'll ever need to make is to trim time from the beginning or end of a multimedia file. The Trim Audio and Trim Video dialog boxes are identical except for the video preview.

1. Insert an audio or video file on your slide.

2. Select the audio or video on the slide so the Audio Tools or Video Tools contextual tabs are available.

3. On the Playback tab, click Trim Audio or Trim Video.

4. Click and drag the green handle on the playback bar to indicate a new start point.

5. Drag the red handle to indicate a new end point.

6. Fine-tune the Start Time and End Time using the input boxes.

7. Click the Play button to preview the trimmed clip.

8. Click the green start handle and use the previous and next frame buttons to move the start point frame by frame.

9. Click the red end handle and use the previous and next frame buttons to move the end point frame by frame.

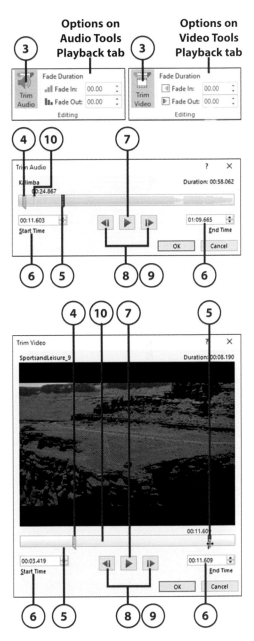

10. Click on the playback bar and use the previous and next frame buttons to move back and forth frame by frame.

Non-Destructive Editing

PowerPoint does what is called non-destructive editing. This means that even though you trim the multimedia file, the trimmed bits are still there so you can go back and reedit at any time. These will be removed if you optimize and compress media on the File tab.

Fade Audio and Video In and Out

Media files sometimes start and stop very abruptly. Fading in or out can help soften that.

1. Insert video or audio onto your slide. If you're working with a video, add a poster frame. (See the next section.)

Video Fade In and Out

The video fade feature fades from the poster frame into the video, and at the end, from the video back out to the poster frame. If you haven't added a poster frame, the fade may look jumpy. If your video includes audio, it will fade in and out from a slightly lower volume.

2. On the Audio Tools Playback or Video Tools Playback tab, enter the Fade In and Fade Out times in seconds.

3. Check the Video Tools Playback tab to ensure that the Hide While Not Playing check box isn't select-ed. (When selected, this setting hides the video until it plays.)

4. Click Play to test the multimedia file.

Add a Poster Frame to a Video

A poster frame is simply a preview image. It's the frame that shows when the video isn't playing. Sometimes the poster frame is actu-ally the first frame of the video. Other times it's the title of the video, some other meaningful image, or even just solid black.

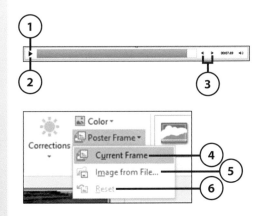

1. Insert a video onto your slide, and click the Play button to start the video. The Play button becomes a Pause button while the video plays.

2. Click the Pause button to pause the video on the frame you want to use for the poster frame.

3. Use the Move Backward and Move Forward buttons to fine-tune your position if necessary.

4. On the Video Tools Format tab, click Poster Frame, Current Frame.

5. Or choose Image from File to use any picture as the poster frame.

6. Click Reset if you want to remove the poster frame.

>>>Go Further

CREATING YOUR OWN POSTER FRAME

Here's an easy way to create your own poster frame.

1. Draw a rectangle the same size as your video. (You can see the size of the video on the Video Tools Format tab.)

2. Format the rectangle. A basic black fill is good. If you want the video to fade into and out of the slide more seamlessly, fill the shape with the same color as the slide background.

3. Type the title of the video or other text in the rectangle if you want.

4. Right-click the rectangle and choose Save as Picture.

Now you can use this picture as your poster frame.

Crop a Video

Cropping a video isn't the same as trimming time; it's actually just like cropping a picture. Insert a video onto your slide to begin.

1. On the Video Tools Format tab, click Crop.

2. Hover near a crop handle, and when your pointer changes to a crop tool, click and drag a corner or edge to crop the video.

3. To help you determine where to crop, notice that you see ghosted areas representing the cropped portions of the video.

4. Click away from the video or click Crop again to crop the video.

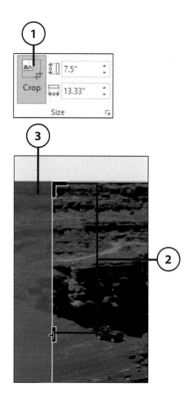

Apply Video Styles and Other Formatting

Video styles are just like picture styles. They let you apply a preformatted combination of borders, shadows, bevels, reflections, and other effects to a video with one click. In fact, many of the picture and video styles are identical!

Of course, you can also manually apply any of these features—shadows, borders, reflections, bevels, rotation, the list goes on. These tools also work just as they do with pictures. Insert a video on your slide to get started with the various formatting tools.

1. Select the video, and on the Video Tools Format tab, click the More button to expand the Video Styles gallery. Click to select a video style.

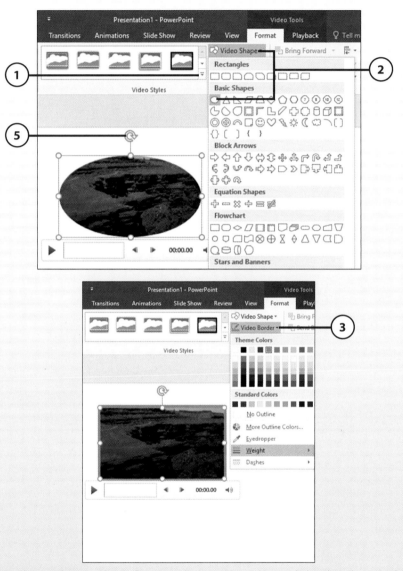

2. To play a video in a shape, for example, an oval or a heart, click Video Shape and then choose a shape from the gallery.

3. Add a border to your video using the tools in the Video Border gallery. Choose a color, change the weight, and select dashed or double outlines.

Video Tools

| w | View | Format | Playback | Tell me... | Echo Swi... | Share |

Video Shape ▾   Bring Forward ▾
Video Border ▾   Send Backward ▾
④ Video Effects ▾   Selection Pane   ⑤

Preset   **No Presets**

Shadow

Reflection   **Presets**

Glow

Soft Edges

Bevel

3-D Rotation ▸   3-D Options...

4. Apply and customize shadows, reflections, glows, soft edges, bevels, or 3-D rotation settings using the various galleries available in Video Effects. (See Chapter 3, "Creating and Working with Shapes," for more details.)

5. Rotation tools are also available along with alignment, order, and group tools on the Video Tools Format tab. Or you can click and drag the rotation handle above the selected video.

All of These Things Are Just Like the Other

Video Effects Presets are similar to the Video Styles you select from the gallery on the Ribbon—they are preformatted combinations of settings you can apply with one click, but they include more bevels and perspectives than the Video Styles do. In fact, all the Video Effects are identical to the Effects available for Pictures and Shapes.

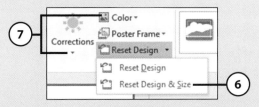

6. If you mess up while formatting the video, click Reset Design to remove all the formatting and start over. Reset Design doesn't affect any cropping, though; if you need to remove crops, select Reset Design & Size.

7. Use the Color and Corrections settings to apply a duotone color and adjust the brightness and contrast of the video. These tools work just as they do when you're working with pictures. (See Chapter 5, "Working with Pictures," for more details.)

Setting Up Audio and Video Playback

When you insert a video in a PowerPoint presentation, it's set to play when you click it. If you remember the animation chapter, you might recall that this is actually a trigger animation, and it's the perfect way to go, especially if you're presenting on a touchscreen device.

However, if you're presenting in a traditional environment where you don't have an easy way to click the video itself to start it, you may find it easier to set the video to play automatically or when you advance the slide. The same goes for audio—it's really all about the environment you're presenting in.

Play a Media File Automatically or When Clicked

Playing a media file when clicked is super easy because when you insert audio and video, PowerPoint sets them to start when you click them on the slide.

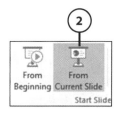

1. Insert an audio or video file on the slide.

2. To start the Slide Show, click the Slide Show tab and then click From Current Slide. Or click the Slide Show icon in the status bar at the bottom-right corner of the screen.

3. In Slide Show view, move your mouse pointer over the video and click it to start the video. Click the video again to pause. Click it again to start.

4. Now move your mouse pointer away from the video and press the spacebar or down arrow just as you would if you were advancing through an animated presentation. Notice that this doesn't play the video; it moves you to the next slide.

Mouse pointer changes to hand

Media controls

5. On the Audio Tools Playback tab or the Video Tools Playback tab, change the Start setting to Automatically. Now the media clip will play automatically after any previous animation on the slide.

>>>Go Further

MULTIMEDIA ON CLICK = WHEN CLICKED

Setting up media to play can be confusing, but it's mainly because of the terminology. Don't let it scare you!

When you insert a video or audio clip, on the Video Tools Playback tab and Audio Tools Playback tab you'll see that the clip is set to Start on Click. But take a second and hover over that setting long enough for the ScreenTip to appear. It tells you the clip will play automatically or when clicked—that's really the key. Or, to think about it another way, the media does start to play on click—on click of the media file itself!

Now you may recall that there is an animation setting called "on click." It animates an object when you advance, whether that's by clicking the mouse (but not clicking a specific object), pressing the spacebar, using the Page Down key, or any of the myriad ways you can move through your slides.

You also might recall there is an animation setting called a trigger animation. A trigger animation is initiated when you click a specific object. That's exactly what's happening with the media clips: They're using triggers. And the trigger is what enables you to pause and start it on click. Without a trigger, the video will restart from the beginning every time you click it.

Trigger lightning bolt ——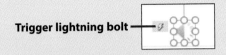

There are a couple of things that will help remind you that the video is set with a trigger. One is the lightning bolt symbol. You'll see this next to the Start setting on the Playback tab and next to the media clip on the slide as well. The other thing is the ScreenTip. Take a second to reread it and remind yourself that the media will begin when you click it specifically, not when you just randomly click as you would to advance typical slides or animations.

If you set the Start value to Automatically on the Playback tab, the trigger is removed, and the media will start automatically after the previous animation on that slide.

Play a Media File "On Click"

Often you'll want to set your media to play just like any other animation so that it starts playing when you advance the slide—in other words, using an "on click" animation. This is definitely necessary if you're in a traditional speaking situation where you're using a slide advancer rather than an actual mouse or keyboard.

1. Insert an audio or video clip onto your slide and select it.

2. On the Animations tab, click Add Animation, and then click Play.

Play Multimedia Automatically

If Play media is the first animation in the Animation Pane, changing the Start action to With Previous or After Previous will cause the audio or video to play automatically when you advance to this slide.

3. Open the Animation Pane to double-check that the Play animation comes before the trigger animation.

4. Click the Play animation in the Animation Pane and change its Start action from On Click to With Previous or After Previous if necessary.

5. Right-click the Trigger animation in the Animation Pane and choose Remove if desired.

Play animation   Trigger animation

Triggers Can Be Helpful

Choosing Play from the Add Animation gallery adds the Play animation setting to the media. Choosing Play from the Animation gallery on the left overwrites the default trigger animation.

Leaving the trigger animation in isn't a bad thing. In fact, it ensures that if you click the video itself by mistake, it will pause and then you can click it again to start playing from that point. Without the trigger animation, clicking the video itself will cause it to start over from the beginning. If there's a chance you might click the video inadvertently, be on the safe side and leave the trigger on it.

Control Other Video Playback Options

Video files have some other playback settings that you may find useful.

1. To turn off the media controls that appear in Slide Show view, go to the Slide Show tab and uncheck Show Media Controls.

2. On the Video Tools Playback tab, click Play Full Screen, and your video will fill the screen while it's playing and then shrink back to size when it's finished.

Media controls

3. Click Hide While Not Playing to hide the video until it plays. Because you can't see it, it's important that you set a Play animation to start the video and don't rely only on the trigger.

4. Click Loop Until Stopped, and your video will continue to play until you move on to the next slide or otherwise stop the video.

5. Click Rewind After Playing, and the clip rewinds to the beginning after it's finished.

6. Change the volume of the video using the options under Volume.

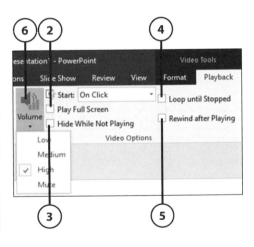

About the Media Controls

If you leave the Media Controls showing, which is the default setting when you insert a media file, you can click in the timeline or click a bookmark to jump to a specific point in the video when you're in Slide Show view.

Unchecking Show Media Controls turns off the media controls on all media throughout the presentation. It's an all-or-nothing setting; you cannot control it for each individual media clip.

Either way, the media controls will still appear in Normal (editing) view. You can use the Play, Fast Forward, and Rewind buttons there while you're editing, and you can click in the timeline or on a bookmark to jump to a point while you're creating the presentation.

Play Audio as a Background Track

Although you may need to play an occasional sound on a slide, a frequent use of sound in PowerPoint is playing audio across slides as a background track. The background music will start playing from the slide on which you insert the audio file.

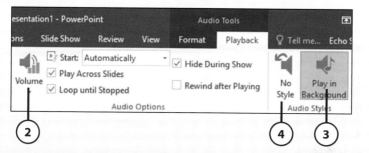

1. Insert an audio clip onto the slide and select it.

2. On the Audio Tools Playback tab, click Volume to adjust the volume if desired.

3. Click Play in Background.

4. Click No Style to remove the Play in Background settings and revert to the default audio playback options.

What Does Play in Background Do?

When you click Play in Background, the following Audio Playback Options are put into play:

- The sound's Start action is changed to Automatically so you don't have to click it to begin. The Start action is also moved to the front of the animation list so the audio will start playing when you come to that slide.

- The Play Across Slides option is checked. This plays the sound continuously as the slides advance.

- The Loop Until Stopped option is checked. When finished, your audio file will start over so you're not left with slides but no music.

- The Hide During Show option is checked so the audio icon doesn't appear on your slide. Because the audio starts automatically, you don't need to see it and click it.

Hiding the Audio Icon

There are a couple of ways to hide the audio icon. One is to check Hide During Show on the Audio Tools Playback tab.

The other is to simply drag the file off the edge of the slide where it won't show in Slide Show view. This has an added benefit of getting it out of your way while you're working.

Regardless of which method you choose, if you hide the audio icon, make sure the sound is set up to play automatically because you won't be able to click it to start it during the presentation!

Add Bookmarks to the Media Timeline

Bookmarks are useful to add to an audio or video clip. Click a bookmark to jump to that point in the media clip.

1. Insert an audio or video clip onto the slide and select it.

2. Use the media controls to pause the video on the frame where you want to add the bookmark.

3. On the Audio Tools Playback tab or Video Tools Playback tab, click Add Bookmark.

4. To remove a bookmark, select it on the media timeline and click Remove Bookmark on the Audio Tools Playback tab or Video Tools Playback tab.

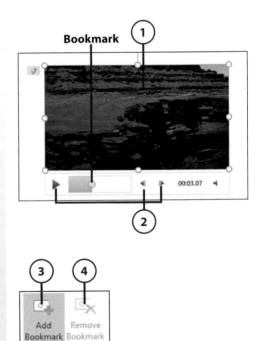

Bookmarks Can't Be Moved

There's no way to move or edit a bookmark; you must delete it and re-create it.

Use Bookmarks to Sync Animation to Your Media

The most impressive thing you can do with bookmarks is use them as a trigger for animations. This lets you sync objects to your media! It's perfect for those times you need to
add captions for audio or point to something in a video.

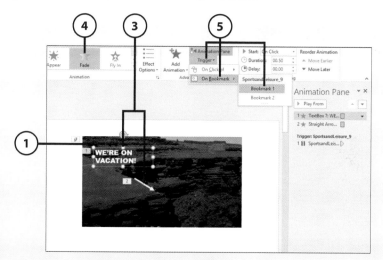

1. Insert an audio or video clip and select it.

2. Add a bookmark where you want text or a graphic to appear.

3. Create the text box or graphic.

4. Apply an animation to the text box or graphic.

5. Select the animated text box or graphic. On the Animations tab, choose Trigger, then
   point to On Bookmark. Choose the bookmark you want from the list.

Bookmarks as Animation Triggers

When the video plays, the object will animate at the bookmark. Note that this
won't really work with sound set up as a background track because the sound
and bookmarks will be available only on the first slide. Of course, if the trigger
animation is also on that slide, you're in good shape! Also, if you delete a bookmark with an attached animation, you'll need to redo the trigger animation
after the bookmark has been re-created.

Making Your Media More Portable

As users upgrade to newer versions of Office, it's getting easier to use PowerPoint files with media embedded in them. The downside is that media files usually make the PowerPoint files extremely large.

If you're running into issues with users running PowerPoint 2007 and 2010, or if you just need to get the PowerPoint file size down somewhat, try the Optimize and Compress features. Or convert your whole presentation into its own video. See "Save As a Video" in Chapter 11 for details.

Optimize Media Compatibility

Use Optimize Media Compatibility if you need to play your presentation on another computer. To begin, create a presentation with embedded audio or video.

1. Save a copy of your presentation before you optimize—just in case.

2. Click the File tab. Backstage should open to the Info tab.

3. Click Optimize Compatibility. When the process is complete, click Close to close the dialog box.

4. Play all the media in the file to ensure that the quality hasn't degraded.

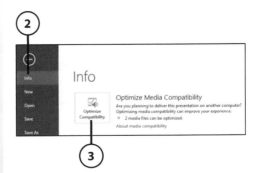

Compress Media

Use the Compress Media command to make your PowerPoint file size smaller. Compress Media removes trimmed parts and compresses to the quality level you specify. To begin, create a presentation with embedded audio or video.

1. Click the File tab. Backstage should open to the Info tab.

2. Click Compress Media and choose Presentation Quality, Internet Quality, or Low Quality.

3. Play all media in the file to ensure that the quality hasn't degraded.

4. If you're unhappy with the results, click Compress Media again and choose Undo.

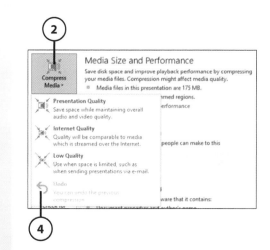

Optimizing and Compressing Media

The Optimize Compatibility and Compress Media commands convert all video files to .MP4 files for maximum compatibility. Audio is converted to .M4A, with one exception: .MP3 audio is already compressed, so those files won't change when you use Compress Media.

If you compress video, you won't have to also optimize it because the process of compression also optimizes.

Optimizing actually uses the presentation-quality compression settings, so if you're planning to use Compress Media for Presentation Quality, you don't have to compress also.

Check for issues

Create and print sections

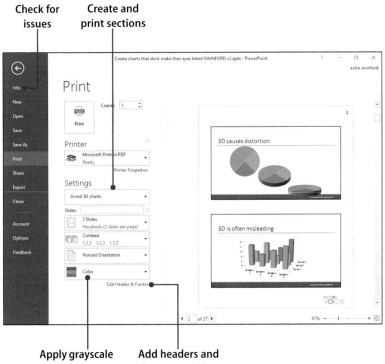

Apply grayscale settings

Add headers and footers to slides and handouts

In this chapter, you will learn about printing your presentation and steps you may want to take as you finalize it. Specific topics in this chapter include the following:

→ Creating sections
→ Adding headers and footers
→ Reviewing your presentation
→ Printing
→ Checking for issues

Printing and Finalizing Your Presentation

It's rare that you'll work on your presentation in isolation. When you're collaborating with others, you'll want to check out how to use PowerPoint's sections to help organize and divvy the work, as well as the sharing options that allow for real-time simultaneous editing.

Other things that come in handy as you put the final touches on your file include running the Document Inspector to ensure you haven't left any private information in the file, adding footer text with identification or confidentiality information, and using PowerPoint's various printing options to create handouts for your audience or speaker notes for yourself.

Creating Sections

Sections can help you organize and structure your presentation. They're also helpful when you're collaborating with others—add someone's name to a section and assign it to him!

You can create and edit sections in either Normal view or Slide Sorter view. Slide Sorter view is usually better when you need to move sections around and reorganize your presentation.

1. Select a slide thumbnail in either Slide Sorter view or in the Slides pane in Normal view. This will be the first slide in the section.

2. Right-click the thumbnail and choose Add Section.

3. Right-click the new section, named Untitled Section, and choose Rename Section.

4. Type a new name for the section in the Rename Section dialog box and click Rename.

5. Click Remove Section if you want to delete the section marker. Your slides will remain in place.

6. Click Remove Section & Slides if you want to delete the section and all slides in it.

7. Click Remove All Sections if you want to delete all the section markers.

Slides pane in Normal view

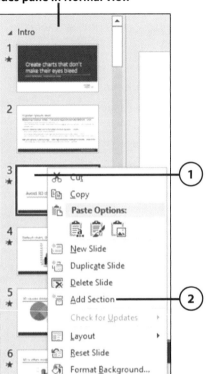

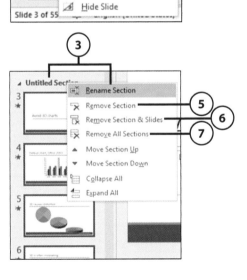

8. Switch to Slide Sorter view and then right-click a slide and click Move Section Up or Move Section Down to reorder the sections.

9. Click the triangle next to any section to expand or collapse it.

10. Click Collapse All or Expand All to collapse or expand all the sections.

11. Click and drag a section ahead of or behind another section to reorder the sections.

12. Click and drag any slide or slides from one section to another, just as you typically work with slides in Slide Sorter view.

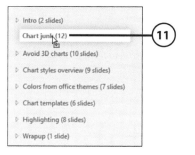

(9) **Slide Sorter view**

Start Slide Show

Intro

Create charts that don't make their eyes bleed

Hipster ipsum text

1   *   2

Untitled Section

Rename Section
Remove Section
Remove Section & Slides
Remove All Sections
Move Section Up — (8)
Move Section Down
Collapse All
Expand All — (10)

Avoid 3D ch

3

(9)

Intro (2 slides)
▶ Avoid 3D charts (10 s...
▷ Chart junk (12 slides)   Rename Section
▷ Chart styles overview   Remove Section
▷ Colors from office the   Remove Section & Slides
▷ Chart templates (6 slic   Remove All Sections
▷ Highlighting (8 slides)   Move Section Up
▷ Wrapup (1 slide)   Move Section Down
        Collapse All
        Expand All — (10)

▷ Intro (2 slides)
Chart junk (12) — (11)
▷ Avoid 3D charts (10 slides)
▷ Chart styles overview (9 slides)
▷ Colors from office themes (7 slides)
▷ Chart templates (6 slides)
▷ Highlighting (8 slides)
▷ Wrapup (1 slide)

>>>Go Further

USING SECTIONS IN PRESENTER VIEW

You can use sections in Presenter view. Click the See All Slides button to see the slide grid, and Sections are listed to the left. Click a section to jump to those slides. Chapter 11, "Setting Up Your Slide Show," has more information about Presenter view.

Presenter view

Adding Headers and Footers

"Headers and footers," often shortened to just "footers," refers to three things collectively: the date, the slide number, and the footer text. You need two things in order for a footer to appear on a slide. First you need the place-holder, and then you need to fill that placeholder.

This means that in order for a slide number to appear on your slides, you need the slide number placeholder, and then you need to turn on the slide number. The same applies for the date. For footer text, you need the placeholder, and then you need to display it and add text to it.

Requirement 1: Add Footer Placeholders

The first step to adding footers to your slides is to ensure that the slide layouts have footer placeholders; otherwise, there won't be any place for the footers to appear.

1. On the View tab, click Slide Master to open Slide Master view.

2. In Slide Master view, scroll up (if necessary) in the Slides pane and select the slide master at the top.

3. On the displayed slide master, check for a date placeholder, a slide number placeholder, and a footer text placeholder.

4. If any of these placeholders is missing, click Master Layout on the Slide Master tab of the Ribbon.

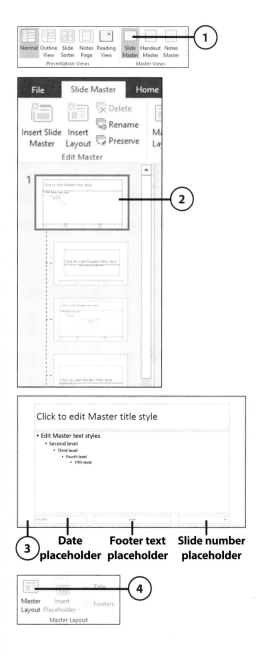

Date placeholder   Footer text placeholder   Slide number placeholder

5. Select all placeholder check boxes in the dialog box and click OK.

6. Position and format the footer placeholders on the Slide Master.

7. Check each individual layout (one at a time) and turn its footer placeholders on or off by clicking the Footers check box on the Slide Master tab.

8. Close Slide Master view by clicking Normal on the View tab. Or if you are still on the Slide Master tab, click Close Master View.

Title Slide Layout

Title and Content Layout

>>>Go Further
TROUBLESHOOTING TIPS

If you're working with an existing PowerPoint file, especially one that's had slides pasted in from a number of presentations, it's pretty common for the footer placeholders to be missing. You may find it helpful to turn the footer placeholders on, then off, then on or off again on each of the layouts.

Also it's not unusual to turn the footer placeholders completely off on layouts such as Title Slide and Section Header. It's tempting to delete them from those layouts, but if you paste in existing slides that do have footers, they'll become orphaned when the new layout has no footer placeholders. Have you ever pasted in a slide and had its slide number or footer text become 18-point black font? That's an orphaned footer. It's looking for a placeholder to live in.

This tends to happen when you don't need all three of the footers. For example, maybe you want to show just the page number and footer text, and you'd prefer to leave the date off. In that case, you might experiment with placing the date placeholder off the edge of the Slide Master so the date won't show on the slide even if the date is displayed.

The biggest benefit to using the footer placeholders is that it gives the presentation author flexibility and control over whether the footers show. If you always want a slide number to appear no matter what, you might consider putting a text box (not a placeholder) on the slide master and then clicking the Insert tab, and then Insert Slide Number. This type of slide number works more like a regular text box or graphic on the slide masters and layouts—you won't be able to select them on the slides, and you won't be able to turn them on or off at will. You can do the same with the date: Add a text box and then select Date & Time on the Insert tab.

Requirement 2: Populate the Footer Placeholders

Now that you have footer placeholders in place, you need to turn them on and fill them with text.

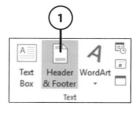

1. In Normal view, go to the Insert tab and click Header & Footer.

2. In the Header and Footer dialog box, check Date and Time. Choose from a date that updates automatically when you open the presentation or a fixed date that will display whatever you type in that field (even if it's not a date).

3. Check Slide Number to turn on slide numbers.

4. Check Footer and type in your preferred footer text.

5. Check Don't Show on Title Slide to prevent the footers from appearing on any slide based on the Title Slide layout. (If you turned footers off on your Title Slide layout, you don't have to worry about checking this box.)

6. Click Apply to apply the footers to the current slide.

7. Or click Apply to All to apply the footers to all slides in the presentation.

8. Click the Notes and Handouts tab to populate footers on the Handouts and Notes Pages.

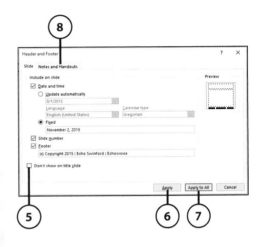

Troubleshooting Tips

Especially if you've pasted in existing slides from other presentations, you may need to reapply footers periodically to clean up any previously existing footers.

If you apply a footer to only one slide, later clicking Apply to All will override any single-slide footers.

Reviewing Your Presentation

Of course, while you're finishing your presentation, you'll want to review it. Sharing via OneDrive is a great way to review with colleagues, and you can all add comments to facilitate collaboration.

Review and Compare is the PowerPoint equivalent of Word's Track Changes, but by necessity you get a lot more information than just text changes. Review and Compare shows you changes to everything from text to formatting to transition timings and animations.

Add Comments

Comments provide an easy way for you and your colleagues to communicate as you col-
laborate on a presentation. Comments don't show in Slide Show view, so you don't have
to worry about them popping up during your presentation.

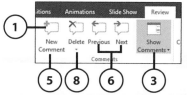

1.   Select a slide or an object on a slide. On the Review tab, click New Comment.

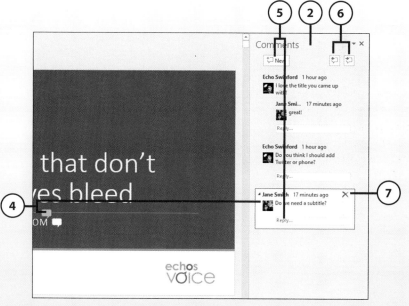

2.   Enter your comment in the Comments Pane.

3.   Turn the Comments Pane on or off with the Show Comments button on the Review tab.

4.   To select a comment, either click a comment bubble on the slide or click a comment
     in the Comments Pane.

5.   Click New to type a new comment in the pane or click and type in the Reply box to
     respond directly to a previous comment.

6.   Use the Previous and Next buttons to jump to the next comment.

7.   Delete a selected comment by clicking the X next to it in the Comments Pane.

8.   Click the bottom of the Delete button on the Review tab to delete a selected com-
     ment or to delete all comments and ink on the slide or in the presentation.

Add Ink

Use the ink tools to draw and highlight objects on your slides.

1. Click Start Inking on the Review tab to open the Ink Tools contextual tab.

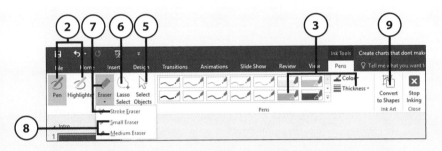

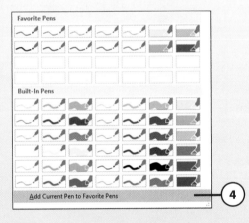

2. Choose a pen or highlighter to work with. Highlighters are automatically semitransparent.

3. Format a pen or highlighter using the Color and Thickness options or choose a prefor-matted pen from the gallery.

4. Click the More button to display the Pens gallery and then click Add Current Pen to Favorite Pens to save a pen you've created.

5. To select a pen stroke after you've drawn it, use Select Objects or Lasso Select.

6. With Lasso Select, click and drag around objects to select them.

7. Click Eraser and then Stroke Eraser to erase individual pen strokes by clicking on them.

8. Click Eraser and then Small or Medium Eraser to erase parts of pen strokes by "rub-bing" that area with the eraser head.

9. Click Convert to Shapes and then draw on the slide. Your rough pen scratchings will become true shapes such as ovals, rectangles, triangles, and arrows. You'll be able to use all the Drawing Tools on them, just as with any other shape.

Ink Equations

The new feature Ink Equation lets you insert mathematical equations using your handwriting. On the Insert tab, click Equation, then Ink Equation at the bottom of the gallery. Write your equation with your mouse or pen and click Insert to convert it to text on your slide.

Share with Colleagues

Instead of emailing a separate file to every person, save the file in a central location and send everyone an invitation to share. That way all changes and comments are concentrated in one place.

1. Click the Share button in the upper-right corner of your screen.

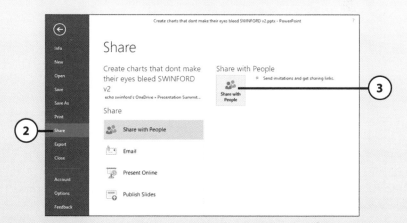

2. Alternatively, click File, Share. You'll be prompted to save your file to OneDrive if it's not already there.

3. After your file is saved on OneDrive, click Share with People. The Share Pane will open.

Test View and Edit Permissions!

Be sure to test the Can View permissions, especially if you're sharing your file with people who you want to be able to view, but not download or edit the presentation. Unbelievably, the Can View setting sometimes allows others to edit the file as well!

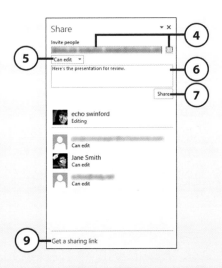

4. In the Share Pane, use the address book or type the email addresses of the people you want to share with. Separate addresses with a semicolon.

5. Change the permissions from Can Edit to Can View, if desired. Can Edit grants editing permission to the others. Can View lets them view the file but not edit it.

6. Add a message. This text will be included in the email.

7. Click Share to send email with a link notifying the others where to go to see the file.

Do I Have to Set Up Outlook to Share?

Nope. The email notification to share will still send even if you don't have Outlook installed. If you'd prefer to use a specific email program, click any recipient in the list and then click the Mail button and choose a different email option.

It's usually a good idea to go through the share process and send the email to yourself as a test before you share with others.

8. Right-click any recipient to remove her from the list after sharing or change her view/edit permissions.

9. If you'd rather just generate a link and share it elsewhere, click Get a Sharing Link at the bottom of the Share pane.

>>>Go Further
REAL-TIME COLLABORATION

Saving your presentation to OneDrive and sharing with others opens the door to real-time collaboration, in which you and your colleagues author and edit the presentation simultaneously. You'll see their changes to text and formatting as they happen, and they'll see yours. You can each choose what device you want to work on (your Mac, your PC, PowerPoint on your tablet, PowerPoint Online in a web browser on your phone, and so on). If one of you goes offline, those changes will be synced back to the document when that person is back online.

Use Review and Compare

Use Review and Compare to merge two versions of a presentation. Then compare them and accept or reject changes.

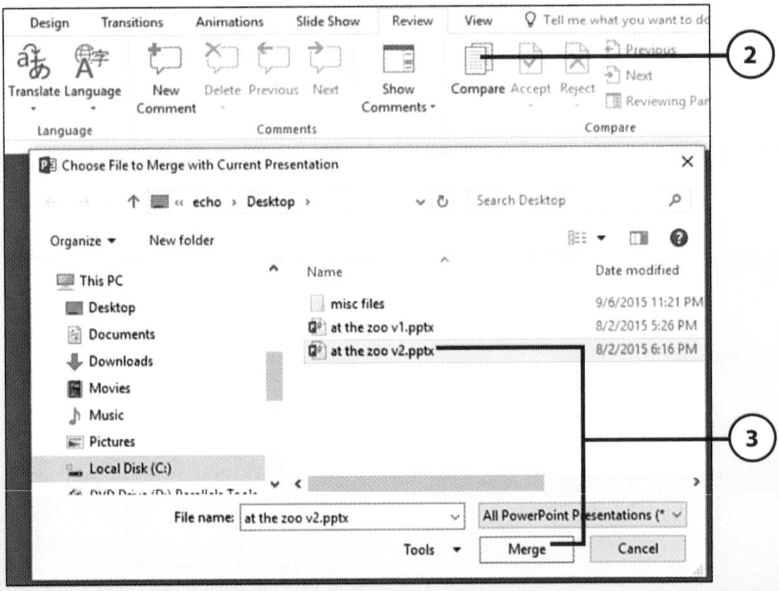

1. Open the original presentation.

2. On the Review tab, click Compare.

3. Navigate to the newer version of your presentation, select the file, and click Merge.

Using Review and Compare

You can start with either the older or the newer presentation; it doesn't really matter. It's usually easier, though, if you start with the presentation you're most familiar with and merge the presentation someone else has been making changes to.

Review and Compare works best when the presentations aren't completely different. If you expect extensive revisions to your presentation, use Review and Compare periodically throughout the revision process. If you Review and Compare only the first and last versions of the presentation, it may be too confusing to be helpful.

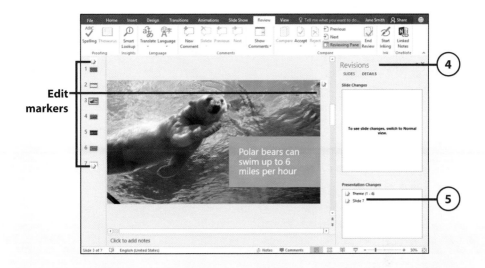

4. The two presentations are merged together. The Revisions Pane opens, and edit markers may appear on the selected slide or in the Slides pane.

5. Changes that affect the overall presentation, such as transitions and deleted or moved slides, are listed in the Presentation Changes area on the Details tab. They also appear with edit markers in the Slides pane.

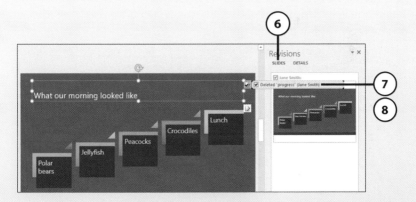

6. Click the Slides tab in the Revisions Pane to select all changes on a specific slide.

7. Point to any of the edit markers on a slide to see details about the change.

8. Click the edit marker to accept a change.

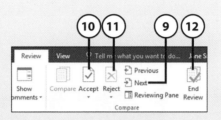

9. Use Previous and Next to move through the changes.

10. Click the bottom of the Accept button and select an option. You can accept all changes on a slide or the whole presentation.

11. Click the bottom of the Reject button and select an option. You can reject all changes on a slide or the whole presentation.

12. Click End Review when you're finished. Any changes you haven't yet accepted or rejected will be discarded.

Printing

Whether you need to print speaker notes for your own use or handouts for your audience, PowerPoint offers you many options. The Print tab in Backstage view hides a lot of useful settings, but after you know the settings are there, you'll use them all the time.

Use Black and White Settings

If you're planning to print in black and white, optimize the grayscale and black and white settings in your presentation first. These settings do not affect the presentation in Slide Show view; they affect slides only when they're printed.

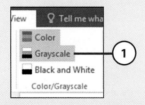

1. On the View tab click Grayscale.

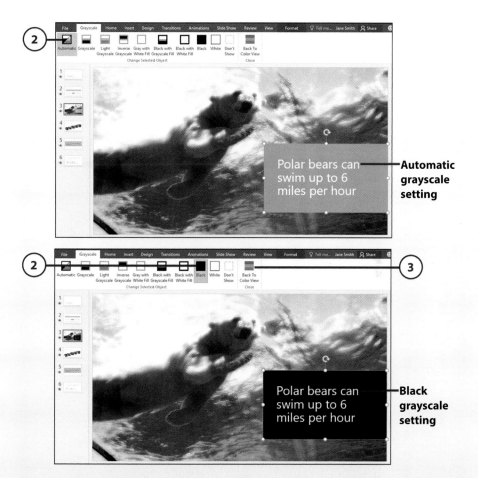

Automatic grayscale setting

Black grayscale setting

2. Select an object on the slide and choose another setting on the Grayscale tab. Note that some objects, such as charts and tables, won't let you change Grayscale or Black and White Settings.

3. When you're finished, click Back to Color View.

Grayscale Versus Black and White

You can print in either Grayscale or Black and White. Both options drop out background colors and picture fills to save toner. Black and White is designed to save as much toner as possible, so it will often give you a wireframe-type outline of an object, whereas Grayscale will give it a grayscale fill instead.

Any changes you make in Grayscale view will also be made automatically in Black and White view, and vice versa. For example, if an object has an automatic dark gray fill and you change it to light grayscale, the object will have a light grayscale fill in Black and White view as well.

Remember, neither of these affects your color slides. They apply to objects only when you print—and even then, only when you print using the Pure Black and White setting or the Grayscale setting.

Print Slides

On the Print tab in Backstage view, you decide what to print and how to print it.

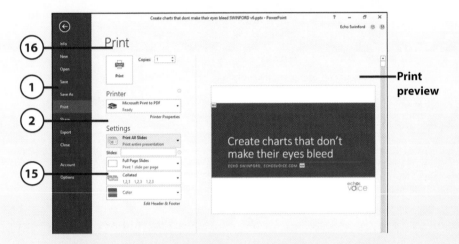

1. Click File and then click the Print tab.

2. To specify which slides to print, click Print All Slides.

3. If you selected the slides you want to print before opening the Print tab, click Print Selection.

4. Choose Print Current Slide to print the slide showing in the preview.

5. Choose Custom Range to specify which slides to print and then type the slide numbers in the Slides box.

6. If you have sections in your file, you can choose a specific section to print.

7. Hidden slides will be printed by default. Uncheck the Print Hidden Slides option if you don't want hidden slides to print.

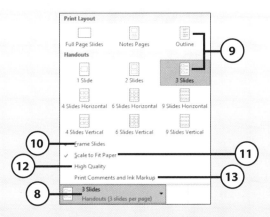

8. If you don't want to print one slide per page, click Full Page Slides to determine what print layout to use.

9. Select from Notes Pages, Outline, or any of the horizontal or vertical Handouts layouts.

10. Select Frame Slides if you want to add a border around full-page slides. Frame Slides is automatically selected when you print handouts so the slide thumbnails have a border.

11. Select Scale to Fit Paper to fit the full slide onto the page. Without this setting, the default widescreen slides will be cut off when printing.

12. Choose High Quality for the best print quality. Uncheck High Quality if you're having trouble printing.

13. If you have comments or inking in your presentation, you can opt to print those by selecting Print Comments and Ink Markup.

Printing Comments and Ink

When you print comments and ink markup, the ink prints on the slides. So do comment bubbles. The comments themselves are printed on the page following the slide.

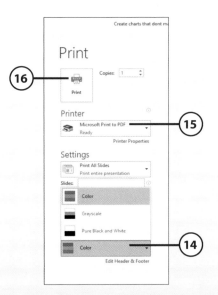

14. To print in grayscale or black and white (even if you're using a color printer), click Color and then choose the appropriate setting.

15. Select a different printer or click Send to OneNote 16.

16. Click the Print button when you're ready to print.

Specifying Custom Print Ranges

When you enter a custom range of slides to print, use these tips:

- 1-12 prints slides 1 through 12.
- 1, 12 prints slide 1 and slide 12.
- 12-1 prints slide 12 through 1 (backward)
- 1, 4, 9-12 prints slide 1, slide 4, and slides 9 through 12.

Print Handouts

Printing handouts is a good way to see a quick overview of your presentation.

1. Click File and then click the Print tab.

2. Click Full Page Slides and choose a print layout.

Print preview

3. Handouts include slide thumbnails in a set configuration. You can print 1, 2, 3, 4, 6, or 9 slides per handout page. The 3 Slides handout option includes 3 slide thumbnails with blank lines beside them.

4. To add logos to your handout pages, put them on the master. On the View tab, click Handout Master. Note that the slide thumbnail and lines position and sizes cannot be changed in the Handout Master.

5. To add or remove the slide number, date, or text footers from the handouts, click Edit Header & Footer, and then click the Notes and Handouts tab and make the appropriate selections.

6. Click the Print button when you're ready to print.

Printing Outlines
An outline will print only text included in placeholders. Any ad hoc text boxes, graphics, or diagrams won't print in an outline.

Print Notes Pages

Notes pages include any speaker notes you've added, along with a slide thumbnail so you know what the notes refer to.

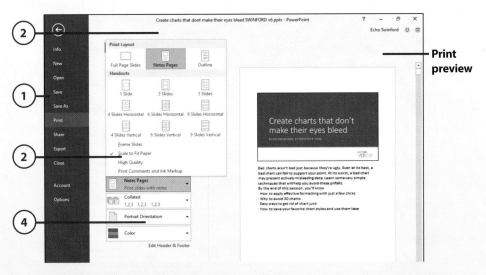

Print preview

1. Click File and then click the Print tab.

2. Click Full Page Slides and choose Notes Pages from the print layout options.

3. To add logos to your Notes Pages, put them on the master. On the View tab, click Notes Master. Resize and reposition the slide thumbnail and text placeholder on the Notes Master as desired.

4. To add or remove the slide number, date, or text footers from the Notes Pages, click Edit Header & Footer and then click the Notes and Handouts tab and make the appropriate selections.

5. Text can be entered into the Notes pane in Normal (editing) view. Or, on the View tab, click Notes Page to enter text directly into the notes pages.

6. Click the Print button when you're ready to print.

Add Color to Notes Text
Although color formatting applied to notes text doesn't show in Presenter view or in the Notes pane in Normal view, it will show in Print Preview and can be printed.

Notes Pages as Leave-Behinds
Notes Pages don't have to be only for the speaker. In fact, Notes Pages can make great handouts and leave-behinds. Add your logo to the Notes Master and make the slide thumbnail and text placeholder bigger or smaller. Instead of typing your speaker notes in the placeholder, type in the information you want to leave behind with your audience. Copy any additional information like tables and charts and voilà! You have a nice handout.

>>>Go Further
CREATE POWERPOINT HANDOUTS IN WORD

You can print handouts with slide thumbnails in PowerPoint. You can even print Notes Pages, which combine a slide thumbnail with its speaker notes. But what if you want to print multiple slide thumbnails per page and include the speaker notes too?

In that situation, use the Send to Word feature. Well, that's what it used to be called back in the day—from PowerPoint 95 through 2003, that is. In PowerPoint 2016, you can find this feature by clicking the File tab, then Export, then Create Handouts.

In the Send to Microsoft Word dialog box, you can choose to create slide thumbnails either with blank lines or with speaker notes beside them, as well as a few other options. The difference in all cases is that these slide thumbnails, blank lines, and speaker notes are completely editable in Word so you can resize and reposition at will.

Here are some best practices to consider when you create handouts in Word.

- Choose Paste Link in the Send to Microsoft Word dialog box. This seems counterintuitive, but it helps keep the Word file size down.
- Save the Word file and then break the links. In Word, click the File tab, and then on the Info page, click Edit Links to Files. In the Edit Links dialog box, break all the links to your PowerPoint file.
- Don't expect that changes in your PowerPoint file will be accurately reflected in the Word document. Send to Microsoft Word doesn't recognize when slides have been reordered, hidden, or deleted, and because speaker notes aren't linked, changes to them also aren't recognized. (So you might as well break those links!)

To see more specifics about these Send to Microsoft Word best practices, check out http://echosvoice.com/4-best-practices-for-powerpoint-handouts-with-send-to-word/.

Checking for Issues

Especially before you send your PowerPoint file to someone else, you'll want to check through it to make sure you didn't inadvertently leave any personal information in the file or include content that's inaccessible to people with disabilities. PowerPoint has some built-in utilities that let you check for these types of things. At the very least, head to the File tab, click Info, and take a look at the list next to the Inspect Presentation header to see a general list of potential problem areas.

Check Compatibility

If you know you'll be sharing your presentation with someone using an older version of PowerPoint, or if you plan to save the file as PowerPoint 97-2003 format, running the compatibility checker will give you an idea of content that won't be editable and may not display the same as in PowerPoint 2016.

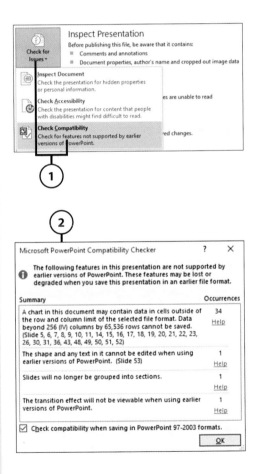

1. Click the File tab and then click Info. Click the Check for Issues button and then click Check Compatibility.

2. The Microsoft PowerPoint Compatibility Checker dialog box displays. Notice the issues presented in the Summary list, if applicable.

Check Accessibility

PowerPoint can help you determine whether your content will be accessible for people using screen readers.

1. Click the File tab and then click Info. Click the Check for Issues button and then click Check Accessibility.

2. In the Accessibility Checker pane, review the errors and tips and make changes as necessary.

3. To add Alt Text to an object, right-click the object and choose Format <Object>. In the Format pane, click Size & Properties, then Alt Text.

4. Type a title and description of the object for screen reading software to use.

The Compatibility Checker

The Compatibility Checker flags content with features that earlier versions of PowerPoint don't support. This doesn't always mean there will actually be a problem. For example, any chart created in PowerPoint 2016 will be flagged because we can now add more than 256 columns and 65,536 rows of data to an Excel spreadsheet. Chances are your chart doesn't have that many columns and rows. And if it does, you shouldn't be presenting it on a PowerPoint slide, anyway!

The newer transitions, mostly Exciting and Dynamic transitions, will become fades, so that's not as bad as it seems in the checker, either.

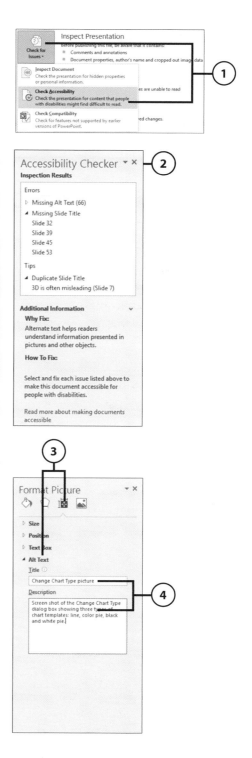

Inspect Document

Use the Inspect Document feature to remove speaker notes, comments and annotations, the cropped area of pictures, and other information. Save your file before running Document Inspector. Better yet, save a copy of your file if there's any chance you may want to get those speaker notes back!

1. Click the File tab and then click Info. Click the Check for Issues button and then click Inspect Document.

2. In the Document Inspector dialog box, choose the types of content you want to check for.

3. Click Inspect.

4. Click Remove All to remove all instances of each type of found content.

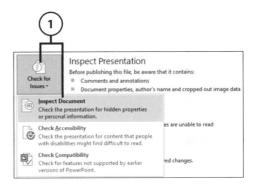

Understanding What the Document Inspector Has Found

Any chart you created in the presentation will trigger the Embedded Documents warning. Think of it as a reminder to make sure that the spreadsheets behind your charts don't include more information than you are prepared to share. Click the More Info button beside Embedded Documents in the Document Inspector dialog box to learn how to turn your charts and other embedded content into images.

When you scroll down in the dialog box, you'll see an Invisible On-Slide Content item, which refers to hidden objects. Open the Selection Pane and check your slides to find them.

The Presentation Notes item refers to speaker notes. This is handy to use when you want to send a copy of your presentation to someone but don't want him to have all your speaker notes. This way you don't have to remove them slide by slide.

>>>Go Further

HOW DO I PROTECT MY PRESENTATION?

This is a question that comes up a lot. You've created an awesome presentation, and you want people to see it; but you don't want to give them a PowerPoint file with slides and objects they can easily reuse in their own presentations.

If you've poked around under File, Info, Protect Presentation, you may be aware of a few features there that look pretty promising.

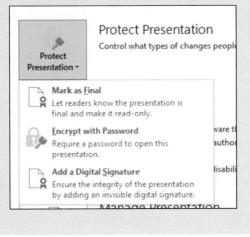

- Mark as Final. This is simply an administrative feature. Click Mark as Final to flag this file as the final version. Click Mark as Final again to unflag it.

- Encrypt with Password. This does add a password requirement to your presentation, but that only prevents people from opening the file. Users without the password won't be able to view it at all; users with the password will be able to see it, but they'll also be able to make changes to it.

- Add a Digital Signature. You'll need a digital ID to add a digital signature. When you select this option, you'll be prompted to get a digital ID from a Microsoft Partner, and you'll be taken to a web page with a list of companies providing digital ID services. These aren't free, but they're not all terribly expensive, either. Digital signatures help verify that your file is legit, but they don't do anything to protect the file.

Other options to consider are to convert your presentation to a video or PDF (see Chapter 11) or to upload it to a service such as SlideShare, SlideShark, Articulate, Office Sway, or Office Mix.

Be careful with OneDrive. Even though you can generate a Share link on OneDrive, and even though that link generator says that people with the link can only view the presentation, all they have to do is view the presentation and click the Edit or Download button and they'll have access to the file for editing.

Whichever option you decide on, just remember that if your presentation can be seen, it can be re-created. Nothing can completely prevent that—but you can certainly make it a little more difficult by using some of the options discussed.

Set up and
start a slide
show

Create hyperlinks
and custom shows
for navigation

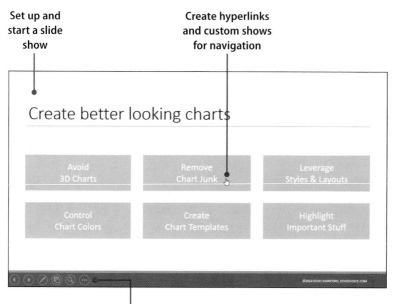

Use various slide show
tools such as ink,
magnification, and
Presenter View

In this chapter, you will learn how to set up and run your presentation as a slide show, as well as different methods to distribute it digitally. Specific topics in this chapter include the following:

→ Setting up the presentation structure
→ Delivering your presentation
→ Other ways to deliver your presentation

Setting Up Your Slide Show

You can give your presentation in a number of ways, and PowerPoint provides you with various tools to support all of them. When you're presenting in the traditional manner, in which you speak and manually advance through the slides, Presenter view may just change your life. It displays your speaker notes, includes thumbnails of your current and next slides, and lets you see a grid of all slides and jump to any of them easily. It even gives you a timer so you don't talk too long!

If you need to deliver your presentation online or as a stand-alone kiosk presentation, you can take advantage of hyperlinks and actions that allow your viewers to jump to specific places in the presentation. Custom Shows can help you tailor your presentation for different audiences. And the Slide Show settings help make sure your presentations all run smoothly.

Setting Up the Presentation Structure

How you plan to give your presentation has everything to do with the underlying slide-show setup. For example, if you plan to create a self-running presentation, you can opt to give your slides automatic transitions and simply set the file to loop until the recipient presses the

Esc key. Or you might want to give the audience the option to click a button when they're ready to move to the next slide or to the home page. Even if you are presenting the slide show, you might want that ability to jump around, too.

Add Speaker Notes

Speaker notes are the place to put all the things you want to remember to say as you present so you don't have to put those cues on the slides. Speaker notes display when you use Presenter view, or you can print them.

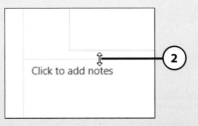

1. If the Notes pane isn't open, click Notes on the status bar at the bottom of the screen in Normal view.

2. Click and drag the top of the Notes pane to resize it if desired.

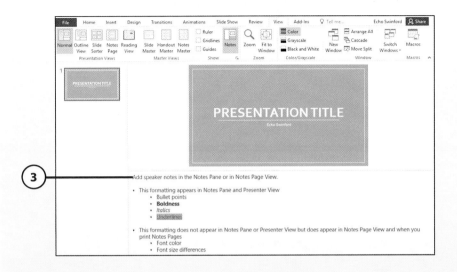

3. Type speaker notes in the Notes pane in Normal view.

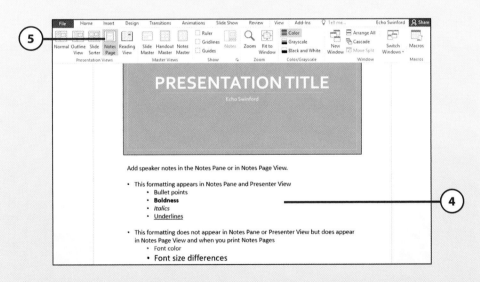

4. Formatting such as bold, italics, underlines, and bullet points will display in all the different Notes Pages views. Font color will not appear in Presenter view or in the Notes pane in Normal view.

5. To see what the notes pages will look like when they're printed, open Notes Page view by clicking Notes Page on the View tab. Text entered in the Notes pane appears here, and text that you add in Notes Page view will appear in the Notes pane.

The Four Faces of Notes Pages

Notes Pages have four views, each of which can be used in different ways:

Notes pane in Normal view. Used to quickly add text to go along with your slide. Displays text only. Displays most text formatting but not color.

Notes Page view. Open by clicking Notes Page on the View tab. Displays all text formatting, including color. Can type or paste in other content. Indicates what Notes Pages will look like when printed.

Notes in Presenter view. Displays text only. Displays most text formatting but not color.

Notes Page Master. Add elements (such as a logo) that should appear on every Notes Page. Position and size slide thumbnail and text placeholder.

Hide Slides

You may want to include slides in your presentation that you won't show. Hiding them is an easy way to ensure they're available but won't get in the way of your primary slides. Hidden slides are printed by default. You can choose not to print them using the Print tab settings in Backstage view (see Chapter 10, "Printing and Finalizing Your Presentation").

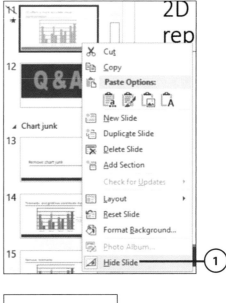

1. To hide or unhide a slide, right-click the thumbnail in Normal view or Slide Sorter view and click Hide Slide.

2. Notice that a hidden slide is slightly ghosted and has a line through the slide number. Hidden slides don't appear in Slide Show view when you advance through the slides.

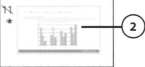

Displaying Hidden Slides

To display a hidden slide during a presentation, input its slide number on the keyboard and press Enter or click on it in Presenter view. After you've displayed a hidden slide, it will continue to display when you advance, as though it were unhidden.

Add Links So You Can Jump Around

Add hyperlinks to slides in your presentation and then click on them during a slide show to jump to that slide. Don't forget to add a link to get back to the original slide! Keep in mind that hyperlinks can be clicked only in Slide Show view. They don't work in Normal view.

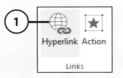

1. To add a hyperlink, select an object or text on the slide, click the Insert tab, and then click Hyperlink.

2. In the Link To area of the Insert Hyperlink dialog box, choose Place in This Document. This lets you link to a slide in the presentation.

3. Select a slide to link to from the Select a Place in This Document list. When you click the slide, a preview will appear. If it doesn't, that link may not work properly.

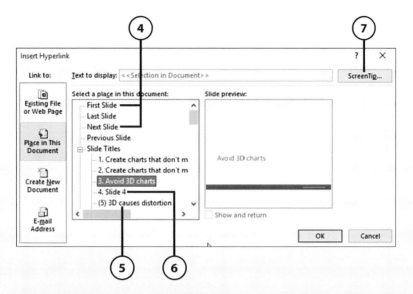

4. Choose First Slide if you want the hyperlink to jump to the first slide in the presentation. Choose Last Slide to go to the final slide in the presentation. Choose Next Slide
to go to the next slide. Choose Previous Slide to jump to the preceding slide in the
presentation, not necessarily to the slide you viewed just before.

5. Notice that a hidden slide is indicated in the list by a slide number in parentheses.

6. The slide names are generated from the text in the title placeholders. If the slide
doesn't have a title placeholder, it will display as Slide 4, for example.

7. Click the ScreenTip button to add identifying text that will appear when you hover
over the link in Slide Show view.

8. Right-click the linked object if you want to edit, open, or remove the hyperlink. The
Open Hyperlink command jumps you to the linked slide in Normal view.

Linking to Sections

You can't use the Insert Hyperlink dialog box to add hyperlinks to specific sections in a presentation, but you can jump to a section or even a specific slide by
clicking on it in Presenter view.

>>>Go Further

HYPERLINKS BEST PRACTICES

Be sure to test your hyperlinks before using them in a presentation; you don't want to be caught unaware when the links do something you don't expect or when you can't get back to your landing page.

Hyperlink applied to text ————

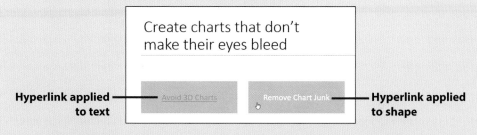

Create charts that don't make their eyes bleed

Avoid 3D Charts · Remove Chart Junk

———— **Hyperlink applied to shape**

Selecting text or a text box when inserting a hyperlink will format the text with an automatic hyperlink color and underline. If necessary, you can change the hyperlink and followed hyperlink colors by editing the presentation color theme. (See Chapter 12, "Creating Your Own Theme," for instructions on editing the color theme.)

For a cleaner look, select a shape and apply the hyperlink to that. Alternatively, place a shape on top of the text you want to link to. Give it no line and no fill so it doesn't obscure the text. PowerPoint 2013 and 2010 will also recognize these as hyperlinks. If you know that your presentation will be run on PowerPoint 2007, give the shape a 100% transparent fill color instead.

During a slide show, after you've clicked to jump to a linked slide, from there you can navigate the presentation with the arrow keys or other options as usual.

>>>Go Further

WHAT ABOUT ACTION SETTINGS?

Actions are much like hyperlinks. In fact, you can add hyperlinks from the Action Buttons listed at the bottom of the Shapes gallery. You can also use actions to do things like run macros, open other programs, and play sounds, and you can set these up to happen when you click an object or even when you just move your mouse over an action button without actually clicking.

Action Buttons

The Action Buttons at the bottom of the Shapes gallery are preformatted to include hyperlinks. The Action Settings dialog box automatically opens when you insert an Action Button so you can easily see the settings and change them if you want.

The Hyperlink To list in the Action Settings dialog box includes more options than the Hyperlink dialog box accessed from the Insert tab. For example, the Actions hyperlinks include Last Slide Viewed and End Show as options.

If you insert the Back or Previous button on your slide, you'll see that its action is set to hyperlink to the previous slide. If you want this button to work like a true Back button, change its setting to Last Slide Viewed. If you want the Home button to return you to the second slide instead of the first slide, which is the default for the Home button, change its Hyperlink To setting to Slide in the Action Settings dialog box and choose your preferred slide from the list.

Create Custom Shows

Custom shows are a great way to set up a presentation when you know you'll want to show different subsets of your slides to different audiences.

1. On the Slide Show tab, click Custom Slide Show. Select an existing custom show to begin presenting that custom show or click Custom Shows to create a new one.

2. Choose a custom show from the list. Click Edit to make changes to it, Remove to delete it, Copy to duplicate it, or Show to present it.

3. Or click New to create a new custom show.

4. If you are creating a new custom show, in the list of slides on the left check the box next to slides you want to include, and then click Add to place the selected slides in your custom show.

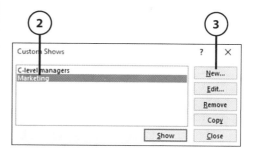

Repeat Slides in a Custom Show

When you create a custom show, you can repeat slides without creating numerous duplicates in your presentation file. Simply add the same slide to your custom show in the Define Custom Show dialog box as many times as desired.

5. Use the Up and Down arrows on the right side of the dialog box to reorder slides in the custom show.

6. Use the X in the dialog box (between the Up and Down buttons) to remove slides from the custom show. This doesn't delete slides from the PowerPoint file; it just removes them from the custom show.

Show and Return

If you hyperlink to a custom show, the custom show begins playing when you click the link in Slide Show view. When you're setting up the link, check the Show and Return option so the custom show will close and return you to the original presentation when it's finished.

Set Up Slide Show Options

Use the Set Up Slide Show command to access settings that are important especially when you're creating self-running presentations. There are other settings here you'll want to be aware of as well. Many are available in Slide Show view, but sometimes it's easier to specify them before you begin presenting.

1. On the Slide Show tab, click Set Up Slide Show.

2. Choose the type of slide show that should be used when you start Slide Show view.

3. Choose Loop Continuously Until Esc to keep your presentation playing continuously. Be sure to add automatic transition timings to your presentation if you plan to loop it. Press Esc to stop the presentation.

What Show Type Should I Choose?

Presented by Speaker is the most common setting. This is a typical full-screen presentation.

Browsed by an Individual opens your presentation in a resizable window. This setting can be helpful when comparing presentations and other uncommon situations because it allows you to run two presentations side by side, each in its own window.

Browsed at a Kiosk is also referred to as Kiosk mode. Kiosk mode eliminates the ability to advance from slide to slide by clicking the mouse or spacebar as you usually would. Instead, with Kiosk mode, you must use automatic transitions or hyperlinks to advance. Press Esc to end a kiosk slide show.

4. If your presentation includes narration or animations, you can opt to turn those off by selecting Show Without Narration or Show Without Animation.

5. If the presentation is not displaying smoothly, for example, animations are jerky or transitions are stalling, try checking the option Disable Hardware Graphics Acceleration.

6. Choose a different pen or laser pointer color here before you begin the presentation.

7. Specify which slides should display during the presentation—all of them, a range, or a specific custom show.

8. Opt to use any automatic transition timings or to advance everything manually regardless.

9. Specify which monitor the slide show will appear on. This is the presentation your audience will see.

10. Enable or disable Presenter view.

11. If your presentation is sluggish when displayed in Slide Show view or you're using a projector that's expecting a specific resolution, you can specify a resolution here.

12. Click OK when you're satisfied with the settings.

13. Notice that you can access some of these settings on the Slide Show tab as well as the Set Up Show dialog box.

Delivering Your Presentation

Most PowerPoint users know you can navigate through your slides by clicking the mouse button or pressing the spacebar, but there are also other methods you can use to advance slides. In addition, you have access to a laser pointer, highlight markers and inking pens, a zoom tool, and a black screen.

Start the Slide Show

Before you can begin presenting, you must put the presentation into Slide Show view. Choose from among many options.

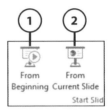

1. On the Slide Show tab, click From Beginning to start the slide show from the first slide.

2. Or click From Current Slide if you want to start the slide show on the currently selected slide.

3. Or click the Slide Show icon on the status bar at the bottom of the screen to start the slide show on the currently selected slide.

Keyboard Shortcuts
The shortcut to start a presentation from the beginning is F5. The shortcut to start a presentation from the current slide is Shift+F5.

Wait! My Slide Show Doesn't Look Right
If you have a second monitor or a projector attached to your computer, PowerPoint will also open Presenter view automatically when you start a presentation. Slide Show view is the full-screen slide your audience will see. Presenter view is designed for only you to see. It shows you thumbnails of your current and next slides, a timer, and various other tools. If the slide show displays on the wrong monitor, click Display Settings at the top of the Presenter View screen and click Swap Presenter View and Slide Show.

Navigate the Slide Show

There are any number of ways to step through the slides during a typical presentation. Most presenters use a combination of keyboard and mouse or slide advancer controls, depending on the situation and the presentation. Refer to the next section, "Use Presenter View," for additional instructions when you're using Presenter view.

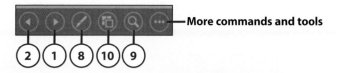———**More commands and tools**

1. Start the presentation. To advance to the next slide or animation, click the mouse button, press the N or Page Down key, press the spacebar, press the right or down arrow, or press Enter. You can also click the Next Slide button on the pop-up toolbar that appears when you move your mouse to the lower-left corner of the screen.

2. To go to the previous slide, press the left or up arrow, or press the P or Page Up or Backspace key. You can also click the Previous Slide button on the pop-up toolbar.

3. If you're using a touch device, you can swipe left to move forward and right to move back.

4. To jump to a specific slide, type the slide number and press Enter.

5. Press B to black the screen. This is a great way to focus the audience's attention on what you're saying. Press B again to return to the slide show. Similarly, W makes the screen white.

6. Press Ctrl+H to hide the arrow pointer. Press Ctrl+U and move the mouse to unhide it.

7. Press Ctrl and click (and hold down) the mouse button to turn your pointer into a laser pointer.

8. Press Ctrl+P to turn the arrow pointer into a pen, and Ctrl+I to change to a highlighter. Press Ctrl+A to return to an arrow pointer. You can also access these options from the Pen tool on the pop-up toolbar.

9. Press the + key to zoom in on the slide. Press – to zoom out. Zoom tools are also available on the pop-up toolbar. On a touch device, stretch and pinch gestures will zoom in and out.

Back to Slide Show view (10)

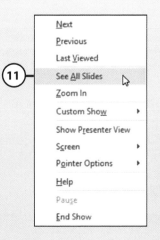

10. To see all the slides in a grid similar to Slide Sorter view, click the See All Slides button on the pop-up toolbar or right-click on the slide and select See All Slides. Click a slide or section to jump to it.

N<u>e</u>xt
<u>P</u>revious
Last <u>V</u>iewed
(11) See A<u>l</u>l Slides
<u>Z</u>oom In
Custom Sho<u>w</u> ▸
Show P<u>r</u>esenter View
S<u>c</u>reen ▸
P<u>o</u>inter Options ▸
<u>H</u>elp
Pau<u>s</u>e
<u>E</u>nd Show

11. Right-click the slide in Slide Show view to see a shortcut menu with all these commands and more.

Presenter View Is for Your Eyes Only

Remember, your audience sees everything that happens on the screen in Slide Show view. If you open the See All Slides grid in a slide show, the audience will see all your slides. If you right-click the slide, your audience will see the shortcut menu. If you rely on the pop-up toolbar, they'll see that too.

Activating the slide grid in Presenter view will keep it for your eyes only; the audience won't know you've opened it.

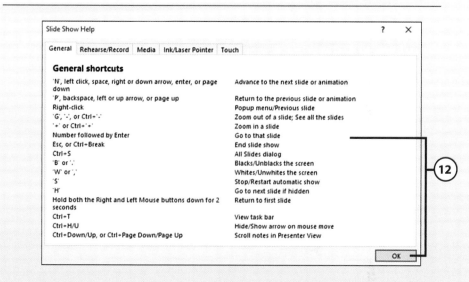

12. When you're in Slide Show view, press F1 or right-click the slide and choose Help to see a list of all shortcuts available during a slide show. This is a good thing to do while you're practicing. Click OK or the Close button to exit the dialog box.

13. Press Esc to exit Slide Show view at any time.

>>>Go Further

I HATE THE POP-UP TOOLBAR

The pop-up toolbar appears in the lower-left corner of the slide-show screen whenever you move your mouse. It will disappear a couple of seconds after you stop moving the mouse.

If you want to get rid of the pop-up toolbar altogether, turn it off in the PowerPoint Options dialog box. In Normal view, click the File button, then Options, and then Advanced. In the Slide Show section, uncheck Show Popup Toolbar. You can also turn off the right-click menu, the prompt to keep annotations when you exit the slide show, and the black slide that says, "End of slide show, click to exit," which appears automatically at the end of every presentation.

PowerPoint Options	
General	☐ Disable hardware graphics acceleration
Proofing	☐ Disable Slide Show hardware graphics accelerat
Save	☑ Automatically extend display when presenting
Language	Open all documents using this view The view sav
Advanced	**Slide Show**
Customize Ribbon	☑ Show menu on right mouse click ⓘ
Quick Access Toolbar	☐ Show popup toolbar ⓘ
Add-Ins	☑ Prompt to keep ink annotations when exiting
	☑ End with black slide

If you turn off the pop-up toolbar, right-clicking the mouse will go backward to the previous slide or animation. Right-clicking on the slide itself will still bring up the right-click menu—unless you also turned that off in the PowerPoint Options dialog box.

Use Presenter View

If you've attached a second monitor or projector to your computer, Presenter view will begin automatically when you start a slide show. Your audience sees everything that happens in Slide Show view, but only you see Presenter view.

1. On the Slide Show tab, make sure Use Presenter View is checked.
2. Start the slide show. If you have just one monitor, press Alt+F5 instead.

I Don't Have a Second Monitor

Lots of people don't have a second monitor or a projector sitting around just to practice with. If that's your situation, press Alt+F5 to begin the slide show (or Alt+Shift+F5 to begin from the current slide), and Presenter view will open on your single monitor so you can practice with it before you really have to present!

Current slide **Preview of next slide Speaker notes**

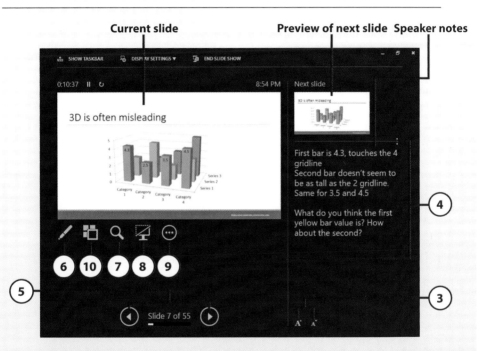

3. Click the Make the Text Larger icon or the Make the Text Smaller icon to increase or decrease the font size of the speaker notes.

4. Click and drag the edge of a pane to resize it.

5. Click the Forward and Back arrows to move to the next or previous slide.

6. Click the Pen tool to access the laser pointer, pen, and highlighter tools. Use these on the current slide thumbnail in Presenter view, and the audience will also see them in Slide Show view.

7. Click the Zoom tool and click an area of the current slide thumbnail to zoom in on the slide. Click the Zoom tool again to zoom back out.

8. Click the Black or unblack icon to black or unblack the screen in Slide Show view.

9. The More Slide Show Options icon provides access to tools such as a white screen, a list of custom shows (if there are any in your presentation), and Help, which displays the keyboard shortcuts you can use. Your audience won't see this if you launch it from Presenter view.

10. Click the See All Slides icon to see all your slides. Click a slide or section to jump to it. Only you will see the grid if you launch See All Slides from Presenter view.

More Zoom

The Zoom tool in Presenter view zooms in only a little. If it's not enough, you can still press the + key to zoom in more. The – key still zooms out as well. Just be careful not to zoom too far out or you'll find yourself in the See All Slides grid!

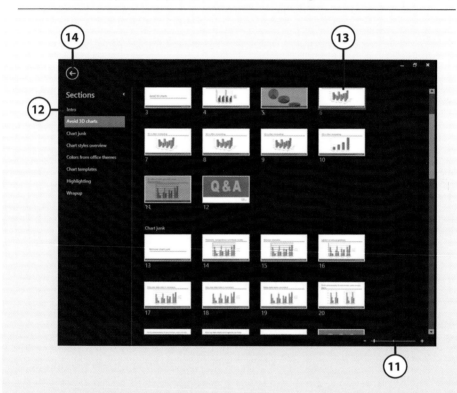

11. Use the slider in the lower-right corner of the screen to resize the thumbnails in the See All Slides grid.

12. Click a section to jump to the first slide in that section.

13. Click a thumbnail to jump to that slide.

14. Click the Back button or press Esc to return to Presenter view. Press Esc again to exit Presenter view and end the presentation.

>>>Go Further

SETTING UP PRESENTER VIEW

If Presenter view displays on the wrong monitor when you start a slide show, click Display Settings at the top of the Presenter View screen and click Swap Presenter View and Slide Show.

To specify this before you begin the slide show, go to the Slide Show tab and choose the monitor you want the slide show to display on. The other monitor will show Presenter view. Generally you want the slide show to display on the external monitor or the projector and Presenter view to show on your laptop's monitor.

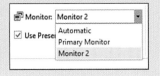

Using Alternative Delivery Methods

If you're giving a traditional presentation, you're more than likely standing in front of an audience while talking and advancing slides on the screen. Although that's still common, it's also common to turn your presentation into a video or deliver it via the Web to an online audience. This section is about saving your presentation for some of those alternative delivery methods.

Present Online

You may have access to screen-sharing software, but if you don't, Present Online is a great way to share your presentation with others on the fly.

1. Open your presentation.

2. Click File, Share, Present Online. You can also click the Present Online button on the Slide Show tab.

Skype for Business

Your File, Share, Present Online screen may look slightly different if you have Skype for Business or another optional broadcast service. You may also see these options when you click the Present Online button arrow on the Slide Show tab. If applicable, select Office Presentation Service from the drop-down list and continue with Step 3.

3. Check the box to allow remote viewers to download a copy of your presentation if you want.

4. Click the Present Online button in the right pane to start the process (or if you accessed Present Online from the Slide Show tab, click Connect).

5. When you click Present Online, PowerPoint generates a link for you to send to the people you want to present to. You can copy the link or send an email directly from the dialog box.

6. Click Start Presentation to begin the slide show.

7. Even after you exit Slide Show view, you're still in Present Online mode. Your viewers will see the last slide you were on until you click the End Online Presentation button to end the online presentation.

8. Click Send Invitations to reopen the Present Online dialog box with the link.

9. Click From Beginning or From Current Slide to restart the online presentation.

It's Not All Good

Present Online Leaves a Lot to Be Desired

Present Online is a free service designed to be used when you want to share a presentation with someone else on the fly. It's great for a quick review with a colleague or friend, but it's generally not robust enough to rely on for use with clients or others you want to impress.

You cannot schedule a Present Online broadcast in advance. It's a strictly in-the-moment proposition.

There is no audio component such as a conference call line. Assuming you want to actually talk to the people you're sharing with, you'll need to use your telephone, Skype, Skype for Business, or another telephony application. Of course, if that application shows up as one of your Present Online options in PowerPoint, then use it along with its audio options.

Although Present Online is supposed to be used in spur-of-the-moment situations, the link to view the file is too long and difficult to read to someone verbally. You will almost certainly have to email it to the people involved right as you begin the Present Online process.

The Present Online broadcast servers have been known to be unavailable, sometimes for months at a time. When they break, free services such as Present Online often don't receive as high a priority as paid services.

Save as a Video

It's super-easy to turn your presentation into a video, which you can later upload to a website for others to view.

1. To convert your presentation into a video, click File, Export, Create a Video.

2. Choose the size and quality of the video. See the following sidebar for additional information on these options.

3. If you've recorded narrations or have automatic transition timings in your presentation, you can opt to use those or not.

4. If you don't have automatic transition timings, specify the number of seconds to remain on each slide before moving to the next.

5. Click Create Video to start the conversion process. The video is rendered in real time, so if your presentation is 10 minutes long, it will take about 10 minutes for the video to be created.

Not All Media Can Be Included

If you have links to online media in your presentation, PowerPoint will warn you that it cannot include that media when you convert your presentation into a video. When this happens, the video in your presentation will be rendered as a static picture with no audio.

>>>Go Further

CHOOSE THE RIGHT VIDEO SIZE

When you convert your presentation into a video, you will choose Presentation Quality, Internet Quality, or Low Quality export settings. Presentation Quality is the highest quality setting; it also creates the largest file size. Internet Quality is medium quality and file size. Low Quality gives you the smallest file size.

Presentation Quality
Largest file size and highest quality (1920 x 1080)

Internet Quality
Medium file size and moderate quality (1280 x 720)

Low Quality
Smallest file size and lowest quality (852 x 480)

By default, PowerPoint creates MP4 (MPEG-4 Video format) videos, but you can also choose WMV (Windows Media Video format) in the Save as Type drop-down list after you click the Create Video button. MP4 is the most universally compatible video for use on both Mac and PC systems.

Presentation Quality videos are saved at 1080p. Internet Quality uses 720p. Low Quality uses 480p. This setting refers to the vertical resolution; the horizontal resolution for each will be determined proportionate to these vertical settings.

Save as a Picture Presentation

One way to semiprotect your presentation is to distribute it as a picture presentation. This saves a copy of your presentation as images on blank slides. It also strips any speaker notes that were in the original presentation.

1. Click File, Export, Change File Type.

2. Choose PowerPoint Picture Presentation.

3. Click Save As at the bottom of the Export page. This opens the Save As dialog box with the PowerPoint Picture Presentation format already selected from the Save as Type drop-down.

PowerPoint File Types

Common formats in the File, Export, Change File Type list (which are also available in the Save As Type drop-down list) include the PowerPoint 97-2003 Presentation format (.PPT extension instead of .PPTX), PowerPoint Show (.PPSX), PowerPoint Template (.POTX), and PNG and JPG images.

---

4. If you don't see the format you want to save as on the Export page, choose Save as Another File Type, and then click Save As. Finally, select the format you want from the Save as Type drop-down list.

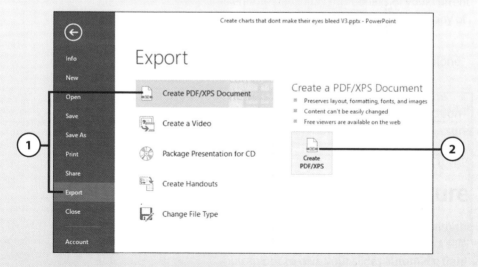

5. Type a name for your presentation in the File Name box and then click Save.

Save a Presentation as a PDF

A PDF is a good choice for distributing your presentation or handouts because it's a universal format. PDFs generally have a small file size, and they can be viewed on most devices.

1. Open your presentation and then choose File, Export, Create PDF/XPS Document.

2. Click the large Create PDF/XPS button to begin the save-as-PDF process.

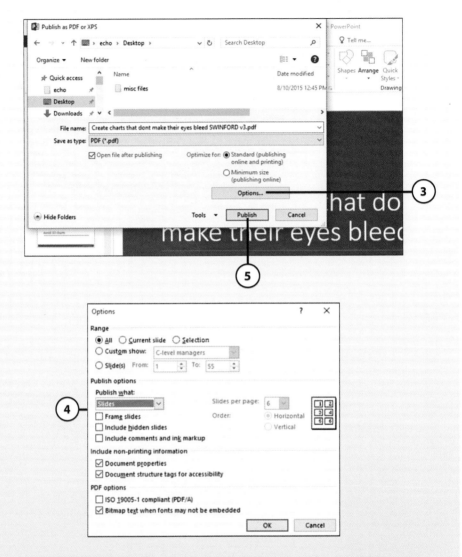

3. In the Publish as PDF or XPS dialog box, click Options. This opens the Options dialog box, which has options similar to print settings.

4. In the Options dialog box, specify which slides you want to print and opt to include hidden slides, include comments and ink, or add a border to the slides. Also select whether you want to publish full-page slides, notes pages, or handouts. After you've made your selections, click OK.

5. Click Publish to create the PDF.

What is XPS, anyway?

XPS stands for Open XML Paper Specification, which is an open, standardized format for Microsoft Office documents. It was introduced with Office 2007 and was intended as an alternative to PDF. In practice, it hasn't gotten much traction so you're better off sticking with PDF. Fortunately, when you choose to publish your presentation as PDF or XPS, PDF is the default format.

What About Printing to a PDF Driver?

If you have a PDF creation program such as Adobe Acrobat, you may have a PDF driver that lets you select PDF as a printer.

Printing to PDF can be a great tool, but you'll often get better quality output if you export or save in the native PowerPoint PDF/XPS format. This seems to be especially true if your presentation uses gradients and semitransparency.

>>>*Go Further*

PRESENTING WITH PDF

If you open the PDF you just created and display it in full-screen mode, it will look just like a set of slides. Adobe Acrobat (the full program, not the free Acrobat Reader) also gives you some presentation tools to apply to your PDFs. Use these to set the PDF to open full-screen and apply page transitions. You can even add video and sound to a PDF!

Many, if not all, of the links in your PowerPoint presentation will survive the conversion to PDF. If they don't, you can also add navigation to the PDF in Acrobat to make it more interactive.

>>>*Go Further*

OTHER WAYS TO SHARE OR DELIVER A PRESENTATION

These days, there are literally countless ways to put your presentation in front of people. Here are a few of the more common options:

- Email your presentation.

- Share via screen-sharing applications such as Skype, Skype for Business, GoToMeeting, Join.Me, WebEx, and others.

- Upload to cloud storage or presentation-sharing services such as OneDrive, Dropbox, and others.

- Use presentation sharing services such as Sway, Docs.com, SlideShare.net, SlideShark.com, and so on.

- Store your presentation on OneDrive and then embed it in your webpage (see instructions at http://tinyurl.com/q7vnyaf).

Always test your sharing service before sending links to the world to ensure it does everything you expect and nothing you don't. For example, you should be aware that most cloud storage options (OneDrive, Dropbox, and so on) allow users to download the presentation, even when the link seems like it should be for viewing only.

>>>*Go Further*

FORGET ABOUT THE PACKAGE FOR CD OPTION

People sometimes ask about the PowerPoint Viewer and Package for CD, but both of these options are virtually obsolete now. The PowerPoint Viewer was designed for use on systems without PowerPoint. It allows you to view a presentation but not edit it. You can still find it in various places online, but why bother now that you can run a presentation in the PowerPoint app on your phone, on your tablet, on your iPad, and on your laptop or desktop computer?

Package for CD is in a similar situation. First, when did you last use a CD? Second, Package for CD was useful partly for gathering any linked media files and resolving the links so the presentation could find the audio and video. Now that we can embed multimedia, Package for CD isn't so necessary. Third, Package for CD used to include the PowerPoint Viewer and create all the files necessary to run the presentation, using the Viewer, automatically from the CD. No PowerPoint required, and no Viewer installation required. Now Package for CD simply gathers the presentation and creates an HTML page with a link you click to open the presentation or to download and install the PowerPoint Viewer. The verdict? Don't waste your time with either the Viewer or Package for CD.

Work in Slide Master view

Create custom layouts

Customize your own theme color set

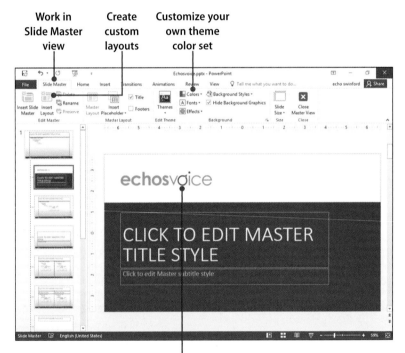

Add graphics to all slides and individual layouts

In this chapter you will learn to create your own theme or template. Specific topics in this chapter include the following:

→ Changing theme colors, fonts, and effects
→ Formatting masters and layouts
→ Saving themes and templates

Creating Your Own Theme

Every PowerPoint file is actually based on a theme, which consists of colors, fonts, effects, and slide background graphics. Microsoft provides a number of stock themes you can base your presentations and templates on, but usually you'll want to make some changes to them to reflect your own style or corporate branding.

Most of these changes will be made on the slide master and layouts. Add background graphics, pictures, and logos; resize and reposition placeholders; or change the default font and bullet formatting in Master view, and you won't have to do it on every single slide as you create it. You can even create your own custom layouts.

Office Themes Versus PowerPoint Templates

Every PowerPoint file is based on a theme. Even the Blank Presentation option on the Start screen uses the default theme named "Office Theme."

The most common question is, "What is the difference between a theme and a template?" The reality is, not much. There are some distinctions you might want to be aware of, but themes and templates are essentially the same. What are those differences? Well, for starters it might help if we call them by their correct names: Office themes and PowerPoint templates.

Office themes use the file extension .thmx, and you can apply an Office theme to Word documents, Excel spreadsheets, and PowerPoint presentations. When you look on the Design tab in Word and PowerPoint and the Page Layout tab in Excel, you're looking at themes—because themes can be used in all the Office applications (the ones that support themes, anyway).

Office themes consist of a color set, a font set, and an effects set that determine the look of your file as well as what formatting options you get in the Shape Styles and other galleries. When you apply a theme to a PowerPoint file specifically, you'll realize that it also includes slide background graphics and layouts that determine placeholder formatting and position.

PowerPoint templates are limited to PowerPoint. (Likewise, Word templates are limited to Word, and Excel templates are limited to Excel.) Templates can also hold content that themes cannot. For example, a PowerPoint template might have sample slides, a Word template often includes AutoText or Building Blocks, and an Excel template may include formulas. Basically, you can think of a template as a theme plus content specific to the application.

The easiest way to create your own theme or template is to start with a theme that is close to the one you want to create and modify it to suit your needs. Or feel free to start with Blank Presentation (based on the Office theme), which has a completely clean background and standard effects.

If you want to learn all the intricacies involved with creating themes and templates, grab a copy of Building PowerPoint Templates: Step by Step with the Experts by Echo Swinford and Julie Terberg.

Changing Theme Colors, Fonts, and Effects

Creating a new template is kind of circular. To begin, you'll usually want to choose or create a new theme color set, a font set, and sometimes even an effects set. After you have determined these, you can apply them to the slide master and begin formatting the individual layouts and placeholders.

If you're working with an existing presentation, you can still change these elements. Anything in the presentation that has used theme colors, fonts, or effects as part of its formatting will update to take on the new look.

Create Your Own Theme Color Set

PowerPoint comes with a number of available color sets you can choose from. Start with one of these and tweak it to your satisfaction.

1. Start PowerPoint and choose Blank Presentation to start a new presentation.

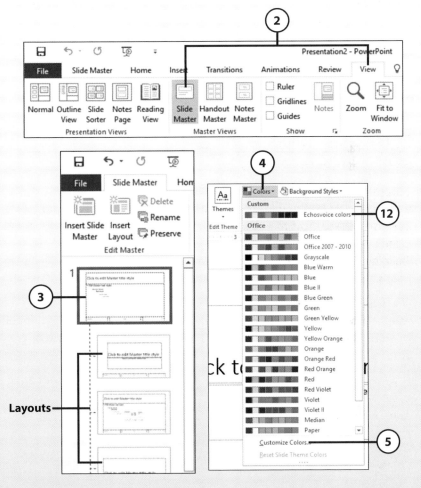

2. On the View tab, click Slide Master.

3. In the Slides pane, scroll to the top and click on the largest thumbnail. This is the slide master, and it controls the formatting for the child layouts below.

4. On the Slide Master tab, click the Colors button. If you want, click one of the provided theme color sets to use as a basis for your theme colors.

5. Or click Customize Colors at the bottom.

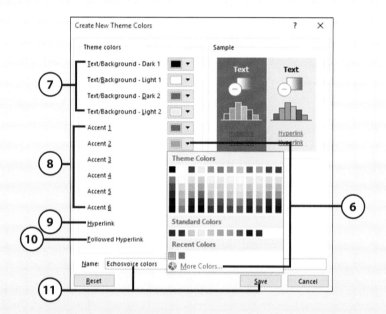

6. In the Create New Theme Colors dialog box, click a color chip to change its color. Choose another color or click More Colors to input your own RGB values.

7. The chips labeled Dark 1 and Dark 2 should remain dark colors. The chips labeled Light 1 and Light 2 should remain light colors.

Choosing New Theme Colors

The Dark 1 and Light 1 colors in the Create New Theme Colors dialog box usually represent the slide background and text colors. The Dark 2 and Light 2 colors are often used for black and white or for additional font and background color options.

SmartArt and tables will all use Dark 1 or Light 1 as their font color. Charts will use a tint of Dark 1 or a variation of Light 1. (If Light 1 is white, the chart font will be white.)

8. Accent colors appear in the Shape Styles gallery, in the Tables gallery, as SmartArt graphics colors, as the default chart data series colors, and in all the color pickers. Your accent colors should be visible against the slide background, and the text colors should contrast with them.

9. Hyperlink color is the color that linked text will be formatted with automatically.

10. Followed Hyperlink is the color that hyperlinked text turns to after you click the link in Slide Show view.

11. Name your color theme and click Save. It will be applied automatically to the slide master.

12. The custom color theme will appear in the Colors gallery on your computer. Click the color theme to apply it to any presentation or theme.

>>>Go Further

COLOR THEMES FOR EXISTING PRESENTATIONS

You can't edit the stock color themes. But you can click Customize Colors to open the currently applied (stock) color theme and tweak it if you want. Then save it with a new name. The new custom color theme will be applied to the presentation when you save it.

To edit a custom color theme you've created, right-click it in the Colors gallery and choose Edit. To delete one, right-click and choose Delete.

When you're working with an existing presentation, find the Colors gallery in Normal view by going to the Design tab. Click the More button on the Variants gallery and then point to Colors. From there the steps are the same as if you were in Slide Master view, and the new colors will be applied to your presentation when you save the customized theme color set.

Choose a Different Font Set

PowerPoint comes with many available font sets you can choose from, or you can create your own. Start PowerPoint and choose Blank Presentation to start a new presentation or begin with the same presentation you used in the preceding exercise.

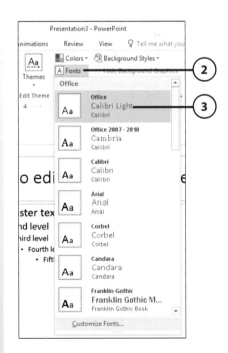

1. On the View tab, click Slide Master. Make sure you've selected the slide master in the Slides pane.

2. On the Slide Master tab, click the Fonts button.

3. Choose an existing font set. The first font shown under each font set name is the Heading font; it will automatically be applied to all title placeholders. The second font is the body font; it will be applied to all other placeholders.

4. To create your own theme font set, select Customize Fonts at the bottom of the Fonts list.

5. Select a heading font and a body font.

6. Name the custom theme font set and click Save. The new font set will be automatically applied to the slide master. You can find the Fonts list on the Design tab in Normal view. Click the More button on the Variants gallery and then point to Fonts. From there the steps are the same as if you were in Slide Master view.

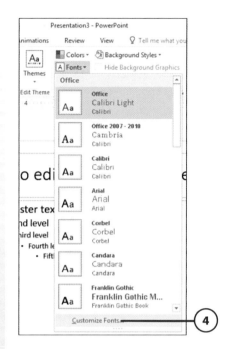

Choose Safe Fonts

It can't be said enough: You're really better off sticking with the stock theme font sets because they generally include fonts that are widely available on many versions of PowerPoint. Don't bother embedding fonts in your template, either. Presentations based on the template don't inherit the embedded font setting.

Select a Different Effects Set

Theme effects control things like the shadows, gradients, outline thickness, and more that you see in the Shape Styles gallery. You can choose a different theme effects set, but creating your own requires an extensive understanding of PowerPoint, the matrix that establishes the effects, and XML. Most custom themes and templates just stick with the default effects that came with the theme they started with.

It's helpful to format shapes on a regular slide so you can see how the different theme effects sets affect them.

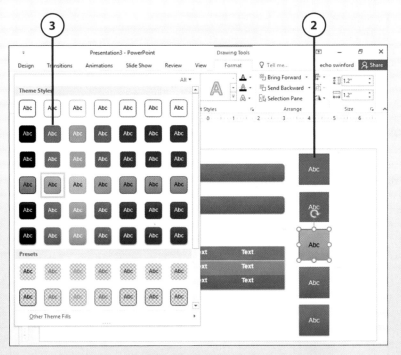

1. In Normal view, create a slide based on the Blank layout.

2. Draw a rectangle about 1" x 1" on the slide master. Copy and paste it so you have five rectangles total.

3. The first rectangle will automatically be formatted using the style on the second row of the Shape Styles gallery. Format another one using the third row, another using the fourth, another using the fifth, and the last one using the sixth.

4. Notice that you can also add a SmartArt diagram and a table, each formatted with one of the formats labeled Best Match for Document.

5. Go to the Design tab and click the More button on the Variants gallery. Point to Effects and then hover over each theme effects set to see how it affects the formatting of the various objects.

6. Click a theme effects set to choose it. This will apply the effects to all slides and the slide master. You can also access the Effects gallery in Slide Master view on the Slide Master tab.

Formatting Masters and Layouts

Slide masters and layouts are the basis for slides in a presentation. This is where you set up the background graphics and format and position the placeholders.

When you look at Slide Master view, the largest thumbnail is the slide master, and the smaller thumbnails are the layouts. These have a parent-child relationship: Whatever you do to the slide master trickles down to all the individual layouts. When you create slides, they inherit their settings from the layouts they're based on.

Apply Colors, Fonts, Effects

Remember those theme colors, fonts, and effects you set up in the previous section? Apply them to your slide master before you start formatting.

1. Start PowerPoint and choose Blank Presentation to start a new presentation.

2. On the View tab, click Slide Master. Scroll up and then select the slide master at the top of the Slides pane.

3. If you want to apply one of the stock themes to use as a starting point, click the Themes button on the Slide Master tab and click to apply a theme.

4. On the Slide Master tab, click the Colors button and choose your custom theme colors or one of the stock theme color sets.

5. Click the Fonts button to choose your custom theme fonts or one of the stock theme font sets.

6. Click the Effects button and select an effects set.

Start Fresh

It's best to start building a theme from a clean file; this is why we're starting with a new Blank Presentation file.

You can actually use any of the stock themes, especially if there's one you can leverage to save a bunch of formatting steps. Just start with that one and modify it.

If you're working with an existing presentation, you can still apply new color, font, and effects sets to the slide master, and those changes will apply to all slide content that uses theme formatting.

Format the Master Background

There's a little-known feature in PowerPoint called Background Styles. Apply a background style to the slide master so the font color contrasts properly. After you've applied a background style to force the font contrast, you can override it to use a different color, gradient, or picture.

For this exercise, continue with the presentation you just applied colors, fonts, and effects to. You should be in Master view with the slide master selected.

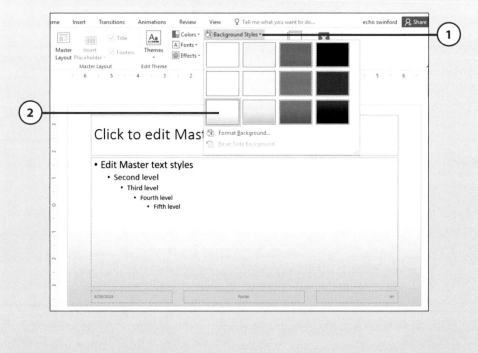

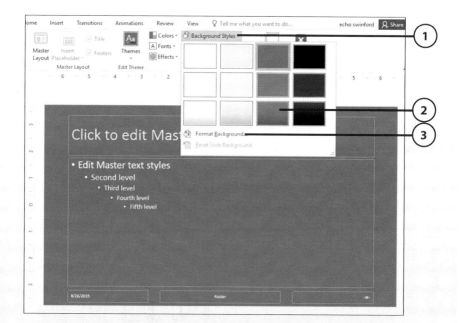

1. On the Slide Master tab, click the Background Styles button.

2. Hover over the different background options. Notice that when you hover over the blue and black options, the font automatically turns white, and when you hover over the white or gray backgrounds, the font remains black. Click a thumbnail to apply the background style to the slide master.

Choosing a Background Style

PowerPoint gives you 12 background styles to choose from. These correspond with the Dark 1, Light 1, Dark 2, and Light 2 theme colors. Usually you'll have four solid color options, a variation of each color, and then a more intense variation for each. The variations you see depend on the theme Effects set you applied.

If you like any of these, go for it! If you don't like them, choose an option that forces your font to be the color you need. So if you plan to use a dark background, even if it's not a black background, choose the black background style because it forces the font to be a light color. Likewise, if you plan to use a light background, even if it's not white, choose the white background, which gives you dark fonts.

It's the same even if you plan to add a picture to the background: Choose a background style that gives you the font color you'll need.

3. Click the Background Styles button again and then click Format Background to open the Format Background pane.

4. Apply a different solid color, gradient, picture or texture fill, or pattern fill. (You can also open the Format Background pane even from Normal view by right-clicking in the slide workspace and selecting Format Background.)

5. Add any graphics, including PowerPoint shapes and pictures, that should appear on every layout. For example, if you want your logo to appear on every slide, put it on the slide master. If you need your logo to appear on only a few specific layouts, add it directly to those layouts.

Apply Background Style to a Single Layout

Later when you're formatting individual slide layouts in Slide Master view, you may want to use a different look for some of them—the Title Slide and Section Header layouts are perfect candidates for a different look. In that case, right-click any thumbnail in the Background Styles gallery and choose Apply to Selected Layouts.

Format and Position Master Placeholders

After you've set the master background, you're ready to format and position the title, content, and footer placeholders. The layouts will pick up the format and positions you specify here on the master, but you can override those settings whenever necessary. Taking care of these on the master saves you from having to reformat and position every placeholder on every layout.

For this exercise, continue with the presentation you just applied colors, fonts, and effects to, and set the background of the slide master. You should be in Slide Master view with the slide master selected.

1. Click the edge of the title placeholder and apply font and paragraph formatting. Change colors, boldness, line spacing, and so on, as desired.

2. Resize and reposition the title placeholder as desired.

3. Format the content placeholder. Apply font color, set up bullet points and indents, specify line spacing, and so on.

4. Resize and reposition the content placeholder as desired.

5. Format and position the footer placeholders.

Forcing All Caps

You cannot use the Change Case button to force slide titles to be sentence case or title case. However, you can force all caps or small caps by clicking the Font dialog box launcher and checking the appropriate setting.

Use Dark 1 or Light 1 for Text

Generally, you'll want to use the Dark 1 or Light 1 color when you format the content placeholder so it matches the text in tables and SmartArt diagrams. You can always update your theme color set with a new Dark 1 or Light 1 color to accommodate this as you're formatting the slide master and layouts, or you can choose a color from the Dark 1 or Light 1 column.

You may find it helpful to know that charts are inconsistent. If the slide background forces a light font, charts will use Light 1, especially if it's white. However, if the fonts are Dark 1, charts will use the third chip down (lighter 25%) in the Dark 1 column as their default font. If you prefer gray text anyway, you may want to set the font in your content placeholder to that color.

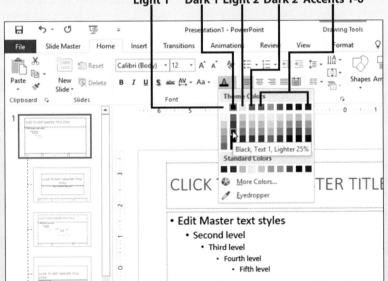

Dealing with Footer Placeholders

Dealing with footer placeholders can be tough. You can turn them off completely on the View tab, and this is recommended for title slide layouts especially. But what if you want the footer text and slide number, for example, but not the date?

One approach is to leave that placeholder on the slide layout and just instruct users not to turn on the date in the Insert, Header and Footer dialog box. Another option is to drag it off the bottom edge of the slide layout where it won't show even if someone does turn it on. You can format it with 1-point text and make it match the slide workspace so it doesn't show much when you're editing in Normal view.

If you deleted a placeholder from the master, click the Master Layout button on the Slide Master tab and check the box to get it back.

6. Save the file if you want. For now you can leave it in Slide Master view, and you can save as a Presentation (.pptx) file until later, when you've finished with all formatting.

Format the Title Slide Layout

You will probably want to change up the background graphics on the Title Slide layout. Using the Hide Background Graphics option will help you with this change.

Continue with the same file you've been working with. Start in Slide Master view.

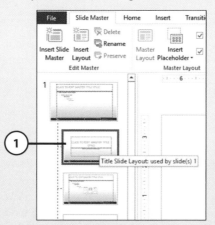

1. Click the Title Slide layout in the Slides pane. It's the first layout under the slide master.

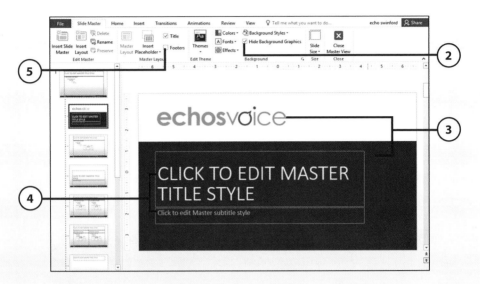

2. On the Slide Master tab of the Ribbon, click Hide Background Graphics.

3. Change the background and add graphics to the Title Slide layout as desired. For example, insert a larger logo and graphics.

4. Position and format the title and subtitle placeholders as desired.

5. Uncheck the Footers option on the Slide Master tab to turn off the footers on all title slides.

6. Repeat this process for any of the other layouts that need graphics different from those on the slide master.

Format Individual Slide Layouts

You may want to reposition the content placeholders on individual layouts. And some of the default layouts have specific quirks. Continue with the same file you've been working with. Start in Slide Master view.

1. Click the Two Content layout in the Slides pane.

2. Check to see that the content placeholders are positioned where you want them. Usually the two will span the width of the title placeholder. If you changed your title placeholder on the slide master, you may need to adjust the placeholders in the Two Content layout.

Set Up Guides

Setting up guides on the slide master can help you as you resize and reposition placeholders on the individual layouts. With nothing selected, right-click the workspace area and choose Grid and Guides to turn them on and add them to the master or individual layouts. For more information about using guides, see Chapter 4, "Aligning and Positioning Shapes."

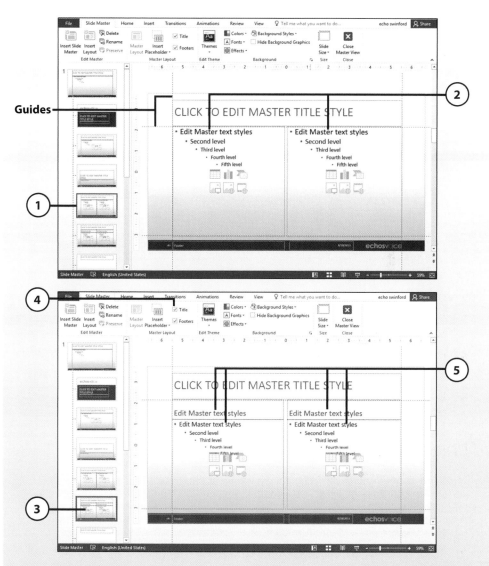

Guides

3. Click the Comparison layout.

4. Click the Title option on the Slide Master tab to turn off the title placeholder. Then click it again to turn the placeholder back on. When you turn it back on, the title placeholder will be in the same position as it is on the master. This technique works with any title placeholder on any layout.

5. Reposition and format the column headings and content placeholders. You may want to make the font smaller since there is potential for so much text on the Comparison layout.

6. Continue through the rest of the layouts, formatting and positioning placeholders as desired.

Can I Delete a Layout?

You can delete layouts you won't need, but be careful. If you have old presentations that use that layout, PowerPoint won't know what to do with them when you paste in those old slides. You'll end up with orphaned layouts.

Many people delete the Title and Vertical Text layout and the Vertical Text and Title layout. These layouts are especially useful for Asian users, which might be a consideration for you. They won't show in the New Slide gallery in Normal view unless you have an Asian language or a right-to-left language enabled.

Create a Custom Layout

If PowerPoint doesn't have a layout with the placeholders you want or need, you can create your own custom layout. Continue with the same file you've been working with. Start in Slide Master view.

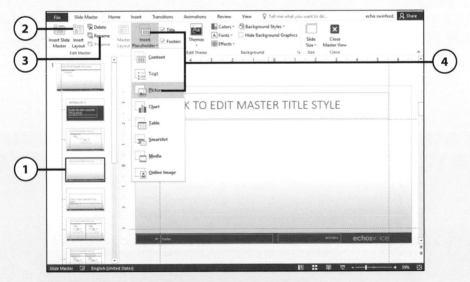

1. Click in the Slides pane where you want to add the layout.
2. On the Slide Master tab, click Insert Layout.

3. Click the layout in the Slides pane and then click Rename on the Slide Master tab. Rename the layout with something descriptive.

4. Click the Insert Placeholder button arrow on the Slide Master tab and then select the type of placeholder to add. Click and drag on the slide to add it.

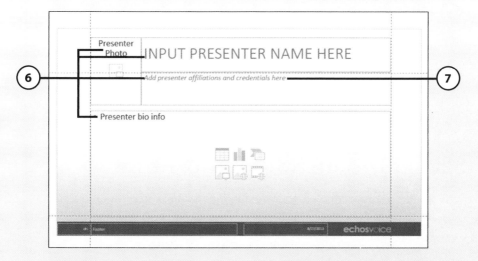

5. Continue adding placeholders and formatting them and positioning them as desired.

6. Click inside any placeholder and type to replace "Edit Master text styles" and "Click to add text" with your own prompt text to help your users know what to do with any placeholder. You can change the prompt text on any placeholder on any layout, but you cannot change the prompt text on the slide master.

7. You can also delete the extra levels of text in a placeholder. They will still be formatted, but they don't have to appear in the placeholder.

8. Click and drag thumbnails in the Slides pane to rearrange layouts, but the Title Slide layout should always be first.

WHEN DO YOU CREATE A CUSTOM LAYOUT?

You really don't want to add or remove placeholders from any of the default layouts. When you do this, PowerPoint doesn't recognize the layout as itself and creates orphaned layouts when you reuse existing slides based on them. If you need more or fewer or a different type of placeholder than a default layout has available, create a custom layout with those placeholders.

You can duplicate a default layout and add or remove placeholders from the duplicate to save some formatting steps. For example, if you need to add a placeholder to the Title Slide layout to accommodate presenter affiliations, duplicate the Title Slide layout and add a placeholder to it. If you need to add a subtitle placeholder to the Title and Content layout, duplicate the Title and Content layout and add a text placeholder and then position it to serve as a subtitle. If you add the placeholder to the Title and Content layout, when you reuse a Title and Content slide, PowerPoint may move all the existing body text into the subtitle placeholder!

To duplicate a layout, select it and press Ctrl+D or right-click the layout and choose Duplicate Layout. Don't forget to rename it after you duplicate, or it will be named 1_Title Slide or something similar, and that's not a very helpful layout name.

Other examples of when you might create a custom layout include presenter bio slides, disclosure slides, agenda slides, full-page pictures, three pictures plus captions, SWOT analysis (quad content), and case studies. The possibilities are truly endless.

Saving Themes and Templates

While you're working on your theme or template, you can save it as a Presentation (.pptx) file so it's easier to open and edit. When you've finished formatting the file, be sure to test it by closing Slide Master view and creating at least one new slide based on each layout to ensure that it looks and works as you expect.

When you're really finished with the file, it's time to save it as a PowerPoint Template file. Add any example or instructional slides you want to make available to users and save as a PowerPoint Template. Finally, save as an Office Theme so you can leverage the theme colors, fonts, and effects you specified in Word and Excel.

Save a Template

The next-to-last step is to save your file as a template. This is more important to do than it was in earlier versions of PowerPoint because doing so also removes any variants that might still be in the file. When you resize slides with the Slide Size tool, PowerPoint will reapply any variants that are left over in the file. If you've reformatted your background and placeholders, you don't want PowerPoint overriding that and reapplying one of the stock variants! Saving your file as a PowerPoint Template (.potx) prevents this situation.

The other thing about templates is that when you double-click a .potx in File Explorer, it opens a new presentation (.pptx) based on the template; it doesn't actually open the .potx, which prevents you from making changes to it inadvertently.

Make sure you are in Normal view, not Slide Master view.

1.   Select the first slide in Normal view, more than likely a title slide.

2.   Click File, Save As, Browse. It doesn't matter which location you choose because PowerPoint will place the template in the correct folder when you save it.

3. Name the template.

4. In the Save as Type drop-down list, select PowerPoint Template (*.potx).

5. Notice that when you select PowerPoint Template, the Save As dialog box automatically points you to the user templates folder, in Documents\Custom Office Templates. When your templates are stored here, they will appear in the Personal or Custom folder on the File, New screen.

6. Click Save to save the file as a template.

Save a Theme

The very last step is to save your file as a theme. You don't have to do this, but it's helpful if you want to use the same colors, fonts, and effects in Word and Excel. You can also use this theme as the basis for a Word or Excel template.

To begin, open the template file (.potx) or double-click it to open a presentation based on the template. Make sure you are in Normal view, not Slide Master view. All slides will be automatically deleted when you save the file as an Office Theme.

1. Click File, Save As, Browse. It doesn't matter which location you choose because PowerPoint will place the theme in the correct folder when you save it.

2. Name the theme.

3. In the Save as Type drop-down list, select Office Theme (*.thmx).

4. Notice that when you select Office Theme, the Save As dialog box automatically points you to the theme folder in C:\Users\UserName\AppData\Roaming\Microsoft\Templates\Document Themes. When your themes are stored here, they will appear in the Custom folder on the File, New screen. They will also appear in the Themes gallery on the Design tab.

5. Click Save to save the theme.

Symbols

A

Index

Q–R

REGISTER THIS PRODUCT
SAVE 35%*
ON YOUR NEXT PURCHASE!

How to Register Your Product

- Go to quepublishing.com/register
- Sign in or create an account
- Enter ISBN: 10- or 13-digit ISBN that appears on the back cover of your product

Benefits of Registering

- Ability to download product updates
- Access to bonus chapters and workshop files
- A 35% coupon to be used on your next purchase – valid for 30 days

  To obtain your coupon, click on "Manage Codes" in the right column of your Account page
- Receive special offers on new editions and related Que products

Please note that the benefits for registering may vary by product. Benefits will be listed on your Account page under Registered Products.

We value and respect your privacy. Your email address will not be sold to any third party company.

* 35% discount code presented after product registration is valid on most print books, eBooks, and full-course videos sold on QuePublishing.com. Discount may not be combined with any other offer and is not redeemable for cash. Discount code expires after 30 days from the time of product registration. Offer subject to change.

quepublishing.com